More than a Monologue

Volume I

CATHOLIC PRACTICE IN NORTH AMERICA

SERIES CO-EDITORS:

Angela Alaimo O'Donnell, Associate Director of the Francis and
Ann Curran Center for American Catholic Studies, Fordham
University

John C. Seitz, Assistant Professor, Theology Department,
Fordham University

This series aims to contribute to the growing field of Catholic
studies through the publication of books devoted to the historical
and cultural study of Catholic practice in North America, from
the colonial period to the present. As the term "practice" suggests,
the series springs from a pressing need in the study of American
Catholicism for empirical investigations and creative explorations
and analyses of the contours of Catholic experience. In seeking to
provide more comprehensive maps of Catholic practice, this series
is committed to publishing works from diverse American locales,
including urban, suburban, and rural settings; ethnic, postethnic,
and transnational contexts; private and public sites; and seats of
power as well as the margins.

SERIES ADVISORY BOARD:

Emma Anderson, Ottawa University
Paul Contino, Pepperdine University
Kathleen Sprows Cummings, University of Notre Dame
James T. Fisher, Fordham University
Paul Mariani, Boston College
Thomas A. Tweed, University of Texas at Austin

More than a Monologue

SEXUAL DIVERSITY AND THE CATHOLIC CHURCH

Volume I: Voices of Our Times

*Edited by Christine Firer Hinze
and J. Patrick Hornbeck II*

FORDHAM UNIVERSITY PRESS
New York   2014

Fordham University Press has no responsibility for the persistence or accuracy of URLs for external or third-party Internet websites referred to in this publication and does not guarantee that any content on such websites is, or will remain, accurate or appropriate.

Fordham University Press also publishes its books in a variety of electronic formats. Some content that appears in print may not be available in electronic books.

Library of Congress Cataloging-in-Publication Data is available from the publisher.

Printed in the United States of America

16 15 14   5 4 3 2 1

First edition

Contents

Acknowledgments

We editors owe debts of gratitude to a great many people and organizations, without whose generous contributions this project would not have been possible. We acknowledge, first, the four institutions who hosted the More than a Monologue conferences in the fall of 2011, at which much of the material comprising this two-volume set was originally presented: Fairfield University, Yale Divinity School, Union Theological Seminary, and Fordham University. Special thanks go to the leaders of the organizing committees that proposed, developed, and carried out the events at each of the four sites, in particular Paul Lakeland at Fairfield, Michael Norko and Diana Swancutt at Yale, and Kelby Harrison at Union. We are deeply grateful to all who supported these conferences: administrators and academic units who contributed resources at Fairfield, Yale, Union, and Fordham, the Arcus Foundation, Geoffrey Knox and Roberta Sklar, and others who provided financial, logistical, and technical support; our many conference volunteers, participants, and attendees; and especially the forty-some speakers and panelists, all of whom generously lent their time, talent, and effort to making the conference series such a great success.

The preparation and publication of this book have been made possible by the talented and dedicated work and assistance of Fredric Nachbaur and his colleagues at Fordham University Press, theology Ph.D. student Amanda Alexander's excellent and timely editorial assistance, financial support from the Fordham University Office of Research, and intellectual and logistical support from Terrence Tilley and the Fordham Department of Theology. We are also grateful to the three anonymous Fordham University Press reviewers for their suggestions and to Tom Beaudoin and Brad Hinze for their work in reading and co-writing a theological response to the complete set of essays. Most of all, we offer abiding thanks to each of the authors who have so generously opened their lives and shared their stories in order to create this unique collection.

Nowadays when things change so rapidly and thought patterns differ so widely, the church needs to step up this exchange by calling upon the help of people who are living in the world, who are expert in its organizations and its forms of training, and who understand its mentality, in the case of believers and nonbelievers alike. With the help of the Holy Spirit, it is the task of the whole people of God, particularly of its pastors and theologians, to listen to and distinguish the many voices of our times and to interpret them in the light of God's word, in order that the revealed truth may be more deeply penetrated, better understood, and more suitably presented.

—*Gaudium et Spes*, no. 44

Introduction

CHRISTINE FIRER HINZE AND
J. PATRICK HORNBECK II

Fordham University

Listening to Voices of Our Times

In the autumn of 2011, four institutions of higher education hosted a series of conferences on sexual diversity and the Roman Catholic Church. Two of the venues—New York's Fordham University and Fairfield University in Connecticut—were Catholic universities in the Jesuit tradition; the other two—Union Theological Seminary in New York City and Yale Divinity School—were nondenominational divinity schools where Roman Catholics comprise a substantial proportion of the student body. The series, entitled "More than a Monologue," featured in total nearly fifty speakers and attracted more than a thousand audience members; many more followed the proceedings online.[1] The high levels of interest generated by the series reveal that the contemporary conversation about sexual diversity within the American Roman Catholic community is vibrant; it is also complicated, sometimes tense, and often fraught with anger, pain, and hesitation on all sides.

This volume, along with its companion, *Inquiry, Thought, and Expression*, seeks to keep alive this difficult yet rewarding dialogue.[2] It contains expanded and updated versions of remarks that speakers delivered at all four of the More than a Monologue conferences; it also includes a number of new voices, chosen because of the pastoral, academic, or personal perspectives that they bring to the topic of sexual diversity in and around the Roman Catholic tradition. While the conferences focused largely on the experiences of people who identify themselves as lesbian, gay, bisexual, transgender, and/or queer (LGBTQ), among other terms, the experiences of heterosexual persons in encountering and responding to sexual diversity are equally important. Their voices, too, were represented at the conferences, and essays by authors who describe themselves as heterosexual appear in both books.

Experience, in all its forms, is the theme and the unifying principle of this volume. In these pages, working professionals, students and teachers, journalists and social scientists, theologians and ethicists, priests and pastoral workers, and the family members and friends of LGBTQ people reflect, from their varied circumstances and points of view, on how sexual diversity and the Catholic Church's teaching and practice concerning it have affected them, their families and friends, and their lives in church and society. This book, like the conference series out of which it has come, aims to provide an opportunity for a wide audience to listen as these writers reflect, attentively and respectfully, upon their experiences of sexual diversity in relation to official and unofficial Catholic teaching and practice in this area.

The experiences our contributors recount are often personally weighty, socially multivalent, emotionally evocative, complicated, and messy. How could it be otherwise? Faith and sexuality, after all, are each enormously powerful—and persistently puzzling—spheres of human life. Both sex and faith engage and touch persons in life-shaping and life-altering ways, for both good and ill. Sexual experience, like religious faith, can delight and intrigue, teach and enrich, heal and console, but, also like faith, can confuse, disappoint, and damage. Both areas of experience are prone to distortion, misuse, and trivialization. Yet in sex and in faith, countless people seek, and many find, both healing immanence—the precious gift of being accepted and affirmed—and a conduit to transcendence that, quietly or dramatically, invites one beyond egotism into larger vistas of truth and love and ultimately toward a horizon that Christian believers name God. At once ubiquitous and exceptional, quotidian and startling, for multitudes of people on our planet faith and sexuality are prime places for experiencing the agony and the ecstasy of being human—and everything in between.

Perhaps this is why, even in cultures or periods of history where there is assumed to exist a sharp separation or contradiction between a vital faith life and a vital embrace of sexuality, there are people who refuse to—or simply cannot—walk away from one for the sake of the other. To put the point in explicitly theological terms: if St. Irenaeus was right to claim that "the glory of God is the human being fully alive," those holding out for something beyond an "either-or" between sexual truth and religious truth, sexual wholeness and religious wholeness, are surely on to something.[3]

Sexuality, Experience, and the Catholic Moral Tradition

Sadly, for many contemporary U.S. Catholics, experiences of disconnection, tension, and conflict between the realms of faith and sexuality predominate. This sense of disjuncture affects wide swaths of everyday believers whose sexual values or practices transgress traditional boundaries. It especially affects Catholics whose experiences of sexuality do not fit within culturally dominant or ecclesially sanctioned heterosexual norms.

Seen from the perspective of Catholic moral theology, dissonance between one's sexual experiences and one's religious faith can have more than one cause. Catholics discover through the practice of their faith perennial truths concerning what a good life before God requires. A sense of estrangement between one's faith life and one's sexual life may be the consequence of failing to acknowledge or to enact such truths and their requirements. When these failures occur because of ignorance or to insuperable limitations—because one truly does not know or cannot do any better—Catholic moralists have tended to deem them more tragic than blameworthy. When, however, knowledgeable and capable Catholics adopt religiously unorthodox sexual beliefs and practices, divergence from church teachings has been typically seen as a sign of a troubled relationship with God and God's law—a symptom of sin.[4]

But Catholic theology also recognizes that in certain circumstances, departing from a moral teaching may signal something other than ignorance, incapacity, or sin. Christians believe that God's Spirit, truth, and goodness, which abide in a special way in the church, are present throughout creation. Every human being is endowed by God with reason, freedom, and the divine image, and by attending to God's created order, we are able to discover, acknowledge, and pursue what is morally good. This theological vision grounds Catholics' conviction that whatever is authentically true and morally good will appear as such, both to church members and to all persons of "right reason" and "good will."[5] When aspects of the church's teachings concerning sexuality fail to appeal, or even to make sense, to large numbers of reasonable, good-willed Catholics and their neighbors, this may indeed be due to the ignorance and sin in which they and their cultures are ensnared. But history has shown that disjunctures between Catholic moral teaching and Catholics' moral sensibilities and practices can also occur when previously unseen or unappreciated facets of God's creation are coming to the fore or when new insights into human reality are emerging. In such cases, maintaining continuity with Catholic orthodoxy may require that some of its older formulations of moral truth be rethought, adapted, or reformed.[6]

A contemporary Catholic experiencing dissonance between the church's sexual teachings and her or his sincerely held sexual understandings and practices, therefore, must engage an informed, receptive conscience to discern among several potential explanations:[7] "Am I experiencing this dissonance because I simply don't, or can't, see the moral truth embodied in my church's teaching? Am I sinfully refusing to acknowledge or to live by that teaching despite the fact that I see its truth? Or is it possible that I am encountering or recognizing an aspect of moral truth that church teaching has yet to recognize and incorporate fully?" Such questions demarcate challenging territory for interlocutors in current debates about sexual morality in the U.S. Catholic Church. Its landscape is riven by disputes over how to distinguish among moral vice that requires correction, moral ignorance that calls for better education, and the eruption of new moral knowledge and insight that call for rethinking how sexual virtue and holiness may best be construed and enacted in our time and place. Negotiating such fundamental matters is fraught with difficulty and risk. Small wonder, then, that in the face of all this, many—including many church leaders—look to the church and its teachings as threatened treasures that must be defended with even greater vigor in an era of questioning, uncertainty, and flux.

But how is "the church" best understood? With its ancient traditions, global institutional presence, and over one billion adherents, Catholicism is well known for the special, divinely sanctioned authority it accords its pope and bishops, who preside over and interpret a clearly articulated body of teachings to which all members are expected to assent.[8] So prominent is this face of Catholicism that many people identify "the Catholic Church" primarily as a sacralized governing hierarchy that proclaims, preserves, and requires members' obedience to religious and moral teachings that are binding and unchangeable. To those who envision Catholicism in this way, publishing a collection wherein persons speak frankly about their experiences of sexual diversity in relation to Catholic faith might seem merely to foment confusion and invite harmful controversy not only about longstanding hierarchical teachings but also about the God-given authority of the church.

Yet no faith tradition, Catholicism included, is wholly reducible to its governing structures, however indispensable or divinely ordained. Nor is any faith tradition fully contained by its official doctrines in precisely their currently articulated forms, however deserving of respect or assent. For Catholics and all Christians, the institutional church, its teachings and practices, remain like St. Paul's "earthen vessels," vessels that, through God's grace, mediate God's presence and enable the message of the Gospel to flow in and through different eras and cultures, catching up the faithful in the mysterious movement toward God.[9] As the Second Vatican Council strongly affirmed, baptism bestows on all Christians the responsibility and authority to receive, to live out, and to pass on this good news. In this work of *traditio*, of handing on, by virtue of their offices, pope, bishops, and pastors play unique, God-given roles, but so too does every member of the laity.[10]

Embracing and proclaiming the Gospel of Jesus Christ thus requires dialogue and collaboration among all the church's members. The current Code of Canon Law puts this well:

All the Christian faithful have the duty and right to work so that the divine message of salvation more and more reaches all people in every age and in every land. Conscious of their own responsibility, the Christian faithful are bound to follow with Christian obedience those things which . . . pastors, inasmuch as they represent Christ, declare as teachers of the faith. . . . The Christian faithful are free to make known to the pastors of the Church their needs, especially spiritual ones, and their desires. In accord with the knowledge, competence and preeminence which they possess, [the Christian faithful] have the right and even at times the duty to manifest to . . . pastors their opinion on matters which pertain to the good of the Church, and they have a right to make their opinion known to the other Christian faithful, with due regard for the integrity of faith and morals and reverence toward their pastors, and with consideration for the common good and the dignity of persons.[11]

Yet simply to point out canon law's allusions to Christians' shared responsibility for the life of the church, an emphasis reflected in many recent works of Catholic theology, leaves an elephant in the room that must be acknowledged. In fact, both the contemporary conversation among Catholics about sexual diversity and more than a few of the essays included here are marked by struggles and disputes over significant aspects of Catholic Church teachings concerning sexuality.

This being the case, it seems helpful at the outset to summarize succinctly, and as accurately as possible, current official Catholic teachings on these matters.[12] These teachings seek to underscore the dignity and respect due to each person, since all are created out of divine love and in the image and likeness of God. They affirm sexuality as part of God's "very good" creation and hold that the dynamics and structures of sexual identity[13] and expression testify to their natural, divinely ordered meanings and purposes.[14] Sexual desire, these teachings stress, is intended to "draw man and woman together in the bond of marriage, a bond that is directed toward two inseparable ends: the expression of marital love and the procreation and education of children."[15] Within this moral frame, regardless of one's sexual orientation, any sexual desire, pleasure, or activity that takes place apart from these God-given ends is judged to be "disordered."[16] Heterosexual persons in a sacramental marriage between one man and one woman enjoy the sole context wherein sexual desires may be virtuously expressed and requited, provided that every sexual act remains open to both the procreative and the unitive purposes of the "conjugal union." For everyone else and in every other context, following official Catholic teaching requires a life of sexual abstinence. At the same time, "homosexual persons" are to be "accepted with respect, compassion, and sensitivity," and any form of "scorn, hatred, and even violence" directed at them "deserves condemnation."[17]

As with any aspect of Catholicism, these teachings do not exist in a vacuum; they are bound up with Catholic convictions about creation, natural law, the self-giving love of God and its reflection in humanity's makeup and calling, the sacraments, gender, sin, forgiveness, and salvation. Catholic sexual teachings also comprise more than a list of moral prohibitions: they seek to champion respect for the beauty of the human body and the power of sexuality; they insist upon the dignity of every person, realized in community; they aim to celebrate committed, fruitful love; and they highlight the role of conscience, discernment, and the cultivation of virtue in Catholics' moral lives.[18]

For many, including many who seek to affirm what is valuable and true in the Catholic moral tradition, key facets of recent church statements concerning sexual diversity have nonetheless evoked disagreement, consternation, anger, and pain.[19] Drawing particular criticism has been the church's language of order and disorder, inherited from the natural law tradition, according to which any sexual desire or practice that does not reflect what are understood to be the maritally bounded purposes of sexuality is deemed intrinsically "disordered."[20] This language, alongside other passages in church documents, has been interpreted by some to imply that bullying and violence are the sad but inevitable result of LGBTQ persons publicly claiming their sexual identities; to endorse discriminatory laws and legal practices in areas like adoption, marriage, and employment; and, in general, to perpetuate what some term "heterosexism," a form of oppression in which heterosexuality is treated as the sole acceptable norm and nonheterosexuals are relegated to the status of deficient persons and second-class citizens.[21] In each of these areas, church leaders have striven to distinguish the content and limits of their teachings from distorted, partial, false, or malicious readings, most recently making special efforts to allay misunderstandings about the documents' use of the language of "objective moral disorder."[22] But historically tight connections between traditional notions of "objective moral disorder" and the traditional categories of "sins against nature" or "unnatural vices"—plus most people's understandable inability to make sense of a teaching that judges someone's sexual self-understanding, desires, and practices to be morally disordered but purports not to condemn the person per se—continue to insure that, while Catholic teaching speaks of all sexual sin as "disordered," certain (nonheterosexual) desires and behaviors are deemed more uniquely and objectively disordered than others.

Method of Approach

Many of the contributors to this book raise questions about aspects of the church's official teachings on sexuality, but, like the Catholic community as a whole, they take a range of views about how that teaching ought to be received or practiced in twenty-first-century circumstances. Some readers may find our authors' questioning of elements of current moral teaching inimical to the obedience to the magisterium that Catholicism requires. To the contrary, we respectfully suggest, this project's aim is precisely to honor the Christian's (and, thus, Catholic's) call to moral discipleship by pursuing "obedience" in its most robust sense. Confronted with church moral teachings, Catholics are called to obey neither blindly nor as automata, but to respond in the root sense of that term, *obedire*, which in Latin means to listen to (*ob audire*), or to heed, and to act on what is true and valuable in what one has heard. For Catholics, *obedire* accords a special place to the moral wisdom of the tradition reflected in episcopal teachings. But the active work of obedient listening does not end when the final page of the *Catechism* has been read. Because their faith teaches that God's Spirit and truth may manifest themselves in myriad ways beyond their church's visible boundaries, Catholics are also obliged to listen for and respond to what is authentically true and good, wherever it may be found. Pope Benedict XVI underscored that Christians' devotion to love in truth (*caritas in veritate*) entails precisely this habit of attentive, capacious, and responsive listening—again, *obedire*—especially to the voices of the vulnerable and marginalized. Benedict writes, "If in my life I fail completely to heed others, solely out of a desire to be 'devout' and to perform my 'religious duties,' then my relationship with God will also grow arid. It becomes merely 'proper,' but loveless."[23]

Refusing either to ignore, dilute, or reject the Catholic tradition on one hand, or to marginalize, reject, or dismiss the experiences and insights of LGBTQ persons and their heterosexual allies on the other, the essays in this volume collectively aspire to tap into the richness of Catholicism, to address points of struggle and disagreement, and to contribute to its vitality and growth. They do so in the knowledge that while Catholic teaching and moral theology value continuity with the past, adhering to the Gospel in changing times and varied cultures has also required the Catholic moral tradition to continue to learn, to adapt, and to develop. Over the course of church history, this story—a story of adaptation in order to better maintain continuity with the Gospel—is clearly reflected in Catholic moral teachings on such matters as slavery, usury, and the status of women.[24] Closer to the present, official documents on the pastoral care of "homosexual persons" issued by Vatican dicasteries and national bishops' conferences over the past few decades evidence small shifts, for instance, toward the (usually tacit) recognition that sexual orientation is largely innate, rather than chosen out of sin or sickness.[25] Some of our authors emphasize and take heart from subtle changes of this kind, which they see as the fruits of an evolving dialogue between some church leaders and Catholics, both heterosexual and LGBTQ, who are striving to honor and preserve perennial Christian affirmations about sex while also incorporating the new knowledge and wisdom that comes from science and the experiences and testimony of people who care about living their lives with integrity and virtue. Some authors emphasize instead the perdurance and permanence of the Catholic Church's teachings about sexual diversity and describe their own encounters with those continuities as moments of grace in some cases, danger and discouragement in others.[26]

We do not pretend to know definitively whether such lived tensions and conflicts of interpretation can be resolved, and we do not know how, over time, official Catholic teachings will continue to evolve. Our aim, instead, has been to capture the voices of those who find themselves living with, without, or despite the teachings of their church in the face of their own experiences of sexual diversity and who are seeking to discover ways in which these teachings and other sources of knowledge and authority might fruitfully inform faithful everyday living. Accordingly, this volume's method is neither doctrinaire nor dialectical: it neither presumes a unified position nor assumes that there are only two possible points of view. This approach will likely dissatisfy those who are convinced that Catholic traditions about and teachings on sexuality, sexual virtue, and the path to sexual wholeness are uniformly valueless—if not in fact toxic—for LGBTQ people. It will also perplex those who are certain that listening attentively to the experiences and conscientious reflections of those who identify as or with LGBTQ persons can in no way help and will likely harm the Catholic Church and its mission. Against both of these sets of objections, we point to impulses that run deep in Catholics' blood and bones: a conviction that all of material reality reflects God, an aversion to stark either-or choices, and a devotion to a God of Love and Truth that impels attention to, reflection on, and reverence for authentic love and truth wherever they are encountered.

This collection's focus aligns with a strong emphasis in contemporary Catholic teaching and thought on *experience*[27] and *practice*[28] as loci for theological reflection. That being said, the questions that these essays pose are rather different from those that one might expect to find in formal theological treatises or works of moral theology.[29] By narrating their stories and opening windows into their lives, our authors ask us to consider how it is possible to receive and live out traditional Catholic teachings when many testify to having discovered things about sexuality that traditional formulations could not have taken into account. Given Catholicism's natural law–based conviction that careful attention to reality can reveal God's designs and intentions for human flourishing, what happens when data of contemporary experience come into tension or conflict with inherited Catholic formulations about sexual truth and wholeness? Further, how do persons of good will communicate with one another when even the words we use to describe our subject matter and experiences—"LGBTQ" or "homosexual," "sexual orientation" or "same-sex attraction," "the gay agenda" or "pro-queer lives"—so often appear to place us on or against a particular ideological "side"? How can respectful dialogue about these matters within the Catholic community avoid being short-circuited by prejudgments against our interlocutors' deeply held convictions or sincere questions concerning sexuality and concerning treasured faith commitments? Such questions animated the conferences from which these essays have sprung. Indeed, they are questions that cannot help but be raised by people who, like our authors, care about and have been touched by these matters, in many cases painfully or traumatically so. God willing, they are questions that will continue to be pursued by all those haunted by the sense that when the power, beauty, potentials, and challenges of sexuality and the power, beauty, potentials, and challenges of Catholic faith and practice are consigned to separate, hermetically sealed worlds, everyone is the poorer.

The Essays

With two exceptions, the essays that follow are revised and expanded versions of presentations delivered at the four More than a Monologue conferences.[30] The more than forty speakers who participated in those gatherings brought with them their experiences of service in academic institutions and seminaries, Catholic, Protestant, and secular; in lay and ordained ministry in the Catholic Church and other Christian denominations; in Catholic religious life; in formal and informal advocacy for LGBTQ persons and groups; in journalism; and as present and former members of Catholic parish communities. There was not room for every speaker to be represented in this book or its companion volume, and not every speaker wished to contribute. Still, we think the writings collected here are broadly representative of a spectrum of Catholic and post-Catholic experiences and points of view concerning sexual diversity. Some contributors write at length about the value for them of church teachings on sexuality and about their commitment to living out those teachings in their own lives; others witness to what for them is the pain and destruction those same teachings have produced and, in some cases, discuss their decisions to leave Catholicism as a result. A number of contributors do not address church teachings at all or do so only obliquely; they reflect instead on the ethical values and cultural heritage that Catholicism represents for them.

In selecting essays for this volume, our primary objective has been to provide readers a snapshot of the conversation about sexual diversity among contemporary American Roman Catholics, their family members, friends, and lay and ordained ministers. Inevitably, there will be groups and individuals who will not find themselves represented in the picture these pages yield. But we hope that the voices collected here suggest some of the breadth and complexity of U.S. Catholics' experiences of and engagements with sexual diversity.

Arranging our essays was a challenging task, in part because reading them *in toto* reveals so many intriguing commonalities and thematic connections. In the end, one overarching impression provided an organizing principle. In varying ways, each essayist locates her or his reflections in careful attention to how contexts and ways of experiencing and speaking about sexual diversity are embodied in and shaped by particular *practices*— familial, interpersonal, professional, ecclesial, cultural, political. Together, the voices gathered here offer readers a multiply located effort to model and to shape practices of ecclesial listening and dialogue about Catholic faith and sexual diversity.

To highlight the crucial importance of listening as a practice and the importance of cultivating deeper listening "as church" that will inform better practices of "being church" in varied contexts, we offer our authors' contributions in four sections. Neither airtight nor mutually exclusive, these areas bespeak four threads that draw together the book as a whole and some essays in particular.[31]

Part I, "Practicing Love," introduces the voices of singles, families, couples, parents, and children who reflect on their experiences of sexual diversity in light of their experiences of Catholicism and of Catholics.

Part II, "Practicing Church: Listening to Voices in Pastoral Ministry," offers the perspectives of clergy and lay ministers, including those of a Roman Catholic bishop and of an Episcopal priest who has served as an ecumenical chaplain at a large public university. Their contributions cast light on what pastoral workers, Catholic and otherwise, encounter as they walk with people who grapple with issues of faith and sexuality and on how such encounters, in turn, shape those pastoral ministers and their theologies of sexuality and ministry.

In Part III, "Practicing Education: Listening to the Voices of Students and Teachers," three writers discuss their encounters with sexual diversity both inside the classroom, on either side of the proverbial desk, and outside the classroom, in the lives, loves, and struggles of LGBTQ college students.

Part IV, "Practicing Belonging: Voices Within, Beyond, and Contesting Ecclesial Borders," spotlights contributions by authors who have struggled with their identities and place within and around the Catholic community. Authors describe their experiences of living in a range of relationships with the Catholic Church and the Catholic tradition. Like the book's contributors as a whole, a majority of these writers describe themselves as Catholics, but for many, practicing church belonging leads them down unconventional, angular, or discomfiting paths. These essays limn several of those paths: some describe crafting new ways of ecclesial belonging; others report painful experiences of marginalization or exclusion; yet others, finding it impossible to reconcile their sexual identities and convictions with Catholic religious identity, recount considering or deciding to leave the Catholic Church.

Theological analysis continues in a brief afterword, where Bradford Hinze, an ecclesiologist, and Tom Beaudoin, a practical theologian, reflect on what has been voiced and heard in the essays as a whole.

Listening for Truth: Catholic Education's Mission at the "Heart" and "Frontiers" of the Church

This publication project had its genesis in a collaboration among four institutions of higher education, two of them Jesuit universities. Before concluding, therefore, it seems appropriate to step back momentarily to view the work of this volume through the lens of education. As theologians who have personally benefited from long associations with Jesuit institutions and who are deeply committed to Ignatian traditions of pedagogy, critical enquiry, and work for justice, we find it most fitting that institutions sponsored by the Society of Jesus have, through their participation in the More than a Monologue conference series that provided the basis for this volume, created space for respectful, honest conversations about sexual diversity in and around the Catholic Church.

Jesuit education aims to cultivate "depth of thought and imagination" for understanding holistically and discerning wisely God's desires and intentions for creation and humanity, as Jesuit Superior General Adolfo Nicolás has recently observed. It "encompasses and integrates intellectual rigor with reflection on the experiences of reality together with the creative imagination, to work toward constructing a more humane, just, sustainable, and faith-filled world. The experience of reality includes the broken world . . . waiting for healing. With this depth of thought and imagination, we are also able to recognize God as already at work in our world."[32] Jesuits take it as their mission to serve at the heart of the church, yet at the same time they have always been sent to work on the frontiers, where the Christian community engages culture and the critical issues of the day. In this spirit, the Association of Jesuit Colleges and Universities has noted, Jesuit institutions promote dialogue between people of different beliefs and values and "seek to bring the gospel which inspires us to our culture, to evangelize and learn from it, and to live with the tensions inherent in walking on the edges of these frontier situations."[33] Most recently, Pope Francis has underscored the Jesuits' mission to be "builders of bridges, not walls" and to make the hallmarks of their ministries "dialogue," "discernment," and faithful presence at the "frontiers."[34] To live and work in this paradoxical space—simultaneously at the heart and on the frontiers—requires a kind of courage and fortitude that continually asks what it means to promote a reality-affirming love and seeks to put this *caritas in veritate* into practice.

We hope that *Voices of Our Times* will contribute to a fuller understanding of what Catholics see as the God-given embodied humanity of all human persons. As befits its very human and complex subject matter, this collection remains in many ways preliminary, limited, and imperfectly representative. But if attending to its assembled voices leads readers to experience moments of surprise, enlightenment, or challenge, then groundwork will have been laid for the conversation to continue. Should this book, further, yield wisps of fresh perspective on how Catholic faith and sexuality may be more wholesomely integrated or on how an ancient tradition can better engage and honor the actual lives of all of God's children, our mutual time and energy will have been spent blessedly, and well.

Part I: Practicing Love

Listening to Singles, Families, Couples, Parents, Children

In this opening section, we hear first from Deb Word, a mother of two sons who has opened her family home to more than a dozen LGBTQ youths who have been abandoned by their families of origin. She writes movingly of the perspective on family and faith that she has gained not only through her interactions with these teenagers and young adults but also through her relationship with one of her own sons, who struggled for years with Catholic teachings before coming out as a gay man. Word describes the efforts that she and other Catholic parents of LGBTQ children have undertaken to draw the attention of church leaders and communities to the experiences, identities, and humanity of their loved ones. Like the writers of the other three essays in this section, Word points to the ways in which experiences of love in sexual diversity often lead people to firmer understandings of themselves, their families, and their intimate relationships.

Eve Tushnet, a young, single woman, next recounts how, as an undergraduate, she came to a decision to live in accordance with the Catholic Church's teachings on homosexuality. She reflects on the "hidden treasure" in Catholicism's spirituality of celibacy, its theology of friendship, and its notion of vocation. She emphasizes that the commitment to celibacy to which the Catholic Church calls its LGBTQ (and other) members is not easy and ought neither to be undertaken lightly nor as a form of rule following. Yet, Tushnet argues, celibacy can offer new ways of expressing one's love for others and for God.

Janet F. Peck and Carol A. Conklin, two of the plaintiffs in the *Kerrigan v. Commissioner of Public Health* court decision that permitted same-sex marriage in the state of Connecticut, tell the story of their "thirty-three-year-long dream to marry." They describe the significance that marriage has held for them both before and after their wedding in January 2009. Conklin, in particular, writes about her upbringing in an observant Irish Catholic household, her family's reaction to her coming out as lesbian, and the lengthy journey to acceptance that her father undertook.

Finally, Hilary Howes, a public relations professional and transgender activist, describes how she came to accept that her birth gender was not her authentic gender. She also narrates her conversion to Catholicism in mid-life, in part inspired by the faith and love of her wife. Howes observes that while transgender Catholics are not as explicitly rejected by the church as are lesbian, gay, and bisexual Catholics, the absence of formal church policies on transgender individuals often renders them even more invisible.

1 This Catholic Mom: Our Family Outreach

DEB WORD

Fortunate Families and the Memphis
Gay and Lesbian Community Center

I consider myself to be a typical Catholic mom and grandmother. Thirty-nine years ago, I married my college sweetheart, Steve, and together we raised two sons. Our faith is important to us: I am a product of twelve years of Catholic education, and four years after we married, my husband became Catholic. As a family, we have always been active in the church. My husband and I have served as ushers, lectors, and extraordinary ministers of Holy Communion, as well as on parish pastoral and financial councils. Our sons participated in activities at church as well as at school. So, in addition to our own ministries, my husband and I were involved with our sons' sports teams and Boy Scout troops and supported them in band and theater. We were typical, busy, Catholic parents—who gradually began to realize that our older son was gay.

By the time Chris was into his late teens, we assumed that he was gay. His brother, Shawn, collected *Playboy* magazines and hid them under his mattress. Chris bought *Men's Health*. While Shawn said girls were "hot," Chris said they were sweet. Chris went to every school dance with a different girl; Shawn was terrified of girls. Mothers eventually figure these things out.

As I began to realize that I had a gay son, I looked carefully at church teaching about same-gender attraction. Because of what I learned, I began to compartmentalize the church and God. I was sure that Chris was loved by God just as much as was Shawn. I prayed that both of my boys would find someone who would love and cherish them, someone to grow old with them. At church, this was obviously not something I heard was possible, at least for Chris.

For the first time, I began to figure out that I needed to trust God in ways my church does not.

Having a gay son did not so much challenge my faith as it made me learn to trust God. There is that quiet spirit, that quiet voice inside, that tells you when to trust your gut. I spent a lot of time in prayer and reading, and my gut told me that Chris is made in God's image and is who he should be.

As Chris grew up, Steve and I waited for our son to come out to us. We did not know exactly what to say to encourage him. We mentioned his friends who we thought were gay, in what we thought was a positive tone. He told me later that when we spoke about others who were gay, he only heard "different"—and he did not want to be different. He did not want to be gay. We stopped asking about girls and made our language gender-neutral: Met anyone lately? How is your love life?

One night at the end of Christmas break, a few years out of college, Chris sweated through a few hours getting up his courage to tell me something. He sat at the end of my bed, obviously nervous. His dad was snoring peacefully, and I was waiting impatiently for him to say whatever he needed to say so that I could go to sleep as well.

"Mom, you're always asking about my love life. Well, I've found someone," he began tentatively.

"What's his name?" I asked.

"Mom, you knew?"

"Honey, you didn't?" There were hugs and tears. I assured Chris that I would tell his dad and added, "But honey, he knows. We are okay with this. We love you."

That relationship did not last long. Though Chris was now out to a few people, his boyfriend was not out at all. This caused friction in their relationship and ultimately the end of it. The relationship was important enough for Chris, however, that he opened up to us and shared his feelings with us. I will be forever grateful for it because of that.

Some years later, we took a family vacation in the Gulf of Mexico. Five of us, Shawn and his wife, Carrie, Chris, his father and I, held on to one another's rafts as we floated peacefully on the water. I said, "I think this must be what heaven is like."

Chris answered quietly, "Except, I won't be there with you."

"Son, where do you get this stuff?"

He smiled, "Mom, it's your club; you know the rules." Later that afternoon, I asked him if this was why he had not come out to us sooner. "Yeah, Mom," he answered. "I had to deal with the going-to-hell stuff first."

Chris attends church with us when he visits. However, he says that a homily preached in his senior year of college that lumped together "the gay lifestyle, abortion, and murder" has made it too uncomfortable, and even too dangerous, to attend Mass in his little Southern college town. He told me, "It's not worth the pain or anxiety, Mom. I know I am safe in your church, but I don't trust them at home." He says that he still feels Catholic, but I do not know if he will ever again practice Catholicism.

Some days I wonder why I stay in a "club" that my child says is dangerous to his soul. The question becomes more insistent when members of the Catholic hierarchy make ridiculous statements, like that of Cardinal Timothy Dolan, who said, in an interview about New York's marriage equality law, "We'll be booed if we don't hire these people."[1] Cardinal Francis George of Chicago even compared the gay liberation movement to the Ku Klux Klan.[2] I might find it humorous that my church seems to be playing the victim if I did not know the harm such statements cause. Every time someone in authority speaks ill of our gay children, that person gives more ammunition to those who would do them emotional or physical harm. It is unfortunate that our bishops have that kind of power. And I absolutely hate it that our kids do not feel welcome.

I know that I could worship in another church. But the Catholic Church is part of my birthright. I am Catholic like I am an Italian-Irish-German American. Besides, if those of us in the pews who have "skin in the game" all leave, who will help our brothers the bishops learn and grow? Our stories, our families' stories, are important. They put a face on the social justice teachings of the church and remind others that justice means making sure that all families have access to the rights we take for granted in our heterosexual ones.

Because of my abiding commitment to the Catholic Church, I joined a ministry called Fortunate Families, of which I am now a board member. This wonderful group was founded by Casey and Mary Ellen Lopata, who are also parents of a gay son. They felt that they needed to do more than was possible within the confines of a diocesan ministry, though our group actively seeks dialogue with parish priests and bishops. We also reach out to Catholic parents across the country through our network of "Listening Parents." We listen to parents who are on the edge and to parents whose children are.

Our network includes parents whose children have attempted or who have perished through suicide. Tom, a board member of Fortunate Families, is one such parent. He blames his own pontificating at the dinner table, repeating what he knew of church teaching, for his son's suicide attempt. After that attempt, Tom, a Catholic father, was able to communicate to his son that he was as God had made him and assured him that he was a wonderful young man. The experience turned Tom into an advocate.

Another former board member was able to dance at her son's wedding a few years ago. She was able to share his joy in having found a soulmate in his partner. But the experience was bittersweet for her because the wedding was not recognized by the church. She has struggled to minister in a Catholic context and finds it hard to remain a practicing Catholic. She is an advocate who has become weary.

The Fortunate Families board members are Catholic parents who are all old enough to remember life before Vatican II. We realize that when the unchangeable makes no sense, it somehow changes. For example, my non-Catholic grandmother, who later converted, could not be married *inside* the church building. She was married in the rectory instead. Years later, she was told she could be excommunicated if she attended her son's wedding ceremony, which took place in a Methodist church. We all remember "meat eaters' hell" and women who were counseled to "go home and be nicer" to their physically abusive husbands. Things change in our church, slowly. But things do change, and so we have hope. If Chris's generation is not to see a change in the church's stance toward homosexuality, then maybe my grandchildren will. We believe that our children, whether gay or straight, bisexual or transgender, who are in loving relationships are happy, healthy, giving, and caring people.

In addition to Fortunate Families, I am involved in a diocesan ministry begun in 2005 by Bishop J. Terry Steib of Memphis. The Catholic Ministry to Gay and Lesbian Persons has over fifty members who gather monthly for prayer, dinner, and a program. In addition, we sponsor an annual day of reflection. We are very active in community outreach. A few years ago, we participated for the first time in Memphis Pride, our local LGBT Pride celebration. We hugged folks who identified themselves to us as "recovering Catholics" and members of "Catholics Anonymous." We invited them to come to the cathedral for Mass and a potluck. It was through Pride that

I learned that if you want to reach out and welcome the marginalized, you must go where they are.

My husband and I also work with LGBT youth in our local community. Our involvement with housing "discarded" gay youth happened acciden-tally. In the summer of 2009, about the same time I began my first term as a Fortunate Families board member, Steve and I stopped by the Mem-phis Gay and Lesbian Community Center (MGLCC) because we heard there were kids hanging out there who were hungry. As a food service professional, I had once been responsible for three thousand meals a day on a college campus: we knew we could help out a few hungry kids. As we soon found out, some of these children were homeless as well. Will Batts, the center's executive director, was the first to notice that the hungry kids who came were sometimes living—camping actually—in apartments with no utilities. One had lived under a bridge, and more than one had slept for a night or two on the deck of the center before the executive di-rector realized it.

Working through the MGLCC, our home became one of the first "safe house" locations in Memphis. My husband and I have had a dozen home-less gay youth as houseguests in the last few years. Some have come to stay with us several times. We still mentor many of them. Most of the gay youth we take in come from either extremely conservative religious back-grounds or terribly dysfunctional homes. Some have been on their own since the age of fifteen. There are no safe shelters for LGBT youth in the Memphis area. No one reaches out to them. By the time the kids get to us, they have exhausted their resources of family, friends, and cash. They usually come into our house humbled, embarrassed to ask help from a stranger, and hungry.

Our first guests were older than the usual MGLCC youth. They were a young lesbian couple with a four-year-old son. Both had worked until the economy had "downsized" them. They were eventually evicted and ended up living in their car. The shelters did not recognize them as a family, so they came to the MGLCC asking if they could stay in their parked car in the center's backyard. At the time, I was on a committee at the center that was trying to design a plan of action for dealing with the problem of home-less gay youth. Recruiting families who would open their homes as "safe houses" for a few weeks or months was part of that plan. We met the couple and invited them to stay with us for the three weeks they had requested.

We were able to help one of the mothers find a better job, and we enjoyed having their little boy in our house. My grandson was also four at the time, and I knew that if his family were in the same situation, I would want someone to help them. Both of the women had families in town. Neither was welcome at their house.

I will not pretend that offering my home as a safe house is an easy commitment. I live in one of the murder capitals of the United States. My younger son, who is a police officer, has cautioned me frequently about the foolishness of letting strangers into my home. I have an alarm system. I used to be fairly careful. Most of our friends have called us either crazy or saints. I don't like these titles. They allow the speaker to disown the problem. Why would you have to be crazy to do this? Why would you have to be a saint? We are neither. We meet the youth; we are empathetic. We have been through hard times when our families were our safety nets; we are just repaying the favor now. Some friends who support our work have at times offered us much needed help. Once, when we were housing two youths and my husband was between jobs, grocery cards appeared, as if by magic. When our guests need shoes for a job, someone offers them a pair. A friend who lives next door acts as the surrogate aunt for the kids who call us Mom and Pop. Despite the risks, we try to make this a family experience. Though the youth to whom we offer hospitality are not welcome in their birth families, we welcome them and include them in our own.

After our first guests and their son were able to move on, we continued to welcome others. One young man came to us after having been kicked out of the Navy. His mother had not known that he was gay or that he was leaving the military. When she dropped him off at the MGLCC, she told him she was leaving him at the gates of hell. We spent a lot of time with this particular young man, reminding him that God loves him. That was a hard sell, given he could not believe his own mother did.

Another guest of ours told us that his mother had thrown him out repeatedly while he was in high school. After aging out of the foster care system, he went to live with his grandmother. On the fourth day of his stay with her, he awoke to her pouring oil over him. She intended to "anoint the gay away." The next day, he was in our home.

One of the youth staying with us attempted suicide in our home. I spent thirty-six hours in the emergency room and intensive care unit, praying and begging God to let him live long enough to understand that he was loved. His parents came to town for a few hours, but we were the ones who visited him during the mandatory stay in a local mental health hospital. We were the ones who welcomed him back home. He survived, and he will always be a part of our lives. Though he had been separated from his family for several years, they are now back in each other's lives. Slowly, tentatively, they are rebuilding their emotional bonds. There is hope!

Financially, there is always a struggle to keep the doors of the Memphis Gay and Lesbian Community Center open. The food pantry is always available to those in need. A clothing closet provides daily wear and interview outfits. However, we are the only "safe" space within two hundred miles and are squarely in the buckle of the Bible Belt. Sometimes the need overwhelms our resources. I would love to see the center build a facility to house and counsel the youth who come to us, but that requires money we have yet to raise.

I sometimes complain that we are only putting bandages on gaping wounds. We work with kids who have been "discarded" or who have escaped violent homes. They need direction; they need shelter; mostly, they need somebody to love them. They think that if their parents cannot love them, then who can? God is an especially touchy subject: many have been told by preachers, family, and even society that they are damned. Why would you work to build a morally productive life if you believed that about yourself? But whenever I start my "Band-Aid" complaint, our executive director reminds me that these youth are still alive and that they all know that someone cares enough to help them stay warm and to keep them from starving. We will not let one of them be left alone in a hospital room. They know that we care, and this buys them time—time to realize that they are indeed lovable.

My work with the MGLCC youth is not part of my diocesan ministry outreach. I was told by a priest at the beginning of our involvement to be sure not to represent it as such. But for me, my work with MGLCC comes from my formation in Catholic social teaching. We house youth who have no place to go, no one to turn to. This is work we should be doing as church, but instead it is done through the MGLCC. The center feeds the hungry, clothes the naked, welcomes the stranger, and houses the homeless. Matthew's Gospel does not tell us to do this for everyone except the gay kids. The Gospel does not permit us to deny hospitality to anyone.

I am therefore always amazed when a Catholic bishop labels us as *activists*, not Christians. It is as if being an activist is a bad thing. We speak for those who have no voice, or at least not one that will be listened to. How is this a bad thing? How is this opposed to the teachings of Jesus?

When our bishops make silly statements, speak mean-spiritedly of our children, or deny one of them communion, I write letters. I share our stories. I ask them to reach out in love. I wrote one such letter to an archbishop who had denied the Eucharist to a group that he knew by their rainbow pins and sashes to be "activists." I turned part of that letter into a postcard and sent it to all the active bishops in the United States. Another Catholic group took up the message of the postcard campaign as part of their Advent Action. They called on all parishioners to wear rainbow ribbons that year, in solidarity with their LGBT brothers and sisters in the pews. What I wrote, and what they supported, was this:

Dear Bishop,

I wear a rainbow because . . .

I believe that the rainbow is a symbol of a promise from God.

I believe we are all God's children, and have an inheritance in that promise. I believe that wearing it reminds those who would deny my child a place at God's table that they don't own the guest list. I believe that wearing it gives hope to a gay youngster that there are adults who can love him/her. I believe that wearing it gives parents an open door to talk to me about their gay children, and that leads to affirmed and healthy children. I believe that it starts the conversation with those who are ignorant of the struggles of gay folk.

So, if you see me in your communion line with a rainbow cross, or pin, or peace sign, I would hope you realize that wearing the pin is my way of reaching out to the marginalized, and reminding them that they are welcome, loved. When I serve as extraordinary minister of the Eucharist, I wear it to remind me not to judge anyone who comes forward, but instead to share with them the table of the Lord.

There is still much work to be done. I have slowed down this past year in order to receive treatment for ovarian cancer. My treatment and recovery has not stopped us from housing youth or from speaking out. It has just slowed me down a little. This is important work: my church hierarchy is saying things that hurt the youth I love and am trying to help. As long as I am able, I will challenge those who think that our children are anything less than God's children, made in God's image, and loved by their creator. We don't look forward to housing more youth, and I would love for our safe house program to become obsolete, but I'm afraid there will always be one more kid looking for a new Mom and Pop to welcome him or her.

O Tell Me the Truth About Love

EVE TUSHNET

http://www.patheos.com/blogs/evetushnet/

I came out when I was about thirteen. When I was twenty, I entered the Catholic Church. Those seven years were pretty interesting—but the years after my conversion have been even wilder and woollier, as I've slowly figured out how much I didn't know about, among other things, the possibilities for a gay life that is faithful to Catholic teaching.

I suspect one reason it was relatively easy for me to become Catholic is that I had led, up to that point, a semicharmed life. I was a very weird kid who went to schools where bullying wasn't tolerated. My parents were progressive but not pushovers; they had gay friends and listened with only the necessary amount of world-weary bemusement when I said I thought I was "in love" with my high-school girlfriend. I had been basically quite comfortable being queer. In queer communities I'd found friends, solidarity, and a corrective to my intense self-centeredness. All of this allowed me to come to the Catholic Church with relatively little baggage.

I became Catholic as the result of a religious quest prompted by my first real encounter with devout Christians. They guided me out of my various misconceptions about the meaning of "original sin" and about the church's attitude toward the body. I began to suspect, darkly, that there was something wrong with me: I was experiencing new, unexpected, and unwanted attractions to a strange woman, the Bride of Christ.

As my attraction to the church grew, some stumbling blocks remained, including, unsurprisingly, the teachings on human sexuality and especially homosexuality. I asked my friends to explain this to me, and they made some valiant if unconvincing attempts. I asked a priest—and I always tell this story, but I should note that the priest in question is a terrific guy who showed me immense patience and care—who explained that lesbian sex was "like trying to turn a doorknob wrapped in barbed wire." (How did he *know*?) This also, as you can imagine, didn't really convince me. But I knew that I had to be Catholic. I asked myself which I believed *more* strongly: that gay sex was morally neutral or that the Catholic Church had the authority to teach me about human sexuality. To my surprise, I was more certain of the second thing. So I became Catholic despite not really understanding the reasons behind the church's teaching. I still go back and forth on how persuasive I find those reasons. I'll read certain explanations that make a lot of sense to me (Christopher C. Roberts's recent *Creation and Covenant: The Significance of Sexual Difference in the Moral Theology of Marriage*[1] is quite good, for example) yet that leave me with unanswered questions. But overall, what matters most to me is being able to receive the Eucharist. I don't think any individual Catholic fully understands the reasoning behind every difficult church teaching, so I'm willing to live in the state St. Anselm called "faith seeking understanding."

Still, when I look back on my conversion, what leaps out at me is how little I knew! I didn't know *anyone* who was queer and celibate for religious reasons. I didn't know anyone who identified as anywhere on the LGBT spectrum who nonetheless accepted the teachings of the church. What made me think I could do it when I didn't know—or even know *of*—anyone else? Well, obviously my deep humility was a big plus here!

No, what I mean is that I had the insouciant self-possession of the privileged undergraduate, and fortunately that kind of idiocy can carry you through some of the storms of life. "God looks out for fools, children, and Americans," as they say. I would be chaste because I'm super-awesome, the church is super-awesome, and together we would make the ultimate Marvel team-up!

Thank God we don't stay in the church for the same reasons, or with the same mindset, that we enter it. I've now met many Catholics who identify as gay, queer, or same-sex attracted (I use all of those terms for myself, depending on context) and who accept the church's teaching on chastity. There are far more of us than you'd think! And we often have to fight for recognition, not only outside the church, but within it. I've been very lucky, but friends have stories of reaching out for support only to be told—by well-meaning straight people in Catholic ministry—either to "just stop thinking of yourself as 'gay'" or (to men) "just find a nice boyfriend! It's not a big deal, you should be happy!" Neither of these responses actually gives what was asked for or what was needed.

In the years since my conversion, I've learned more about the trials celibacy brings. Many people struggle with loneliness, the question of how to deal with crushes, and sometimes jealousy, as friends get married or move toward marriage. There's anger at the church or at God, and there is the terrible destruction caused by spiritual pride, a self-righteousness born of the belief that what gay people are called to do is somehow much harder than what anyone else is called to. For me personally, the hardest aspect of celibacy has been the lack of accountability: Living by myself, it was easy to feel as though nobody knew what I was up to except God—and maybe sometimes God would blink? I've tried to address that issue by working with a spiritual director and by being much more honest with my friends than I'd like to be, talking more plainly with them about my difficulties.

There are few obvious resources for queer Catholics seeking fidelity to the Catholic Church. The book I've related to most on these topics is actually by a Protestant, Wesley Hill's *Washed and Waiting: Reflections on Christian Faithfulness and Homosexuality*.[2] There's also David Morrison's *Beyond Gay*[3] and Melinda Selmys's *Sexual Authenticity: An Intimate Reflection on Homosexuality and Catholicism*,[4] which are flawed but which many people have found valuable. (Morrison's explication of the "theology of the body" may not resonate with all readers, and Selmys tends to overgeneralize from her own experience. Both authors can at times portray gay communities and gay experience as negative in a way that may alienate readers whose experiences, like my own, were more positive. However, we are not so surfeited with good books on this topic that good or interesting books can be ignored because they aren't perfect. Selmys also writes a blog at http://sexualauthenticity.blogspot.com that reflects her more recent and in my opinion more nuanced thinking on these subjects.) Most of the rest of what I've read can be summed up by a friend's exasperated comment, seeing yet another book cover: "Oh God, not the bandaged heart!" Too many books on homosexuality and Christianity treat gay people as damaged goods, rely on a painfully presumptuous secular psychology, or present a merely negative picture of chastity in which it can seem like the whole point of devotion to God is not having sex.

When it comes to community, too, Catholics aren't where we need to be. In most U.S. dioceses, if there's a ministry for LGBT/SSA Catholics at all, it is either Courage—which has done good for many people but which is much too cozy with the ex-gay movement and the psychological under-pinnings of that movement—or a gay and lesbian ministry that dissents from church teaching either openly or covertly. I've been immensely lucky, yet again, that the gay and lesbian ministry at my own church falls into neither of these categories. It attempts to support people wherever they are in their journey and has many members who accept church teaching as well as many who don't.

But beyond the resources offered directly to gay Catholics, there's so much hidden treasure in the church. I've learned so much more, since I converted, about the spiritual resources the Catholic Church offers to Her queer/LGBT members. We have a rich spirituality of celibacy, a beautiful theology of friendship, and a startling history—dating back to the first days of the "Uranian" movement, which ultimately became today's gay culture—of queer converts. Frederick S. Roden's fascinating *Same-Sex Desire in Victorian Religious Culture* gives a quite sensitive queer-theory read-ing of these conversions, exploring the ways in which the incarnational, sensual, and stigmatized or marginalized nature of the Catholic faith was especially powerful for people whose identities were shaped in part by shame and longing.[5] I've learned a lot from reading articles on celibacy in journals aimed at men and women in religious life, since those journals tend to focus on developing a healthy and adult sexuality within celibacy. A friend of mine pointed out that although when we hear the term "heal-ing" used with reference to homosexuality, we often think in "ex-gay" terms, a loving and grown-up celibacy *also* requires healing. I look to St. Aelred of Rievaulx's terrific, uncompromising *Spiritual Friendship*,[6] which it seems every generation of queer Catholics must rediscover. Aelred speaks to everyone, and our entire culture would greatly benefit from a renewal of devoted friendship. However, the context of devoted, chaste same-sex love in which Aelred develops his theology makes him perhaps especially intriguing and challenging for gay people. Aelred's vision of friendship as an arena of love and sacrifice in which friends are deeply, startlingly honest and vulnerable with one another has been a huge help to me personally in learning to get past my temptations to hide my faults and struggles.

Catholic tradition offers intensely vivid prayers like the Anima Christi, with its imagery of the Word Incarnate, which can offer healing for people who have felt shame or stigma because of their responses to physicality.

The tradition offers saints like Joan of Arc for times when the actions of the church hierarchy seem like a counterwitness to the Gospel. And in our tradition we can pray as well for the intercession of Oscar Wilde. (He came home to the church late, but he did come home.)

Perhaps most importantly, I've reframed my questions. I no longer think of myself as trying to understand the reasons for the church's teaching (even though I still read about that and gnaw on the theology now and then) or even trying to live chastely. I think of myself primarily as trying to discern and live out my vocation.

I think of a vocation as the form in which you are called by God to pour out your love for God and for those around you. This vocation can take the obvious forms of marriage or religious life, but it can also take many forms that aren't as easily recognized or acknowledged in our society. A gay man may be called to love another man chastely—that man may indeed be part of his vocation, part of the way God is calling him to fill the world with love and beauty. Or we may be called to serve those in need: For those of us without the obligations of partner and children, there's a radical freedom along with our radical vulnerability. When I was living alone, I was able to take in pregnant or homeless women who needed somewhere to stay for a night, a brief respite from the storm. I could do this more or less on a whim, reacting with a flexibility that few spouses or children could embrace without resentment. Celibate people are made available to love others through hospitality and through service. Our vocations may include caring for aging parents, teaching children, or ascetic practices that focus our love directly on God. I expect that for most queer/LGBT Catholics, deep friendship will be a major part of our vocations.

This reunderstanding has allowed me to see celibacy not as a regrettable necessity, not as a concession to the rules, not even as an end in itself, but as a tool I can use in my vocation. I don't view my celibacy as a vocation in itself but as something that frees me up to serve others. More importantly, a vocation is always a positive call to love, not a negative call to refrain from some way of expressing that love. So reunderstanding the task of LGBT Catholics as a task of vocational discernment helps us focus on what we can and *should* do, the love we are being called to bring into the world, rather than on what we can't. I often say that sublimation is the opposite of repression: I think I do sublimate my attractions to women into friendship, service to women in need, and writing. That isn't to say

I'm sexually attracted to my women friends or to the women whose poverty and loneliness I try to alleviate. (Or to my words!) But these chaste forms of love do become ways of expressing my love for women and my need for what the 1970s lesbian-feminists called "women's energies."

A couple of years ago I received a poignant e-mail from a man who said, among other things, that he did accept the church's teaching and was trying to live up to it. But he still wondered: What happens if I change my mind? What happens if, years from now, I look back on my celibate life—will I regret it? Will it seem like an enormous waste?

I think it depends. If one's celibacy is purely rule following, then yes, once you no longer believe the rules I think probably you'll regret the sacrifices you made to follow them.

But if you pour out your love for others in friendship and service, if you offer your struggles and your need for surrender as a sacrifice to Christ, if you love God and those around you as deeply as you can in the best way you understand right now—I think even if you change your mind later, that won't be something to regret. One of the most important truths about love is that it's never a waste of time.

3 Our Thirty-Three-Year-Long Dream to Marry

JANET PECK AND CAROL CONKLIN

Plaintiffs in Kerrigan v. Commissioner of Public Health

Janet Peck writes:

Thirty-seven years ago, Carol and I fell in love and began to share our lives together. For thirty-three of those years, we dreamed of getting married but were denied that civil and human right.

That changed on October 10, 2008, when the Connecticut Supreme Court ruled in *Kerrigan v. Commissioner of Public Health* that same-sex couples had to be allowed to marry in our home state. Carol and I were one of the plaintiff couples in that lawsuit. We were represented by Gay and Lesbian Advocates and Defenders, a legal rights organization working for the rights of the gay, lesbian, bisexual, and transgender community in the New England states. As plaintiffs, we were asking for and were granted the right to a civil marriage—the right to be married in the eyes of society and the law.

When a couple decides to get married, they first go to a town hall to apply for a marriage license. Then, actually to get married, they can have either a civil ceremony presided over by a justice of the peace or other legal agent or a religious ceremony presided over by a member of the clergy. In the United States, clergy are empowered by the state to act as legal agents in the signing of a marriage license. Without that legal signature, authorized by the state, a religious ceremony would not be legal. When a couple gets married in a civil ceremony, it is called a civil marriage, although that term is not used in everyday language. Regardless of their choice of ceremony, the couple's marriage license is issued by the state.

In seeking to marry, Carol and I were not asking to be granted a special right. We were asking to be included in a civil right that already exists. Neither were we asking for a different or lesser status, such as a civil union. Our life together has always reflected what a marriage is supposed to be: a relationship of mutual fidelity, love, commitment, and responsibility. We have always felt married in our hearts. We were simply asking for the legal and social recognition of that truth.

As plaintiffs, we were not asking for the right to be married in any religious community, although there are religious denominations that support our right to marry, and there are clergy who would willingly and joyfully sign a marriage license for a same-sex couple. Religious communities are free to marry or not marry whomever they choose. We have no argument with that. To us, that's what freedom of religion means. However, to us, freedom of religion also means that no religious denomination should be able to decide who can obtain a civil marriage or who can be married by a faith community that wishes to marry same-sex couples.

Three months after the *Kerrigan* decision, on January 24, 2009, after thirty-three years in a deeply loving and committed relationship, Carol and I were finally married in front of all our family and friends. It was truly a dream come true for us and one of the happiest days of our lives.

People have asked us why marriage was so important to us. Carol and I wanted to marry for the same reasons everyone else does—because we love each other, and that's what you do when you share the kind of love and commitment Carol and I have. We wanted to pledge our love and commitment to each other in the presence of our family and friends. We wanted to give each other publicly the greatest gift a person can give—the ultimate expression of love and commitment. In cultures around the world, this bond is called marriage. No other word or status carries the same meaning to us or to anyone else.

———————

Like most people, Carol and I learned a lot about marriage from our parents; in fact, it was our parents who taught us the true meaning of marriage. Carol's parents were married for fifty-one years when her mom died of breast cancer. They taught us that marriage is forever.

Unfortunately, my mother died when I was very young. I was four years old when she died, and I really don't have memory of her. But I have an old 16mm film taken on my parents' wedding day that shows my mother smiling at my father in a way that never fails to touch my heart and bring tears to my eyes. It shows my dad looking happier than I remember him ever being. It's as if my mother left me a message on this film, showing me how important it is to bond in this very special way with the person you love.

Carol is that person for me. She is the love of my life and, without question, the person I was meant to marry. I know I have the same love for Carol that I saw between my parents in that old film. I wanted to follow in their footsteps by getting married.

Family members have told me of my father's love and devotion to my mother as he took care of her through a very long and difficult illness. Knowing this, and having had our own experiences of supporting each other through illness and struggles over the years, the words "in sickness and in health, 'til death do us part" had tremendous personal meaning to us as we recited these words as part of our wedding vows.

For us, as for most people, marriage is not just the glue that holds two people together; it's the glue that connects entire families, generation after generation. Before we were able to be married, Carol and I lived outside of that special family bond. For thirty-three years, Carol and I watched as many friends and family members got married. We were always happy for them but sad that we could not get married ourselves. Being excluded from the possibility of marriage set us apart from everyone else and made our relationship feel less than or not as good as everyone else's.

Now that we are married, we are a part of rather than separate from everyone else. We no longer live outside of that special family bonding called marriage, and we feel connected to the generations of family that have come before us. I now feel that I have carried out the message from my mother in that old film. I feel connected to her in a way I had not felt before.

At this point in our lives, although we still carry many of the values taught by the religious denominations of our upbringing, Carol and I do not belong to any faith community. I was raised an Episcopalian, and Carol was born into a very religious Irish Catholic family. One reason we do not practice a religious faith is the negative messages that many religious denominations have preached about homosexuality and, over the last decade in particular, against marriage for same-sex couples. It is very difficult to remain part of a church where you are not supported for who you are and where your relationship is condemned.

Because of this, we did not have a religious ceremony when we married, instead opting to be married in a civil ceremony. But that does not mean that our wedding held any less meaning for us. Honoring and celebrating our love and commitment to each other through marriage in the presence of our family and friends had tremendous personal meaning to us, just as it does to everyone else who marries. We wear our wedding bands proudly and with the utmost respect for what they represent to ourselves and to everyone else. I believe that in every way, our marriage reflects what a marriage is supposed to be and honors its tradition.

Although the most important reason Carol and I married was because we love each other and wanted to honor and celebrate that love in the way that is recognized throughout the world, as we got older we realized we also needed the rights and protections of marriage.

This became painfully clear to us about fifteen years ago, when I began to have health issues and required a number of surgeries and medical treatments. Before one surgery to remove a tumor from my head, as I was being wheeled to the pre-op room, I was told that Carol could not accompany me because the room was too crowded on that particular morning. However, when I got into the pre-op room, I saw that everyone else had someone standing by their gurney. Although I can't be sure, I assumed other patients were allowed to have their spouses with them and that Carol could not be with me because we were not married. This was the first surgery I had ever had, and I was frightened beyond words. If Carol had been able to be with me, she would have calmed me, and I would not have felt so frightened and alone.

The next year I was in the hospital again, this time to remove tumors from my liver. This was life-threatening, major surgery, and Carol had promised that she would be in my room in intensive care when I got out of recovery.

Unfortunately, she was not—she was out in the hallway fighting with the staff nurse to get into my room. When the nurse asked Carol who she was, Carol said she was my partner. Because the word *partner* has so many meanings, the nurse asked Carol what the word partner meant. Carol told her that we lived together, we loved each other, we were lesbians—all of which is kind of personal information to have to divulge in a hospital corridor. But as it turned out, it really didn't matter what Carol said; the nurse insisted that only family members were allowed into intensive care, and Carol was not family. At the time, we had been together over twenty years. Just imagine how that might feel. The person you love most in the world has just gone through major surgery, and you can't get into his or her room.

Carol then pulled out and showed the nurse the copy of the Power of Attorney that we thought would protect us during these times. But after taking a look at it, the nurse said that although the Power of Attorney did say that Carol could make decisions on my behalf, it still didn't prove that she was family. If we had been married, all Carol would have had to say was that she was my wife or my spouse, and she would automatically have been allowed into my room—with no more questions and no proof required.

Carol describes this experience as one of the most frustrating and upsetting moments in her life.

Before another surgery, I was asked to name my next of kin. I named Carol, but when I identified her as my partner, I was told I had to name a legal or blood relative, since Carol was neither. If I had died in surgery, the hospital would not have been able to release my remains to Carol, and she would not have had any legal authority to sign for organ donations or to make funeral arrangements. The Power of Attorney would not help: Power of Attorney ends at death.

It was our deep love and commitment to each other—along with these and many other experiences—that led us to become plaintiffs in the *Kerrigan* case.

All of these experiences would be different now that we are married. I have had some additional minor surgeries since our marriage. It has been a big relief to be able to identify Carol as my wife. No one has asked what that meant. The word *marriage* has power and confers status in a way that no other relationship does. Being married brings us peace of mind and has given us a sense of security that we lacked before—at least in Connecticut and in the thirteen other states, plus Washington, D.C., that allow same-sex couples to marry.

Even though we are married in the same way everyone else is married, until recently, Carol and I and other married same-sex couples were denied access to the federal benefits that are automatically granted to different-sexed couples when they marry. This was because of the Defense of Marriage Act (DOMA), a bill enacted by Congress in 1996 that defined marriage under federal law as being only between one man and one woman and that required the word *spouse* to be used only to refer to opposite-sex husbands and wives.

There are over one thousand rights and protections attached to marriage on a federal level that Carol and I and other same-sex couples were denied because of DOMA. For example, because we were married under the laws of the state of Connecticut, we filed our state income taxes as a married couple but had to file our federal taxes as single individuals. Not only did this feel insulting to us and our marriage, it made the paperwork more cumbersome and expensive, and we paid more in taxes than we would have if we had filed as married. Before we were married, neither of us could carry the other on our employers' health insurance policies, at considerable expense to us. Since I am now Carol's spouse, she is able to carry me on her health insurance, yet still, under DOMA, the cost of my premium was added to her income, and she had to pay federal taxes on that amount. The health insurance premium is not taxed for a married different-sexed couple. Also, under DOMA we did not have access to each other's Social Security benefits, and we would not have had access to our investment accounts in the same way as a married different-sexed couple.

Fortunately, this changed recently when, by a five-to-four decision in the 2013 case *United States v. Windsor*, the U.S. Supreme Court struck down the portion of DOMA that precluded married same-sex couples from receiving the federal benefits of marriage. Carol and I and other same-sex couples are now equal under the laws of our federal government and are now entitled to the benefits and protections of marriage on a federal level. What a wonderful moment in this nation's history and in the lives of legally married same-sex couples! We are no longer second-class citizens.

Carol and I happened to be home together on the day that the decision was announced. We were sitting together, holding hands in front of the TV with my laptop set to the Supreme Court's website, when the ruling came down. When it was announced that the Supreme Court had ruled that Section 3 of DOMA was unconstitutional, Carol and I looked at each other and cried. We had always believed that DOMA was discriminatory and went against this country's promise to treat everyone equally under the law, but to have the Supreme Court affirm that was incredible. As I began reading the words of the decision to Carol, the tears were streaming down our faces. We have always felt proud that the state of Connecticut, the state where we both were born and have lived our entire lives, ruled in our favor in *Kerrigan*. We were thrilled that after thirty-three years together we were able to marry in our home state, but that joy was tempered because the federal government did not recognize our marriage. Now, after being together for thirty-seven years and married for four, we are thrilled that our marriage is now also recognized as equal in the eyes of the federal government.

Unfortunately, this ruling did not in any way create marriage equality throughout the nation, and we feel for the many same-sex couples who do not have the freedom to marry in their home states. At this time, it is unclear how the federal government will treat legally married same-sex couples who have wed in a marriage equality state but who reside in an anti–marriage equality state. In other words, if Carol and I decide to move to an anti–marriage equality state, we may lose the federal rights and protections we have just won.

If you are a different-sexed couple, and you get married in any state in this country, your marriage is automatically recognized in every other state in the country. If we travel to an anti–marriage equality state, our marriage license still means nothing and does not afford us the rights and protections it carries. This puts us at risk when we travel, something we will soon be doing extensively in our retirement years. We should not have to worry about this as we travel in this country. We should be able to travel freely, free of the worry of what might happen to us if our marriage is not recognized and respected. It is our hope that the decision in *Windsor* will set the stage for same-sex couples to win the freedom to marry in all states. It is only then that we and our relationships will have the true equality and the dignity and respect that we deserve.

Whether or not the federal government or other states recognize our marriage, I think if most people came to our home, they would leave thinking we were a happily married couple. I don't think our lives look much different than most couples who are married. We pay our bills, pay our taxes, and do upkeep on our home. Our lives are pretty ordinary, maybe even a bit boring to some people. We are happy in our careers. Carol works as an electrician for the state of Connecticut, and I am a professional counselor with a private practice doing individual, marital, and couples counseling. In our free time we hike, bike, kayak, camp, and visit with family and friends. For thirty-seven years, we have supported each other through the ups and downs of life, and our love and commitment to each other have remained strong, even in a world that has not always recognized it or supported it.

Early on in our relationship Carol and I came out in all aspects of our lives, in our families, our social circles, and our workplaces, because we wanted people to see that we are just as human and that our relationship is just as loving and committed as everyone else's.

I came out to my family soon after I began my relationship with Carol, and I was very fortunate that my family was and continues to be very supportive. Although my father died many years ago, he accepted and supported our relationship and would have been happy to witness our marriage. My other family members added to the tears and smiles on our wedding day. Even my eldest brother, who became a Mormon as a young adult, supported my right to marry. He and members of his family attended my wedding, even though his church has been one of the most vocal opponents of our freedom to marry. My brother realizes that his religious beliefs should never infringe on anyone else's religious belief or practice or deny any one their civil rights. My brother knows that my relationship with Carol should be treated equally under the law. He also recognizes our love and devotion to each other. He recognizes that what we have is a marriage, even though his church actively fights against this truth.

Being born and raised into a Catholic family made Carol's coming out, especially to her father, a very different experience. The following story, told in Carol's words, describes her family's experience on this journey.

I was raised in an Irish Catholic family. My father's sister, my Aunt Mary, Sister Margaret Mary, was a nun; my father's brother, my uncle Bill, was a priest. My parents had eight children. My Dad went to Mass almost every day of his life.

Most of my brothers and sisters and I went to Catholic schools, and we were encouraged to be involved in the church. It was expected when we got older that we would marry.

When Janet and I were first together, my father was transferred to the state of Florida for work. Just before my parents moved, my Dad found out that I was lesbian. He didn't talk to me for about six years after that. That was a very difficult time for me. He would come up for business trips and visit my brother but would not call me. When I talked to my mother about it, she would say that he was just too busy, but he wasn't too busy to play golf and go out to dinner with my brother. When I went to Florida to visit, he was very distant.

After about six years of this, my mother and father came up for a visit, and we were invited to my brother's home to have dinner with him and his family. When I asked my mom if they were staying at my brother's, she said they hadn't been invited, so I invited them to come stay with us. That seemed to break the ice with my dad. After that they always stayed with us on visits, and in turn we would go down to their winter home in Florida and their summer home in North Carolina to visit with them. Over time, I think my father began to see that we were good and caring people. I think he began to see that who we were and what we shared together was something different than what his church had taught him.

Janet and I had a party for our twentieth anniversary, and I wanted to invite my parents. Although by this time it had long been clear to my parents that I was a lesbian, that I was not going to change, and that Janet was my partner, I had never come out to them in so many words. Even after all this time, I was nervous coming out to them and worried about their reaction. I was relieved and happy when they responded positively and agreed to come and participate in our anniversary celebration. Having this conversation lifted a huge weight off my shoulders. I did not invite my Aunt Mary, the nun, because I wasn't sure how she'd take it. But my parents invited her, and she also attended.

Just before the party, my mom and dad sat us down and said that they loved us both very much and would do anything for us. But, they told us, because of the church, they couldn't condone our relationship. I was happy that they came to the party and said that they loved us, but disappointed that they still could not get beyond their religious beliefs and fully accept our relationship.

A few years after that, my mother had developed breast cancer and was dying. I knew she didn't want to be in the hospital and would rather be home, so my eldest sister and Janet and I went down to Florida to take care of her. Knowing that he wasn't able to take care of her by himself any longer, it made my father very happy that, thanks to our care, he was able to have my mother home with him when she died. I know that he appreciated that we were able to do this for him.

After my mother died, my father chose to live in North Carolina full-time. After one of our visits, we realized that my father should not be living alone. So my sister and I talked with him about whom he would want to be near to or live with. We gave him the choice to either live in Florida, where most of my siblings lived, or to come to live with us. He decided to come live with Janet and me.

That was when I realized that my father had come a long way in his acceptance of me and my relationship with Janet.

Soon after my father came to live with us, we became plaintiffs in the *Kerrigan* case, and I told my dad about it. I was unsure how he'd react, but when I told him, he said, "Good luck. I think you should be able to get married because you have the same kind of relationship that your mother and I had." His only regret was that we would not be able to marry in the church. My only regret was that neither my mom nor my dad lived long enough to attend our wedding.

It meant a great deal to me that my father was able to come to a place of acceptance of me and my relationship with Janet. Janet and I were able to share some really wonderful times with my dad before he died. His acceptance of us was a great gift, and the time we had with him was very, very special. I think, had he lived, he would have been proud and happy on our wedding day.

I think my father, in his journey to acceptance and his support for our desire to marry, is a good example of how someone who is so involved in a church that actively preaches against marriage equality can come to see that what we and other same-sex couples share and are talking about is simply love.

The church was a big support for my father all of his life, but on this issue, I think it failed both him and me.

Carol and I agree that a positive aspect of most faith communities is their ability to bring families together. But in Carol's case, Catholic doctrine separated her from her father for many years. Although Carol's father eventually came to a place of acceptance, it took many years—years that were painful for Carol and for him.

In my private practice as a professional counselor, I have seen families come together when their gay or lesbian family member announces their intent to marry. In some of these families, the gay or lesbian family member had never previously spoken to their family about their sexual orientation for fear of rejection. For many of these persons, announcing their intent to marry changed the discussion: they were no longer talking about their sexual orientation but were announcing to family and friends their love and commitment to another.

Everyone understands what someone means when they announce their intent to marry. Everyone understands that marriage is a special bond between two people who love each other. My brother realized this, even though his church fights actively against marriage for same-sex couples. And, over time, Carol's father also realized that what Carol and I had was something different than what he had been taught by the Catholic Church. He realized that we have what he and Carol's mother had—a marriage.

Being married has filled us with incredible joy and has connected us to an energy greater than ourselves. Although our marriage is still not fully recognized, many of the wounds of the past have begun to heal, and the love that we have always held in our hearts feels complete and is at peace.

4 Mother, Father, Brother, Sister, Husband, and Wife

HILARY HOWES

The Center for Lesbian and Gay Studies in Religion and Ministry, Transgender Roundtable, Pacific School of Religion

Blessed by our Creator with male genitalia and a female brain, I struggled to relate to a society that saw me as male until I transitioned to live as a woman. I share a birth year with Disneyland, so for my fortieth we—my wife, daughter, and I—planned a family trip there, with a special treat for me: I could dress as a woman the whole time. I had been cross-dressing in private since childhood, on occasions with a support group during the previous three years, and in the year before the trip I started adding feminine touches to my male wardrobe. During that year, I had been trying to avoid transition by seeing if just expressing my feminine side while maintaining my male identity could work for me. I'm six feet tall, and I had always doubted that anyone would accept me as a woman. In a far-off vacationland, we wouldn't have to worry about rejection from anyone we would ever have to see again. My lifelong fears of rejection and shame, as well as my family's concerns about the social awkwardness of our all-female family unit, gradually dissolved as absolutely none of our fears came to pass. I had a wonderful time with my family, relating to them and to the world as a woman for the first time. Disneyland really became "the happiest place on earth" that week as I came to understand that it wasn't about "enjoying feminine things" for me. I was a woman, treated with dignity and acceptance by virtually everyone, and it felt so right.

On the drive home, the tears started to flow as we talked and came to believe that I would have to transition in real life, too. I struggled to understand how I could be a woman, a husband, and a father. It took the right therapist; good friends; the wisdom of children; the unconditional love of Mary, my wife; and ultimately just trusting in God to find our path. Now I do live as a woman, my marriage bond is strong, and I'm an honest, authentic parent—as well as the daughter my mother wanted after giving birth to two boys.

Integrating my mind and body was an authentic midlife transition that many who knew me supported and even called courageous, inspiring, and ethical. But in the eyes of the 99.9 percent of people who are blessed to have their gender and sex match, this uniquely personal act has been seen as a political statement, a psychological disorder, a character flaw, a weakness, a perversion, and a sin.

In the seventeen years since my transition I have become active in working for equality of people of all genders and have found that many in the LGBT community question my Catholic identity. Many seem to believe that being transgender and Catholic is incompatible. I believe that reconciliation is the mission of religion, so I have researched church policy on transgender people for the past two years. In the Catholic Church, as a transsexual woman, I don't officially exist. That is to say, the Catholic Church does not have an official, *public* policy with regard to the range of gender expression, but considering the church's policies on gay men, lesbian women, divorced women, women priests, and women who abort, perhaps I should count myself as lucky that this is the case.

But the unfortunate reality is that, like in most churches, the Catholic hierarchy defers to the most socially conservative views concerning sexuality in an effort to maintain its aging power structure. In contrast, in a recent survey, lay American Catholics, who have learned well that Jesus always cared for the marginalized, show overwhelming support for the protection of transgender people.[1]

The popular assumption is that, as a transsexual person, I can expect to be treated poorly by the institutional church hierarchy. Unfortunately, this assumption is borne out in recent news reports of a Vatican document secretly sent to bishops and by the pope's own words. As Jeff Israely reports in a 2008 *Time* article:

> Without actually using the word, Benedict took a subtle swipe at those who might undergo sex-change operations or otherwise attempt to alter their God-given gender. Defend "the nature of man against its manipulation," Benedict told the priests, bishops and cardinals gathered. . . . "The Church speaks of the human being as man and woman, and asks that this order is respected." The Pope again denounced the contemporary idea that gender is a malleable definition. That path, he said, leads to a "self-emancipation of man from creation and the Creator."[2]

Respecting the order of men and women is very important to an organization that is controlled solely by persons of one gender. Consider, however, that the Creator does make transsexual (mind/body incongruity) and intersexed (anatomic incongruity) people and that medical science can allow us to lead more normal lives alongside the 99.9 percent of people who have such trouble understanding these variations. Beyond anatomy, rigid gender stereotyping is important to a controlling patriarchy. For those who seek to maintain patriarchal power, accepting any transgender expression (cross-dressers, transvestites, drag queens and kings, and androgynous, bigendered, or gender-queer people) is unacceptable for organizational justification, not a question of morality.

So Why Am I Catholic?

I was raised with no religion and identified as an atheist or agnostic the entire time I was male. But over the course of my life, Catholic teaching and Catholic people have touched me deeply. As a design student, Jungian art therapy opened windows to my soul that I had shuttered in my attempts to be the man people expected me to be. Over time I came to understand how much Jung's lessons are supported by his understanding of Catholicism as a universal faith. Seeing every Bible character as an expression of the masculine and feminine in me helped me get past what some see as sexist or gender oppressive in those stories.

At the age of twenty-two, I married a thinking Catholic whose father had been a Jesuit seminarian for ten years and who had raised her with a well-reasoned faith. I came to see her as a conduit of God's unconditional love as we raised a child and, later, as she supported me through my gender change. Her strong grasp of the core principles of Catholic teaching, rather than superficial dogma, allowed us to remain faithful to God, ourselves, and each other through the mysterious and complicated spiritual journey of gender change.

That journey was broken open when, in 1994, I read *Healing the Shame That Binds You* by John Bradshaw. Bradshaw attended a Catholic seminary and has advanced degrees in theology, religion, and psychology. He writes about the concept of the false self that we create out of the shame and guilt we feel when we believe that our real self is unacceptable to society. This has resonance for many with addiction issues, but it is the elephant in the room for the gender-variant. Bradshaw's work provided me with a lens and a vocabulary that illumined and helped make sense of my experience. At a young age my effeminate nature was discouraged, so I learned to suppress anything that might be seen as feminine, like emotions. I did allow myself to express anger and tried to harden myself into what I believed would be acceptably masculine. Imagine examining everything you say or do to hide who you really are and to play a role constantly. Completely separated from your true self and true emotions, you slip into a functional depression that keeps you distanced from friends, family, and your true identity. In my case, once I had female hormones in my body, I discovered an access to emotions and spiritual awareness that was unimaginable when I lived a false-self life of a man. I've heard that some menopausal women credit hormone therapy for restoring their emotions, too. Bringing my mind, emotions, and public persona into alignment was the starting point for my spiritual growth.

During this new stage of my life, my wife and I have also discovered new and meaningful ways to be Catholic. In particular, five years after my transition (and after some spiritual searching), I was blessed to find a Catholic Intentional Eucharistic Community. This lay-organized but priest-led group features a shared homily during which people reflect on how they live the gospels in their daily lives. It was through this group that I was able to get past the false religiosity of some Catholics and truly appreciate the miracles of shared Eucharist. After three years of attending, I was baptized and confirmed as a Catholic woman, twenty-five years after marrying one. Five years later, during a retreat focused on Thomas Merton, his ideas about the false self came up: "In order to become oneself, one must die. That is to say, in order to become one's true self, the false self must die. . . . [This involves] a deepening of new life, a continuous rebirth, in which the exterior and superficial life of the ego-self is discarded like an old snakeskin and the mysterious, invisible self of the Spirit becomes more present and more active."[3] It was at that time I came out to my community as transgendered, explaining how my path of discarding the exterior and superficial life as a false man allowed my formerly invisible female true self to be reborn, present and ever deepening in my relationship to God. Making my life a parable about the spiritual path we all walk has enriched my community and others I speak to.

The Problem

But as real as these blessings have been, most Catholic transsexual persons experience the institutional church less as a blessing than as a stumbling block. The problem with a secret position on transgender people, such as the Roman Catholic Church seems to have, is that members of the church hierarchy are empowered to follow the most reactionary course in their words and deeds on the subject, without public justification, debate, or challenge. According to a 2003 Catholic News Service article, the

> Vatican's doctrinal congregation has sent church leaders a confidential document concluding that "sex-change" operations do not change a person's gender.
>
> Consequently the document instructs bishops never to alter the sex listed in parish baptismal records and says Catholics who have undergone "sex-change" procedures are not eligible to marry, be ordained to the priesthood or enter religious life, according to a source familiar with the text. . . .
>
> "The key point is that the (transsexual) surgical operation is so superficial and external that it does not change the personality. If the person was male, he remains male. If she was female, she remains female," said the source.[4]

Those familiar with transsexuals will see the irony of the "key point" since, in fact, the truth is the reverse. Transitioning allows us to share with society the gender personality that we have had from birth and to leave behind the false selves we developed to live as others expected us to live based on our external bodies. In the United States, a transsexual can have a surgical procedure only after an extensive psychological evaluation, much soul-searching, and living for at least two years in their perceived gender. The vast majority of transsexuals never have surgery because the cost (up to $50,000) is covered by only a handful of healthcare policies. Interestingly, surgery does not define one's gender for passports or many state drivers' licenses; rather, a doctor's psychological evaluation does. Still, the assertion that one's genitals are superficial could only have come from someone committed to celibacy.

Furthermore, focusing on surgery effectively negates the spiritual path that most transsexuals report their journey to be. Having had no religious upbringing, I used psychological terms to describe my progress toward my true self. But having lived for twelve years now in a community where we seek to follow Christ, I understand that this was always my path of transfiguration, of revealing my true self to my community. Hearing and saying the Nicene Creed each week, I came to understand that my path followed that of Christ, who, we would say, "suffered, died, and was buried." As a transgender person, I suffered alienation, died of shame, and was buried in guilt. Though transition, I rose again in accordance with God's will for me and am now leading a transfigured life.

Unfortunately, according to reliable reports, those armed with this confidential Vatican document regarding transsexual persons have expelled a music minister, a priest, a nun, a lay counselor, a college student, a parochial school student, and even a substitute teacher.[5] They have also torn families apart by teaching that transsexualism is a psychological disorder: parents are counseled to suppress transgender children and to reject transitioning adult children; transsexuals are forbidden the sacraments of marriage (that is, they are forbidden to marry anybody) and holy orders and are barred from religious life. Some bishops even wrote to Congress to oppose the Employment Non-Discrimination Act (ENDA), which would add gender identity to the list of protected classes in employment law.

The Possibility

It doesn't have to be this way. Our faith calls us to follow our consciences, accept mystery, and love one another without exception. Reaching out to my marginalized, extreme minority is not only possible but also enriches the faith communities who do so. Reconstructionist Judaism, Reform Judaism, and various Quaker groups openly allow transgender worshippers in their congregations. Certain Christian denominations, including the Presbyterian Church (USA), the Ecumenical Catholic Church, the United Church of Christ, the Metropolitan Community Church, and the Unitarian Church, openly accept transgender individuals. I hope that having no public Catholic policy in this rapidly evolving field may make it possible for the Catholic Church to avoid the kinds of mistakes it has made with the teachings concerning sexual orientation and contraception that have divided its members so deeply.

This year, I joined a group of transgender ministers and theology students to develop a curriculum for a school of religion. We were challenged to create our own mission statement and goals. We spent the first day discussing the background of our being called together, testing a workshop by two of our members on gender in a faith group setting, and getting to know one another. The next day we would need to do the "real work" of determining just what our organization was going to do. I went to sleep that night wondering what we could do that would be any different from the many programs of "radical inclusion" that ask churchgoers to accept the marginalized LGBT community. The next morning I awoke and dashed this off:

> The mission of the trans round table is to testify to the transfigurational power of spirituality and religion to nurture dignity for people of all genders.

It felt as though God had written through my hand, and I feared that I would have to fight to be sure the statement remained intact. I was frightened and felt unworthy. Very uncharacteristically, I knelt down and prayed first to be spared this task, then for the eloquence to do it.

When I read the statement to the group, everybody immediately supported it. Anyone who has done committee work of any kind will understand what a miracle this was. All of us, we discovered, believed that transgender people have a spiritual story, a story that, when shared, can help heal what is broken about gender for the church and what is broken about the church for queer people. By framing our mission and educational work in this way, transgender believers can choose to use the power of our powerlessness to build our faith communities from the margins.

While the Roman Catholic hierarchy has taken no public position concerning transsexual or transgendered persons, there is hope that ordinary Catholics will be accepting. A 2011 survey by the Public Religion Research Institute found that 93 percent of American Catholics believed that transgender people deserve the same legal rights and protections as other Americans.[6] Even the confidential Vatican document on transsexual persons, according to the Catholic News Service article I mentioned, accepts that life goes on for those who transition. It provides that:

> Priests who undergo a sex change may continue to exercise their ministry privately if it does not cause scandal. (This makes it abundantly

clear that the Vatican's real concern is not morality but being caught in their unsupportable exclusion of women from the priesthood.)

Surgery could be morally acceptable in certain extreme cases if a medical probability exists that it will "cure" the patient's internal turmoil. (Far from extreme, transition is the only medically approved treatment for people diagnosed as transsexual. Reassignment surgery can be the final step in the process that provides for a person's social integration and personal safety.)

Marriages in which one partner later transitions may be affirmed as valid. (Marriages like mine are affirmed by U.S. courts as well.)

I hope that Catholics would look at the body of scientific and medical evidence to develop a loving acceptance of those of us who are gender-variant. The intentional Eucharistic community I belong to has done this. My priest has noted how the unique perspective I have on gender issues that comes from seeing life from both sides now, and how my path to my true gender has parallels in the process of Ignatian discernment, which helps us understand God's desires for us.

I understand that my journey, though personal, touches what is universal about gender and change for everyone. Perhaps your notions of father, mother, brother, sister, husband, and wife will be opened a little by meeting someone who has been all of those at different times in her life. Maybe you can take it from someone who has been there that looking at everything in oppositional terms—"us and them," "black and white," "male or female"—is limiting and dangerous. Ultimately, welcoming the mystery of diversity in God's plan is a starting point for healing in our church, and it is that for which I most hope.

Part II: Practicing Church

Listening to Voices in Pastoral Ministry

The first essay here, contributed by Detroit bishop Thomas Gumbleton, illumines the world of the pre–Vatican II seminary and parish and describes the ways these contexts shaped and limited priests' pastoral approaches to questions of sexuality in general and homosexuality in particular. Shortly after Gumbleton was ordained a bishop in the late 1960s, his younger brother, who had been married to a woman for fifteen years, announced to his extended family that he was gay. This revelation, we learn, became the catalyst for a long familial and personal process that eventually led Gumbleton to new perspectives on church teaching concerning sexuality and transformed his ways of understanding, supporting, and accompanying gay and lesbian Catholics in their faith journeys.

Providing a seasoned voice from lay pastoral ministry, the sociologist and professor Sheila Nelson next describes her experiences with sexual diversity and the church as a Catholic lesbian woman living in the rural Midwest, as a teacher at a Catholic college, and as a lay leader who actively works to ensure the provision of pastoral outreach and care for Catholic LGBT persons and their families across the country. Echoing a number of the themes raised by Jeanine Viau's study of queer youth in Part III, Nelson's practically and spiritually focused reflection lifts up five challenges that must be overcome in order to uncover the God-given light—moving it "from closet to lampstand"—that LGBT Catholics bring to their communities of faith.

Turning to Catholic clergy, Donald Cozzens's essay portrays the multilayered and often painful difficulties faced by the many gay priests in active ministry who are charged with representing and upholding church teaching on sexual diversity while often finding themselves consigned to a complex form of closetedness that Cozzens likens to the recently rescinded military policy of "don't ask, don't tell." Cozzens shows how the "plight of gay clergy" influences current seminary training and priestly practice, with direct consequences for priests' lives, for those whom they are called to serve, and for the spiritual and moral well-being of the church.

To Cozzens's picture of clergy laboring under complicated codes of silence, the diocesan priest and moral theologian Bryan Massingale's contribution adds a critique—based on his own experiences as a university teacher, parish minister, and pastoral advocate—of the deleterious effects of what he calls "the pervasive climate of fear" and reactivity that surrounds even modest attempts at open conversation among Catholics about sexual diversity and the church. Massingale finds this climate of fear debilitating and dangerous, especially within a faith community charged by Jesus to "be not afraid." Left unaddressed, Massingale contends, this fear has wide-ranging effects that threaten the well-being not only of LGBT Catholics but of all Catholics and indeed the very mission and identity of the church.

Our final essay from the perspective of pastoral ministry comes from the Episcopalian priest Winnie Varghese, who shares what she has learned about sexual diversity and the church through her experiences of growing up as a lesbian Christian woman and, later, of ministering as an ordained priest. Invoking the ancient links between Christian prayer, belief, and practice, Varghese proposes that participating in the liturgical language of the Revised Book of Common Prayer has drawn LGBTQ Episcopalians and their fellow congregants to see better and to embrace more fully their dignity and worth in God's eyes and thus in their own eyes as well. Varghese acknowledges continuing struggles for the full recognition and participation of LGBTQ Christians in her own church as well as in the Roman Catholic Church. But she sees positive resources for moving forward in Catholics' and Episcopalians' shared commitment to honoring the truth as it is disclosed in human realities and as that truth is manifested and encountered in liturgy, especially in the community's celebration of the Eucharist.

5   A Call to Listen

The Church's Pastoral and Theological Response to Gays and Lesbians

THOMAS GUMBLETON

Retired Auxiliary Bishop, Detroit

Over the course of many years of pastoral experience, I have come to a deeper understanding of what is meant by the words recorded by Matthew as the conclusion of the Sermon on the Mount: "You must be perfect as your Father in heaven is perfect" (Mt 5:48).[1]

This is not a call to what is impossible. We are not expected to become "God." But just as God is fully and completely God in the fullness of what it means to be God, so each of us is called by God to be fully and completely the human person God has made us to be. Obviously, this does not happen at once. The original blessing of creation has been diminished, sometimes to what seems an almost unredeemable degree, by sin. Redemption takes a long process of being healed, of being loved into a new fullness of humanity, by the God who first loved us into existence, into life.

We have various sources of guidance to help us grow into full human persons as we live out our time on earth. God's Word in Scripture, and especially in Jesus, is the first source to which we look. The community of Jesus' disciples and its tradition is a second source. In addition, we have the insights of other human persons who have prayerfully and consistently pondered God's Word and who can share their insights in directing us. Finally, as the Second Vatican Council reminded us, we have the divine voice echoing in our own depth, within our own spirit as a law written by God in human hearts. This is the voice of personal conscience.

This essay springs from my deep conviction that persons, regardless of sexual orientation, can be "perfect" in the Gospel sense. Homosexual persons can be all God calls them to be as human beings, just as heterosexual persons can be fully human. There is extraordinary diversity in the ways that human creatures image God, in whose image and likeness they are created. Of course, regardless of sexual orientation, every person must struggle to reach as full a form of human development as possible, and in so doing each of us has the right and obligation to use the sources of guidance offered to all Christians. As each person does so, we Christians owe it to one another to respect each other's honesty and integrity in their journeys toward full humanity. And as we make our ways in response to the divine invitation to be "fully alive," I am confident that the loving God who made each of us and who knows each of us in the depths of our being will bring us to an ever fuller sense of peace, love, and life.

———————

My awareness of the spiritual needs of homosexual persons and my deepening involvement in ministry to homosexual persons began in 1992. In March of that year, I was invited, along with two other bishops, to speak at a national meeting of New Ways Ministry. The three of us were asked to serve as a panel of bishops offering a pastoral response to gay and lesbian persons in the church.

Prior to the meeting, each of us was contacted directly or indirectly by the papal nuncio, who suggested that we ought to withdraw from the program. However, after talking it over together, we decided that participating in the work of New Ways Ministry was an appropriate and important pastoral outreach. I am very grateful that I did attend that meeting, because it became a significant turning point in my own life.

Prior to my presentation at the New Ways gathering, I had thought very carefully about what I was going to say. In fact, I had two presentations prepared in my mind. One was a rather generic sort of presentation in which I would indicate how pleased I was to be there, how grateful I was for the invitation to speak, and how appropriate it seemed to me that bishops would engage in some fashion in this clearly identified ministry to the homosexual community within the Catholic Church. I would insist on the need for gay and lesbian persons' full inclusion in the church and on the need to eliminate all overt and subtle discrimination against homosexual people; I would emphasize how I as a bishop would be committed to this in my own personal attitude and actions and how I would work for this in every way possible. I hoped to leave my gay and lesbian listeners with the confidence that they would no longer have to hide their identities in order to be fully welcome in the church—that a new era was opening up in the Catholic Church.

The other presentation I had in mind would be much more personal. I would share my own story of confronting within myself a deep homophobia and working my way beyond it by having to deal with it, not in an academic or theoretical way, but personally, within my own immediate family. Still debating within myself as I walked to the podium, and not sure if I was ready to do it, I found myself saying to myself, "I'm going to do it. I am going to tell my own story."

It is obviously very hard for gay and lesbian people to come out. Though not totally comparable, it is also hard for many of us who are not gay or lesbian but who have in some cases a child, or in my case a brother, who is homosexual to acknowledge this publicly. I was hesitant, primarily because I was not sure how publicly acknowledging and affirming my brother would affect my own ministry or the public esteem accorded to bishops and their role in the church. Obviously, this concern reflected my own ignorance and even fear of homosexual persons. This attitude, often called homophobia, is very much present in our church and our society. But I did not want to be guided by ignorance or fear. That day, I chose, for the first time publicly, to tell my story.

I grew up in a very Catholic family, the sixth of ten children—eight boys and two girls. We grew up during the hard times of the Depression, through the Second World War and its aftermath. My parents were very faithful Catholics, and following their example, I went to parochial school and was very close to the church. At the age of fourteen I entered Sacred Heart Seminary to begin high school and continued through four years of college, followed by four more years studying at St. John's Seminary.

I took to seminary life very readily. I enjoyed it, I did well, and I was very much influenced by the kind of training I had there. But as I look back now, I realize how unprepared I was after my ordination in 1956 to be a pastoral minister to gay or lesbian people. I can remember hearing confessions for hours at a time as a young priest, in the very large parish where I was stationed in the 1950s. Periodically, men would come to confession who were gay, though I didn't know the term then—even the idea of sexual orientation was unknown to me. When they would confess committing sexual acts with other men, I remember how dogmatic and how decisive I was in telling these penitents that their behavior was wrong and that they would have to stop it. I thought I was giving them good advice by telling them to separate themselves from the places where it happened. In reality I had not even a minimum understanding of their situation. While I thought I was being pastoral and helpful, I was actually being totally insensitive and, in many cases, very hurtful to people who had come to me and to the church for help. I was in no position to give that help.

Much later, I read an interview with Andrew Sullivan, a gay Roman Catholic man, printed in *America* magazine in May 1993. One paragraph in particular made me realize how inadequate and even hurtful my efforts had been:

> I grew up with nothing. No one taught me anything except that this couldn't be mentioned. And as a result of the total lack of teaching, gay Catholics and gay people in general are in crisis. No wonder people's lives—many gay lives—are unhappy or distraught or in dysfunction, because there is no guidance at *all*. Here is a population within the church, and outside the church, desperately seeking spiritual health and values. And the church refuses to come to our aid, refuses to listen to this call.[2]

I was, I see now, so clearly a part of the church that "refuses to come to our aid, refuses to listen to this call."

As I look back, I can understand why. In my own Catholic family, you just did what the church said: follow the rules. And while one would hope that seminaries would educate priests-in-formation about sexuality, this was not the case. In fact, in these all-male institutions the training only intensified the homophobia with which I was raised. Several times each year during conferences with my spiritual director, there would be talk about "particular friendships." Only later did I realize we seminarians were being warned to be careful not to enter into a relationship with another student. We were warned against being seen too often with the same person, chatting in the corridor, or having someone in our room. Once in a while a student would leave suddenly. Years later, I could discern the reason. He was gay. But at the time it never dawned on me because no one ever spoke in open terms about sexuality, let alone homosexuality.

I learned how to be a priest out of that experience, ensconced in the narrowly Catholic cultural ghetto I grew up in and the closed seminary life and training that followed. There were, of course, positive aspects of that life and that training. But what should have been a major part of it was not there. For all practical purposes, we were given a thorough education in how to repress our sexuality in order to be faithful to our promise of celibacy. Questions of human intimacy and of healthy affectionate behavior were never raised. We were expected to cope with our sexuality on our own, as best we could. The goal was simply to avoid sin and eternal damnation. For the majority of priests, this resulted in serious personal and pastoral underdevelopment, which made it almost impossible for us to minister effectively, especially in guiding people, whether homosexual or heterosexual, toward fully accepting their sexuality and integrating it fruitfully into their persons and lives.

My younger brother, Dan, had also entered religious life and was in the Holy Cross seminary. As I look back I can see a pattern in his life that I didn't pay any attention to at the time. After a few years he was suddenly dropped from the seminary; there was no explanation, and he never said much about it to anybody. When I called the provincial of Dan's religious order to ask what had happened, he was evasive. I had a suspicion about why Dan was dropped, but I preferred not to explore further. The truth was, he was gay but did not want to admit it, even to himself. Later Dan married. He and his wife had four daughters and seemed to have a good relationship. Then, after they had been married for about fifteen years, he and his family moved to the West Coast, away from where he was known. The truth was, we later learned, Dan had been hiding who he really was, and his marriage really wasn't working out. In retrospect, it's clear that he had come to the point where he knew he had to be honest about his sexual identity. Eventually, when his older kids were in their early teens, his marriage broke up. Fortunately, he and his wife were able to separate amicably, and their children remained in a good relationship with both of them. Throughout that time, Dan and I continued to be in contact.

Then, in the mid-1980s, my brother sent a lengthy and detailed letter to my mother and to all of us siblings. That letter was his coming out, telling us he was gay, telling us his whole situation. By this time he was living with his partner in California and finally had a very humanly enriching life. He wrote that he had come to complete acceptance of himself as a gay man. He no longer had to deny or run away from his most basic identity. He was at peace within himself, and he knew he was loved by God, who, of course, had always known exactly who he was. He had learned how to integrate his sexuality into his life in a psychologically and spiritually healthy way.

When I received Dan's letter, however, my reaction was very negative. I am not happy with myself for reacting this way, but at the time the letter made me angry. I never read it. I threw aside my brother's most personal revelation. After being ordained a bishop in 1968 I had been much more in the public arena in the diocese and even beyond it. Part of my anger upon receiving my brother's letter was rooted in a selfish concern about myself. If my brother became known as a gay person, people in the church would wonder about me, too, and what would that mean? Could I be seen publicly with my brother? Would I have to shun him? Would negative judgments be made about my family? Would society's negative attitudes toward homosexual people be transferred onto me?

All this was more than I wanted to deal with. Even though I knew all of us had received the same letter, I never spoke to my mother or any of my siblings about it. The silence went on for about a year. It was finally broken, at least indirectly, when one of Dan's daughters was married. Some of us went to California for the wedding. We all acted very normally, and by our actions we, in a way, communicated that it was all right. We accepted Dan as he is.

After that, I presumed the whole family was at peace about Dan, but I was wrong. Our elderly mother was still having a very hard time. A life-long Catholic, she had understood that being homosexual meant you were a sinner and not able to be loved by God. She knew that she could accept Dan and that she would never stop loving him. But she nonetheless could not reject the church or what she thought was the church's teaching.

I discovered how much this conflict between her love for Dan and what she thought the church was teaching about him troubled my mother some time later, when she raised the question with me at the end of one of our weekly visits. As I was leaving, I stepped out of the front door, and she followed me. We chatted for a few minutes, and then she asked the question she had been struggling with: "Is Dan going to hell?" For her, someone who was gay was evil and was going to hell. I'm sure she could not be at peace with that question about her son on her mind.

Even though I had not dealt with the whole thing very well myself, by this point I had begun to explore my own feelings and had done much reading and reflection about homosexuality and church teaching. I knew that I had to answer her question truthfully. And I was ready. "No, of course not. God made Dan that way, and God won't put Dan in hell because he is a gay person. Dan didn't choose it. That's the way Dan is; that's who he is. God doesn't send us to hell because of who we are." I know that what I said was very consoling to my mother, but when I said it, it wasn't just to be consoling. I knew that what I said was the truth.

My mother's question opened my eyes to the pain and anguish that many, many good people continue to experience in the Roman Catholic Church and in other churches as well. This pain is caused by a narrow, negative attitude toward homosexual persons. For too long the church has allowed prejudiced judgments, expressed in a variety of negative descriptive words and discriminatory actions, to go unchecked. As a mother of a lesbian woman described it in a published letter about her daughter, the church offered her daughter "condemnation instead of compassion. She fears the judgment of most of those who love her because they have been 'programmed' to perceive her real identity as being perverted." This mother goes on to say, "My daughter is still honest, charitable, and loving and, I am certain, treasured by God who has always known her secret. I am filled with dismay that my church insists she is anything less, while it strives to convince others that she is a threat to society."[3]

I could experience my own mother's anguish in everything this other mother felt about her daughter. And I realized that, as a pastoral minister in the Catholic Church, I had to act to change this.

The New Ways Ministry national meeting offered the first opportunity. Before this meeting I had not been public about my experience. In fact, I had not spoken to anyone about it. I decided it was time to speak publicly, to say: I am a bishop, and I have a gay brother. He is still my brother, he is still part of our family, we fully accept him, and we believe God does also. As soon as I finished speaking, I realized how important it had been to do so: my talk seemed to have an immediate impact on all who heard it. Subsequently, what I said at the conference was written up in the *National Catholic Reporter*, and a journalist interviewed me and wrote a feature story for the *Detroit Free Press*'s widely distributed Sunday edition. As I told that journalist, far from being angry with my brother, I had come to admire him for the way he came to self-acceptance and to the realization of God's love for him. I also admired his courage in risking rejection in order to open the eyes of others. I was proud of him.

After telling my story publicly, a whole new area of ministry opened up for me. I have had the gift of being able to respond to many people who contact me from across the homosexual community, as well as their family members. Where Andrew Sullivan found nothing in the church, I hope I have been able offer some compassionate listening and some careful guidance.

For me, this has been an enlightening and enriching experience. I have heard from people who have gone through very hard times: gay people, lesbian people, parents, priests afraid to tell their bishop they are gay. They hadn't known where to turn but now felt they could share their stories with me. I have had opportunities to listen and offer understanding to an extraordinary number of people. I have been able to counsel many who were in much turmoil. And I have met many good people who, by their honesty and witness, have helped me understand even better. I have realized in new ways how important it is to reach out pastorally and to make the church a truly welcoming and inclusive community.

At the end of the U.S. bishops' pastoral letter "Always Our Children," we state:

> To our homosexual brothers and sisters we offer a concluding word. This message has been an outstretched hand to your parents and families inviting them to accept God's grace present in their lives and to trust in the unfailing mercy of Jesus our Lord. Now we stretch out our hands and invite you to do the same. We are called to become one body, one spirit in Christ. We need one another if we are to ". . . grow in every way into him who is the head, Christ, from whom the whole body, joined and held together by every supporting ligament, with the proper functioning of each part brings about the body's growth and builds itself up in love" (Eph 4:15–16).
>
> Though at times you may feel discouraged, hurt, or angry, do not walk away from your families, from the Christian community, from all those who love you. In you God's love is revealed. You are always our children.[4]

For us bishops and for all Christians, this genuine reaching out—inviting our homosexual brothers and sisters to journey with the whole community in shared awareness that God's love is revealed in all of us—is the first step in making our church a truly inclusive church.

Further steps are also suggested in this pastoral letter:

1. The teachings of the church make it clear that the fundamental human rights of homosexual persons must be defended and that everyone must strive to eliminate any forms of injustice, oppression, or violence against them.

2. It is not sufficient only to avoid unjust discrimination. Homosexual persons "must be accepted with respect, compassion and sensitivity" and must be nourished at many different levels within our communities.[5] This includes through friendship, which is a way of loving essential to healthy human development and one of the richest possible human experiences.

3. More than twenty years ago we bishops stated that "Homosexuals . . . should have an active role in the Christian community."[6] What does this mean in practice? It means that all homosexual persons have a right to be welcomed into the community, to hear the word of God, to contribute their gifts, and to receive pastoral care.

4. Nothing in the Bible or in Catholic teaching can be used to justify prejudicial or discriminatory attitudes and behaviors. We bishops reiterate here what we said in an earlier statement: We call on all Christians and citizens of good will to confront their own fears about homosexuality and to become proactive in denouncing and curbing the patterns of harassment and discrimination that gay and lesbian persons so often experience.[7]

However, we still need to do more. We need to face the reality that there is a basic incoherence in the church's teaching on homosexuality. This is brought out very poignantly by Andrew Sullivan in the interview cited above. He makes the point that, according to official church teaching, homosexuality has no "finality," that is, no God-given purpose. He puts it this way: "It is bizarre that something can occur naturally and have no natural end. I think it's a unique doctrine."[8] He goes on to note that the church concedes in the *Catechism* "that homosexuality is, so far as one can tell, an involuntary condition." It is an orientation, "and it is involuntary. Some people seem to be constitutively homosexual."[9]

The contradiction or incoherence within the teaching arises in its approach to the expression of the condition, when one acts on what he or she is constitutively as a human person. As Sullivan puts it:

> Yet the expression of this condition, which is involuntary and therefore sinless—because if it is involuntary, obviously no sin attaches—is always and everywhere sinful! Well, I could rack my brains for an analogy in any other Catholic doctrine that would come up with such a notion. . . .
>
> You see it even in the documents. The documents will say, on the one hand compassion, on the other hand objective disorder. A document that can come up with this phrase, "not unjust discrimination," is contorted because the church is going in two different directions at once with this doctrine. On the one hand, it is recognizing the humanity of the individual being; on the other, it is not letting that human being be fully human.[10]

The Catholic Church's teachings about moral questions regarding marriage and sexuality—questions of intimacy, of one person loving another— have undergone enrichment over the centuries. This has happened especially in modern times, as moral theology began to draw upon insights taken from the lived experiences of married men and women. An early example of church teaching on marriage, and specifically on the place of sex, is found in a directive from Pope Gregory I to Augustine, the first archbishop of Canterbury, in the beginning of the seventh century. "Since even the lawful intercourse of the wedded cannot take place without pleasure of the flesh, entrance into a sacred place shall be abstained from because the pleasure itself can by no means be without sin."[11] Such a directive clearly expresses a negative attitude toward sex in marriage and the pleasure to be found in married love. The church was officially teaching that it was sinful to enjoy and relish sexual love. According to Pope Gregory, the sexual enjoyment of married persons was sinful and thus precluded participation in the Eucharist!

Today, many people writing moral theology textbooks and treatises are lay people, many of whom are married, and many of whom are women. This development offers opportunities for new perspectives. In fact, Pope John Paul II gave us lyrical and beautiful writings about married life and married love, writings that thoroughly transcend what Pope Gregory said.

This is just one example of how we Catholics have evolved substantially in what we understand and teach to be morally good and morally healthy when it comes to sexuality.

What God really wants for each of us is that we become as fully human as possible and that we avoid those things that diminish us and make us less than fully human. In this perspective we realize the importance of integrating our sexuality into our development as persons. Each of us faces challenges in our efforts to integrate sexuality in the framework of our particular lives and callings. As a celibate person, I have had to discover the way I can be healthy psychologically and learn how to love other people, including having intimacy without physical sexual intimacy. I feel I am called to celibacy but that I have to struggle within that framework. Married people have to integrate their sexuality into their relationship with each other. Their coming together in sexual love must be a way of total giving to each other. It must be a way for them to express their total communion of life, a sacrament bringing the presence of God who is Love into their relationship. As married, single, and celibate persons grow in love, they grow into full humanity.

Gay and lesbian persons must struggle to learn how to love also. They too must learn how to integrate their sexuality into genuine intimacy with another person. We do know what God wants for all of us: God wills that each one of us becomes a fully human person, fully developed as a human person, and, therefore, a person who is at peace within oneself, one who develops the talents and skills that one is given. This will happen through and be expressed in our loving relationships. And for most people it will involve a special loving, nurturing relationship with another person.

From this it seems clear that the most important way to judge what is morally right or wrong in our actions is to discern what makes us more or less a fully flourishing, loving human person. This discernment is very important as we are drawn into sexual relationships, but it is also crucial in any human relationship in which we are trying to develop intimacy. What is morally right will always make us better persons. An early church axiom put it this way: "The glory of God is the human being fully alive."[12]

To deepen our understanding of homosexual love, we must listen to the experience of homosexual people as they struggle to become fully the person each is called to be. Just as moral theologians began to use the insights of married people in developing guidance for the living out of married love, so must moral theologians begin to draw from the experience of those who are called to integrate their homosexuality into their lives in a fully life-giving way. Once again I turn to Andrew Sullivan. His own experience is very enlightening and serves as a concrete example of what I am suggesting:

> Being gay is not about sex as such. Fundamentally, it's about one's core emotional identity. Fundamentally, it's about how one loves ultimately and how that can make one whole as a human being.
>
> The moral consequences, in my own life, of the refusal to allow myself to love another human being, were disastrous. They made me permanently frustrated and angry and bitter. It spilled into other areas of my life. Once that emotional blockage is removed, one's whole moral equilibrium can improve, just as a single person's moral equilibrium in a whole range of areas can improve with marriage, in many ways, because there is a kind of stability and security and rock upon which to build one's moral and emotional life. To deny this to gay people is not only incoherent and wrong from the Christian point of view. It is incredibly destructive of the moral quality of their lives in general.[13]

So, we must ask, does our church's moral guidance to gay and lesbian persons make sense? Does it make sense to teach people to avoid loving, intimate relationships when the result for so many is frustration, anger, and bitterness? That was what resulted for Andrew Sullivan, and it negatively affected his whole life, including his relationships with his family and friends. His experience in trying to live the way the church had taught him to live was not healthy; it was not life-giving.

Asked about the contradiction between trying to be Catholic and trying to be homosexual and active, Sullivan said:

> There is a basic contradiction. . . . I really do not believe that the love of one person for another and the commitment of one person to another, in the emotional construct which homosexuality dictates to us—I know in my heart of hearts that cannot be wrong. I know that there are many things within homosexual life that can be wrong—just as in heterosexual life they can be wrong. There are many things in my sexual and emotional life that I do not believe are spiritually pure, in any way. It [one's sexual and emotional life] is fraught with moral danger, but at its

deepest level it struck me as completely inconceivable—from my own moral experience, from a real honest attempt to understand that experience—that it was wrong.

. . . As soon as I allowed myself to love someone—all the constructs the Church had taught me about the inherent disorder seemed just so self-evidently wrong that I could no longer find it that problematic. Because my own moral sense was overwhelming, because I felt, through the experience of loving someone or being allowed to love someone, an enormous sense of the presence of God—for the first time in my life.[14]

In the Christian context, what Sullivan is saying echoes the First Letter of John: "God is love, and where there is love, there is God" (1 John 4:16). He is saying: "When I really allowed myself to love and be loved, for the first time in my life I deeply experienced the presence of God because God is love!"

But the really difficult problem for gay and lesbian people as they try to grow into full human persons is how to deal with the clear, present teaching of the church. In our letter "Always Our Children," the U.S. bishops teach:

First, it is God's plan that sexual intercourse occur only within marriage between a man and a woman. Second, every act of intercourse must be open to the possible creation of human life. Homosexual intercourse cannot fulfill these two conditions. Therefore, the Church teaches that homogenital behavior is objectively immoral, while making the important distinction between this behavior and a homosexual orientation, which is not immoral in itself. It is also important to recognize that neither a homosexual orientation, nor a heterosexual one, leads inevitably to sexual activity. One's total personhood is not reducible to sexual orientation or behavior.[15]

This is clear church teaching. But there is also within the Catholic tradition a fundamental moral teaching that comes before anything else. It is the teaching regarding "primacy of conscience." That is to say, each of us has the responsibility to form our conscience and make judgments as to what is life giving or not. That means that the judgment I make in my conscience is the final arbiter of what is right or wrong for me. This confers a heavy responsibility, one that some people would rather not take upon themselves.

The Second Vatican Council speaks of this teaching. The Pastoral Constitution on the Church in the Modern World (*Gaudium et Spes*), no. 16, describes one's conscience as the divine voice echoing in our own depths, within our own spirit, as a law written by God in human hearts. In other words, we have been given this sense of what is good and what is bad. So when we are trying to discern what is right or wrong in the depth of our hearts, we have to listen as deeply as we can to what God speaks in our hearts. We look within ourselves and try to determine what is our experience. We must reflect on this inner experience in the context of what has been revealed in Scripture. We must also consider Catholic tradition, which for two thousand years has reflected on the teaching of the Word of God; we must take into account our experience in prayer. Finally, we can discern what is right with the help of another person, a spiritual guide who can provide counsel and direction for us. On the basis of this discernment, we can come to a decision in conscience. A person must always obey the certain judgment of his or her own conscience. That decision is what we must act on, and that is what will make us grow spiritually and personally.

A clear example of the practical application of the primacy of conscience within the church is the moral question of the intent to use nuclear weapons. Catholic moral teaching from the Second Vatican Council has condemned their use without exception:

> With these truths in mind, this most holy Synod makes its own the condemnations of total war already pronounced by recent Popes, and issues the following declaration: Any act of war aimed indiscriminately at the destruction of entire cities or of extensive areas along with their population is a crime against God and humankind. It merits unequivocal and unhesitating condemnation.[16]

The teaching is very clear. Yet no Catholic on a Trident submarine, a Strategic Air Command plane, or based at a missile silo has ever been officially condemned for carrying out the United States' policy of deterrence, which includes the clear intent to use such weapons. No Catholic in the whole military chain of command who obeys this policy has ever, to my knowledge, been refused the Eucharist because he or she is a public sinner. In fact, these persons in the military are provided with Catholic chaplains who provide them the full ministry of the church. Obviously, what is happening in this situation is an acceptance that each person is exercising his or her right to make a decision in conscience, by which they are justified in acting contrary to the clear moral teaching of the church.

I am convinced that as our whole church struggles to understand sexuality's many facets, including the phenomenon of homosexuality, gay and lesbian people can be an important resource for us. As gay and lesbian Christians struggle within their own consciences to discern how to integrate their sexuality into their lives in the most humanly and spiritually enriching way possible, the Word of God, the tradition of the church, their own deep prayer life, and careful discernment with a director/spiritual guide are all available resources. As gay and lesbian Christians undertake their individual human journeys, the church needs to improve its pastoral ministry so that the alienation, hurt, and pain they have experienced will be eliminated, and our gay and lesbian brothers, sisters, sons, and daughters will know that they are fully welcome within our church communities. As we welcome one another, love one another, respect one another, and deeply listen to one another, we will come to be more manifestly the living presence of Jesus that his community of disciples is called to be.

Over the centuries a listening church was enriched by a deeper understanding of married sexual love. Is it not possible that our gay and lesbian brothers and sisters will enrich our church today with a deeper understanding of homosexual love? We can hope for the day when the Andrew Sullivans of our church will feel fully welcome and fully included in communities and ministries that recognize their gifts and are responsive to their needs.

6   From Closet to Lampstand

A Pastoral Call for Visibility

M. SHEILA NELSON

College of Saint Benedict / St. John's University

Christ's ministry was all about inclusivity. He left no one out of the circle and excluded no one from the banquet. But two thousand years later, we, the Body of Christ, often sound much like the Pharisees Jesus criticized—arguing about who belongs, whose lifestyle makes them worthy to approach the altar, who has a right to participate in the sacred. While our culture does not see closets as healthy places for people to live, many in the church still insist that when it comes to persons of certain sexual orientations, invisibility should be the rule, regardless of whether or not a person is sexually active. These voices promote the closet as a necessary safeguard—to protect the homosexually oriented individual from temptation but also to protect children and adults "lacking spiritual maturity"[1] from seeing that persons who identify as lesbian, gay, bisexual, or transgender (LGBT) are for the most part healthy, happy, grace-filled, contributing members of the community. *For God's sake* (so this line of thinking goes), *we need to prevent the impressionable from thinking that LGBT persons are normal!*

Thankfully, more and more of us are refusing to live in the closet, even if we occasionally find it necessary to hide out there. Still, most LGBT Catholics live in parishes and faith communities characterized by institutional closetedness. Our young people grow up in a religious world where questions of sexual orientation are largely ignored: sexual orientation is not talked about in any depth in most Catholic religious education and confirmation programs; except in a handful of welcoming parishes in a few major cities around the country, homosexually oriented persons are invisible and therefore, in the minds of most Catholics, nonexistent. That is why those of us involved in ministry to LGBT Catholics hear repeatedly from parents that when their son or daughter came out to them, they themselves went deep into the closet, fearful of letting anyone know the truth about their child. Yes, these parents feared for the child's safety and well-being, but they also feared for themselves, their reputations, and their ability to participate in and minister to their Catholic parishes, all of which this new realization seemed to threaten. Can a deacon or director of religious education be effective or continue as a church employee when people learn about her or his gay child? Will the friends and co-workers think differently of the person who accompanies a lesbian daughter and her partner to Mass? Many are too afraid to take a chance.

In this essay I discuss the dangers of the closet both from my perspective as a committed lesbian Catholic and as a sociologist who for the past four years has served on the board of the Catholic Association for Lesbian and Gay Ministry (CALGM). In this latter context I have come to know diocesan and parish ministries around the country and have been privileged to see the wonderful work they are doing with and for those marginalized on account of their sexual orientation or gender identity. My message is primarily a plea that all Catholics heed Christ's words:

> You are light for all the world. . . . When a lamp is lit, it is not put under the meal-tub, but on the lamp-stand, where it gives light to everyone in the house. And you, like the lamp, must shed light among your fellows, so that, when they see the good you do, they may give praise to your Father in heaven.[2]

I believe that this Jesus, who proclaimed, "I came that you may have life and have it in all its fullness,"[3] wants us to tear down the closets in our church communities and free one another from lives hidden in shame and fear. When we view each life in the splendor of Christ's love, how can we refrain from giving thanks to God for the genuine beauty of God's LGBT children and for the good that they do? In what follows I will reflect, first, on my own experience as a lesbian Catholic who came of age during the Second Vatican Council; second, on what I consider to be the major challenges or difficulties facing LGBT Catholics today; and third, on the impact of the current state of affairs on the broader church, especially how all of us are weakened and diminished when we fail to welcome our LGBT brothers and sisters and see the ways the Spirit is alive and at work in them.

"When a lamp is lit, it is not put under a meal-tub . . ."
Searching for the Closet Door

I am who I am because of the Catholic Church. My hunger for justice, my commitment to the poor and marginalized, my understanding of the Gospel, even my choice of sociology as a tool for building a better world— all of these are gifts that have come to me through the church. The Catholic community is my home, and it has shaped every aspect of my being. I grew up during the era of Vatican II, a time when opposition to the Vietnam War and the establishment of the Peace Corps dovetailed with the appearance of documents like *Pacem in Terris* and *Gaudium et Spes* and with the emergence of the theological notion of the preferential option for the poor. During these years, civic culture and church culture came together for me in a powerful call to build a better, more just, more peaceful world. I was captivated by this vision for society, and my commitment to it has only grown stronger over the years.

What was missing during this formative time were resources for understanding who I was as a lesbian—what my sexual orientation meant and how to integrate my sexuality with my spirituality, as the *Catechism* says I must.[4] During the 1960s, in my Midwestern city of fifty thousand, this wasn't a *church* problem; it was a *cultural* problem. Sexual orientation was something no one understood or even considered talking about. Without the visible presence of others with whom I could identify, whose life choices and relationships resonated with me, I was unable at the time to understand and come to terms with my reality. Today, LGBT persons see themselves reflected in the broader civil society: they see examples and models of what their lives can be, among them wonderful models of health and wholeness, of commitment and positive relationships. It remains, however, much harder to find reflections of one's reality within the church. When I first came out to myself, I was sure I was the only lesbian Catholic in Wisconsin. In many parts of the country, that feeling of isolation persists today. One can find many lesbians who are "recovering" Catholics but few "out" lesbians who are active in their parishes. It is this invisibility, I believe, that for many of us who are LGBT, and for our families, is even more problematic than the church's moral teachings about sex.

Another problem for me and for many like me is that even when we find a welcoming parish home, our experience at the magisterial and national levels fails to match our experience of local church. This creates a painful cognitive dissonance. I belong to a vibrant parish where the Gospel is central and where my pastor knows and respects me and welcomes my participation in parish life and ministry. My heart thrills when we sing hymns with lines like: "All are welcome," "No one need go hungry," and "Saints and sinners are friends at the table of plenty." Yet in many parishes, people are turned away or denied Eucharist simply because they are wearing rainbow pins or equality buttons. More frequently, LGBT persons simply don't approach the Eucharistic table, because they feel they are not welcome. Some of us have found a church home, but many others experience only judgment and alienation and hunger in the church, despite the songs about a table of plenty providing for all that we need. This disconnect is painful and can be very alienating.

My identity is thoroughly Catholic. I love my church. Yet my sexual orientation forces me to acknowledge, even as a celibate person, that while I can say I own my Catholicism, the Catholic community is not always willing to own me or to acknowledge the gifts that I bring.

"Put it on the lampstand, where it gives light to everyone in the house"

Five Challenges for LGBT Catholics—Threats to the Light We Bring

Through my work in LGBT ministry, I have identified five major challenges facing LGBT Catholics, all stemming in large part from fear and ignorance. These are invisibility, the failure to take seriously people's life experiences, people feeling forced into exile from their church homes, problems about language, and the fear of secularism.

Invisibility. I am convinced that a primary challenge and the root of a great deal of ignorance and fear is the invisibility of the Catholic LGBT population. Ignorance and fear within the community in turn reinforces the invisibility. People choose to remain invisible because they do not feel safe. Tragically, what was true for me in the 1960s remains too true for others today: for LGBT persons in the Catholic Church, silence and invisibility are the norm. One is acceptable only if one remains hidden, closeted, unknown. Most parishes give no indication that LGBT persons are—or even might be—part of the community. We are not included in the petitions at Mass or mentioned in homilies or Confirmation classes; those who do know we are there are often afraid to acknowledge our presence publicly. All of this perpetuates negative stereotypes and hostility. So, for instance, at a workshop on diversity, when asked what would need to change in order for the various categories of "other" to become acceptable to us, a former professor of mine said about homosexuals: "There's nothing that would make them acceptable. If God cannot accept them, then certainly I can never accept them." Another time, as I approached the hotel where a conference on pastoral ministry to LGBT persons was to be held, I was met by a group of protesters holding signs saying: "Tell them, Bishop, that they're going to hell." This certainly is not official church teaching, yet most LGBT persons have heard this kind of talk. Very few of us, however, have ever heard spoken aloud the words of the U.S. bishops' 1997 pastoral letter "Always Our Children": "Though at times you may feel discouraged, hurt, or angry, do not walk away from your families, from the Christian community, from all those who love you. In you God's love is revealed. You are always our children."[5] What a difference it would make if we were to hear those words from the pulpit!

The silence around the issue of homosexuality in our parishes keeps people locked in the closet and breeds despair, especially in our young members. Parents, too, often feel forced to stay closeted about their gay children. I vividly recall one evening when I shared my story with a parish group. After everyone had left at the end of the meeting, one woman, who at first had driven away so no one would see her approach me, returned to tell me about her gay son. She had never shared that information with a single soul in the parish. This kind of silence and invisibility is not of God—putting the lamp under a bushel basket not only results in darkness, but the basket is also likely to catch fire. Trying to hide who one is can only lead to shame and, often, destructive behaviors, a fact to which many who have left the closet for the light will attest.

Failure to discern the movement of the Spirit in people's lived experiences. A second major problem is that in most of its current practice, the church fails to take people's realities seriously, to listen to how they experience grace and divine gift in their lives. If we take seriously the words of Jeremiah, "I will place my law within them and write it upon their hearts . . . All, from least to greatest, shall know me, says the Lord,"[6] we must take seriously people's experience of God. As Christians, we are called to discern the presence of the Spirit in our lives, to examine whether our lives are filled with grace—with peace, patience, generosity, whether our relationships are just and loving, fruitful and life giving. A former female student once e-mailed me in obvious agony, saying: "I have been in a relationship for two years, and it has been God's greatest gift to me. But I'm going to hell because she's a woman." What image of God have we communicated to that young woman? In the same sentence she talks of God's greatest gift to her *and* of God sending her to hell because she accepted that gift. Both these things cannot be true, but because of the messages she had heard as well as those she had not, she was left fearful and confused, unable to reconcile two seemingly contradictory things that she knew to be true. She needed someone in her church community to listen to her with compassion and to help her talk through and make sense of her experience.

What was the gift this young woman was experiencing? She was not talking only about sex but rather about having someone love her as she is, with all her faults and failures, strengths and weaknesses, in all her beauty and all her pettiness. She was talking about having someone know her and not turn away, but rather walk with her through it all, believing in her best self and revealing that best self to her. She was speaking of the gift of mutuality in love: the joy of seeing another person come to life, open up, burst into blossom in the light and warmth of her love. It is in community that we are able to figure out what is real and what is not, what is the gift and how best to embrace it. But that can only happen if the community of faith does as Jesus did: listen and take seriously people's experience. Grace must build on that. Too often, even in the church, love is reduced to sex, and when young people have experiences like my former student's, many panic and then either leave the church or let their fear of sexual behavior freeze them into loneliness and isolation, denying themselves what really *is* God's gift. I recently conducted a sociological survey of people connected to organizations working with homosexuality in the Catholic community.[7] These quotes express sentiments common among the respondents: "Listen to our stories!" "Take us seriously!" "Treat us as individuals, as faith-filled people whose desire to be productive partners in the People of God is no different from that of our heterosexual sisters and brothers." "See the people."

Exiling members of our faith family. In too many cases, LGBT Catholics and their allies feel forced to leave a church home that they love. At a meeting of Catholic parents of LGBT persons, one mother spoke of her young gay son, who came home from Confirmation class saying, "I can't be confirmed. If they can't believe in me, how can I believe in them?" Both the son and his parents stopped going to church. Almost all the other parents at the meeting had also stopped attending Mass, and they spoke tearfully about what they missed most about parish life. These families had not left their parishes because they found church participation to be without meaning. Rather, they felt forced out, not so much by what was said but by what was not said, because of the silent but apparently real denial of their children's existence as well as their faith community's failure to acknowledge in any kind of public way what the parents saw most clearly: the image of God shining through their LGBT child, that child's goodness, giftedness, and love. This experience of exile is not limited to LGBT persons and their families. Recently, one of our CALGM board members shared a similar story of a heterosexual Confirmation candidate in his parish who came home after her Confirmation class and said that she did not feel she could be confirmed because of the Catholic Church's treatment of LGBT persons.

Alienating language. A separate, very painful problem within the Catholic Church today is that we are caught in an apparently intensifying battle over the very words we use to speak about the identities and experiences of nonheterosexual persons. Over the past few decades, the Catholic hierarchy has increasingly been speaking a language distinct from that used by most Catholic laity when it comes to sexual orientation. Official church documents use language that is foreign and often offensive to Catholics in the pews: "intrinsically disordered" and "inclined to evil" mean something very different in official Catholic moral parlance than the phrases do to a nontheologian like me. In a similar way, many church leaders cringe at people identifying as lesbian and gay, because they associate those simple words with a specific political agenda. The national office of Courage,[8] a Catholic ministry for persons experiencing same-sex attraction who are striving to live celibately, declined to participate in my survey of organizations serving the Catholic LGBT population because of language difficulties. Fr. Paul Check, the director, wrote in an e-mail response to my invitation:

While I wish you the best with your work, I am not inclined to agree to Courage's involvement. . . . [W]e begin from a very different premise than the starting point of your work, i.e. that there exist "GLBT Catholics." Courage begins from the idea that there are men and women with same-sex attraction. That distinction in the mind of the Church, as I understand it, is fundamental and shapes everything else that follows.

Bishops now rarely use even the term "sexual orientation" but prefer to talk about "same-sex attraction," often prefacing the phrase with "suffering from." Most of us who identify as gay or lesbian find this language demeaning and not at all descriptive of our reality. Until Catholic leaders and laity break the silence, however, and begin talking not *about* one another but *to* one another and are able to listen respectfully, we will never even understand the extent to which we are speaking different languages, much less learn how to translate them into a common vernacular.

Lack of engagement with contemporary learning out of a fear of secularism. As a social scientist myself, it is my observation that when it comes to LGBT issues, the sciences, including the social and behavioral sciences, are too often seen today as enemies of the church instead of partners in the quest for truth and understanding. John XXIII and Vatican II called us as church to take secular knowledge seriously. If we trusted Christ's method of judging a tree by its fruit, we would discover the many ways we could collaborate with the work of the sciences on these issues, rather than treating them as hostile to faith and the Gospel. Science, too, has good news to proclaim, and research being done in the areas of sexuality, gender, identity, and culture is yielding knowledge that is already enriching the lives, the well-being, and the physical and psychological health of many in Christ's body. We need to be open to and welcome what psychology, sociology, medicine, and theology are teaching us about what it means to be human, and then to let our light shine. Not everything that society embraces is good, but we can look, for instance, at how heterosexual relationships, marriage, and family have changed over the centuries and see that many of these changes have strengthened our relationships, made us better, more whole, more integrated, more holy—and yes, more happy.

Impact of the Status Quo on the Catholic Church

"There is nothing concealed that will not be revealed, nothing hidden that will not be made known. Everything you have said in the dark will be heard in daylight; what you have whispered in locked rooms will be proclaimed from the rooftops."[9]

All three synoptic Gospels include the parable of the lamp and the lampstand. Luke has Jesus tell this story twice (in Chapter 8 and then again in Chapter 11), and each time he follows the parable with the proclamation that everything will be revealed; there will be no secrets when God's reign comes to its fullness. While there are many levels of meaning to this, as a lesbian Catholic I see a promise that all closets will be torn down. There will no longer be a need for anyone to hide; all of us will be welcomed into the light.

The Catholic Church today, like much of secular society and our political establishment, is, in the area of sexuality, stuck. We seem caught in gridlock, frozen in place, polarized. Genuine dialogue is impossible when one side—or both sides—is convinced it has a corner on truth, a direct line to God, or nothing to learn from anyone who disagrees or dares to question its position. To get beyond stalemate, to break free of impasse, will require an abundance of commitment to the difficult practical and spiritual work of mutual compassion and forgiveness.

During Lent 2011, while reflecting on the call to forgive from the heart, I wrote these words:

> For me, it's not the fiery furnace that's hardest to forgive
> the passion, the anger, the red hot emotion . . .
> For me it's the ICE,
> the frozen hearts, the cold shoulders
> the blindness that comes from being frozen in place
> locked in position
> rock hard ideas
> beliefs that leave people COLD,
> frozen to the bone
> life and energy sucked out of them . . .
> It's the ICE—
> Sharp as shards of glass tearing into people's Spirits . . .
> Frozen—locked—hard as rock—unmoving . . .

BUT STILL YOU CALL ME: *FORGIVE*—70 × 7 *times* . . .
Help me, God.
Teach me empathy for icy hearts, frozen spirits . . .

What are the consequences for the church if we do not learn to come out from under our respective bushel baskets, to forgive, to enter into dialogue? What will be the costs if we remain trapped in invisibility and silence or continue to speak past one another? I fear that pastoral ministry will become increasingly difficult and that the voice of the official church will lose credibility not just with the gay community but also with great numbers of the laity. When a Catholic pastor refuses to baptize the child of a same-sex couple,[10] or denies that child a place in the parish school four years later,[11] or publicly turns a woman away from Eucharist at her own mother's funeral and then refuses to listen to the daughter's eulogy or to officiate at the burial,[12] Catholics are prompted to question how such behaviors can be God's will, so contradictory do they seem to the ministry and teaching of Christ. Those of us who identify as Vatican II Catholics believe not only in the *right* to follow our consciences but the *absolute necessity* of doing so, especially when it comes to caring for those in our midst who are most alienated and marginalized. We realize how much we have received from the church, and many of us will continue to choose to remain, speaking our piece of the truth and trusting the Spirit at work in the church.

But how much harder this is for our younger brothers and sisters. Unless we open the closet door and invite one another into the light, I fear that the beautiful light of Christ burning so brightly in our young will be lost to us. The darkness that might have been dispelled by their light will continue to obscure our vision. The bullying and humiliation will likely persist, and the rash of teen suicides will likely continue. For, if the acceptance of LGBT persons in our church is made conditional upon our remaining in the closet, the message the church will be conveying to LGBT young people is that, contrary to what so many in society are trying to communicate, "it *will not* get better."

I have a cherry tree in my yard. It lost several big branches during an ice storm a couple of years ago. The broken places are still weeping sap. For me, that tree is a powerful image of what is happening in the church today. Many of the branches that could have carried our future are instead being snapped off, torn away by the weight of ice that refuses to melt.

A significant source of the life of the church, its energy, the sap that enables growth and fruitfulness, is being drained away. Many of our youth—straight as well as gay—and some of our most active and dedicated adults are leaving and going elsewhere. They are not leaving primarily because of differences in beliefs about morality or theology but because of the lack of dialogue, because we are afraid to judge a tree by its fruit or to invite people to share their experiences or to trust the work of the Spirit in their lives. The message that LGBT people and those who support them often hear from the church, whether the message was intended or not, is: "Go away. You are a problem and we cannot be bothered with you."[13]

In closing, I ask us to remember that we are the church. We must respond to these challenges in our own circumstances and not wait for someone else to do it: "Lord, to whom shall we go? You have the words of eternal life."[14] Let us commit ourselves to the difficult but vital work of reconciliation and dialogue, recognizing that we all need one another. These are the tools by which we will tear down the closet walls, break open the walls of silence, and walk out together into the brilliant light of Christ. It is time to let our light shine . . . the Christ light entrusted to each of us! It is time to stand on the rooftop in the full light of day and to proclaim clearly what God is doing in our lives. As we do, we will begin to experience God's reign, where there will be no more secrets, no more shame, where all in God's household will live together in peace and harmony.

7 Gay Ministry at the Crossroads

The Plight of Gay Clergy in the Catholic Church

DONALD B. COZZENS

John Carroll University

Author's note: My ministry as a priest has included a half-dozen years as vicar for clergy and religious in a large Midwestern diocese. Following that assignment, I served for another six years as rector of a major seminary. These two assignments in particular helped me see the struggles that gay priests face in today's priesthood—struggles that are deeply imbedded in both the structure of the church and the church's teaching on homosexuality.

A front-page story in the September 20, 2011, edition of the *New York Times* reported an event that was noted by virtually every media outlet in the United States: The U.S. military's policy of "Don't Ask, Don't Tell" for gay and lesbian servicemembers had been ended. During the eighteen years the federal law held force, 14,500 military personnel were discharged, and countless thousands were led to see themselves as somehow second tier in terms of their loyalty and trustworthiness. A dispiriting era of secrecy and denial was finally, mercifully, terminated.[1]

While Federal Law no. 103–160 prohibited military personnel from discriminating against or harassing closeted homosexual or bisexual members of our armed forces, it also barred openly gay, lesbian, or bisexual persons from military service. The policy prohibited people who "demonstrate a propensity or intent to engage in homosexual acts" from military service because their presence "would create unacceptable risk to the high standards of morale, good order and discipline, and unit cohesion that are the essence of military capability."[2] Moreover, the "Don't Ask, Don't Tell" law prohibited any homosexual or bisexual person from disclosing his or her homosexual relationships while serving the U.S. military.

I find an eerie analogue of the now repealed "Don't Ask, Don't Tell" government policy in the Catholic Church's unspoken policy of "Don't Ask, Don't Tell" for gay clergy and vowed religious. The church, I'm convinced, will take a major step forward when gay clergy and religious who choose to claim their orientation to friends, family, and parishioners will feel free to do so.

In my book *The Changing Face of the Priesthood*, I reported estimates of gay men in the priesthood that ranged from 30 to 50 percent and raised the disturbing question, "is the priesthood becoming a gay profession?"[3] I recall two bishops with backgrounds in seminary work telling me privately they believed the percentage of gay priests to be higher, perhaps as high as 70 percent. Whatever the actual percentage might be, we are addressing a pastoral issue that touches the lives of many Catholic priests.

So let me try to imagine the plight of gay priests ministering in the Catholic Church.

As priests, gay clergy, like all of the ordained, are official spokespersons charged with presenting church teachings, including the church's teaching on homosexuality, as clearly as they can and in as compelling a manner as possible. For many, this is a plight in itself. When asked about homosexuality, they have an opportunity to make a fundamental point that is often missed—sexual orientation as such is not a matter of morality. Gay or straight, bisexual or confused—we are all God's children. Orientation is not to be confused with so-called sexual preference. Gay and lesbian individuals no more choose their orientation than straight people choose to be straight.

But how does a gay priest deal with the church's position that his sexual orientation is objectively disordered? Must he accept that his sexuality is flawed, skewed in a perverse direction, and that any intimate same-sex behavior is always intrinsically evil?

We can assume that some gay priests experience little or no interior conflict in their preaching, teaching, and pastoral counseling around these issues. For these priests, gay and lesbian individuals are as capable of living lives that forgo sexual fulfillment as are straight priests and Catholics who aren't married. If these priests struggle with their celibate chastity, those struggles appear to be manageable. In fact, many gay priests claim the charism of celibacy. Most of the time, for them, the church's teaching that same-sex orientation is disordered, I suspect, is bracketed or buried.

But other gay priests, as the work of Jeannine Gramick, Robert Nugent, and others has made clear, choke at the thought of instructing gay and lesbian parishioners that the church expects them to lead lives of celibate chastity. For these pastors it remains difficult to impose the burden of celibate living on the shoulders of gays and lesbians in committed partnerships. Many pastors, both gay and straight, find themselves boxed in. Their pastoral and personal experience and the church's teachings on homosexuality are in conflict—a conflict that easily leads to a crisis in integrity.

A Mother of a Gay Son

One morning after I celebrated Mass at a Carmelite monastery, a woman I knew remained seated quietly in the chapel. She looked troubled, so I sat down next to her and asked if she was alright. She confided that one of her sons was gay. "I'm hanging on by my fingertips," she said. "The church is telling me my son doesn't have the right to fall in love."

That's really what the church is saying to gay and lesbian Catholics. Avoid falling in love—the temptation to engage in sexual intimacy will be too strong to overcome if you fall in love. This argument follows from the church's perennial teaching to avoid the "near occasion of sin." For gay priests as well as for the larger population of gay and lesbian Catholics, friendships are to be always platonic.

The plight of gay priests took a significant turn in the fall of 2005, when the Vatican's Congregation for Catholic Education issued an Instruction to bishops, religious superiors, and seminary rectors. The document's wordy title is in itself telling: "Instruction Concerning the Criteria of Vocational Discernment Regarding Persons with Homosexual Tendencies, Considering Their Admission to Seminary and to Holy Orders."

Here is heart of the Instruction: "This department, in agreement with the Congregation for Divine Worship and the Discipline of the Sacraments, holds it necessary to confirm clearly that the church, while profoundly respecting the persons in question, may not admit to the seminary and Holy Orders those who practice homosexuality, show profoundly deep-rooted homosexual tendencies, or support the so-called gay culture."[4] How should a gay priest respond to such an Instruction, an Instruction explicitly approved by the pope? How might a gay bishop or religious superior or seminary rector respond? Is the Catholic Church suggesting in this Instruction that the ministry of a gay priest or bishop is inferior to the ministry of a straight priest or bishop?

Five years before the 2005 Instruction, Father David Trosch wrote on his blog, objecting to an article he had just read that had cited my position on the ordination of gay men.

> Unfortunately, "Cozzens is not against ordaining gay men, and concedes some effective bishops and even some popes may have been gay." I totally disagree with his position of not being against ordaining gay men. I personally believe that it should be incorporated into the *Code of Canon Law* that homosexual orientation invalidates ordination. . . . I further believe that an active homosexual cleric or religious should incur a totally reserved automatic excommunication that remains unforgivable while remaining in such position. Such sin would be a permanent impediment in regard to returning to religious life.

But Father Trosch isn't finished. He goes on to write, "While the expulsion of active homosexuals would possibly, even probably, cause a significant temporary decline in the number of available priests, I believe that in the long run the Church would have a great increase in vocations with a correspondingly healthier Church and world."[5]

In light of the Vatican Instruction and the position represented by Father Trosch—that the ordinations of gay priests are invalid—a number of Catholics might ask themselves: Would God call a sexually disordered male to the dignity of the priesthood? To the exalted dignity of the episcopacy? Apparently so. And because the Vatican Instruction can be read as a de facto admission that the percentage of gay priests is significant, how is it to be explained that God has called and continues to call so many sexually disordered men to Holy Orders?

Before we put the Instruction to rest, I want to consider some of the difficulties seminary officials are likely to encounter when implementing this document.

Do admissions committees for seminaries and religious orders expect candidates, gay or straight, to admit that they may until recently have been sexually active but that they, nonetheless, believe they can lead a celibate life? Do admissions committees believe that they and their candidates can discern between profoundly deep-rooted sexual tendencies and rather shallow homosexual tendencies? Do we expect that straight candidates for seminary admission have weak or shallow heterosexual tendencies? And how do seminary officials measure support for "the so-called gay culture"? The Instruction does not define or describe "gay culture." But I think we understand what the authors of the Instruction are getting at.

Addressing the plight of seminary admissions committees, Mark Jordan writes: "Gay men are assigned to implement policies designed to screen out or cure gayness. . . . Seminary admission decisions are the occasions not only for acts of survival, or cultural reproduction, but of cultural repetition."

Jordan then explains, "Seminaries are and have been finishing schools for a certain kind of homoerotic identity. Efforts to weed out gay candidates, to cure them or teach them concealment, repeat the oldest conditions for producing homoerotic identity in Christian Europe. A Catholic seminary, especially a conservative seminary, is one of the few places left in modern society for building baroque closets. . . . Seminary education is often enough training in how to be homoerotic the old-fashioned way."[6]

After the release of the Instruction, I looked for at least a few bishops to affirm the dignity and ministry of priests in their diocese who were gay. I found none.

———————

Besides having affinities with the U.S. military's recently rescinded "Don't Ask, Don't Tell" policy, it occurs to me that the plight of the gay priest might also be analogous to the plight of Jewish men, women, and children in Europe during the Third Reich. To escape the Nazi death camps they had to hide—and perhaps even deny—their identity as Jews. I suspect there is a good deal of denial and hiding among gay priests.

It's easy to imagine gay priests going about their pastoral duties with diligence and competence, believing that most of their parishioners probably don't suspect their sexual identity. We can only imagine what it's like for the gay priest, keenly aware of his church's teaching on homosexuality, to celebrate Mass, tend to the sick, counsel the confused—and do all of this well—and then hear the lofty voice of the Vatican insist that he is disordered.

Does anybody ask him about his experience? Does anybody care?

This much is certain: The denial or closeting of a core component of one's identity is not good for the soul. It inhibits the joy of spiritual freedom that is at the very heart of the Gospel.

I turn now to "gay ministry at the crossroads," my chosen title for this essay.

I suspect that many church authorities stirred uneasily with our government's remission of "Don't Ask, Don't Tell." It's precisely the unspoken rule they want kept in place for gay clergy. The recent repeal of "Don't Ask, Don't Tell" might by itself bring gay clergy to a crossroads—and a moment of existential truth, a moment to affirm one's personal integrity.

Do homosexually oriented priests sense the inner freedom to confide their gay identity to friends and family—and even to their parishioners?

Writing about vowed religious gay priests, the Dominican theologian Donald Goergen argues:

> Religious communities do not benefit from closeted homosexuality. I do not mean that men need to be public about their sexuality, a notion that seems to be an odd bane of our period of history. By closeted homosexuals I mean men who are closeted as regards their own selves. That is, they are significantly out of contact with their sexuality and thus unable to accept the degree or kind of homosexuality present in them; as a result, they are men who live in denial and fear and self-hatred. For homosexual men to live in religious communities, they need to be comfortable enough to be unafraid of their homosexuality, and they certainly need to be able to acknowledge who they are to trusted friends.[7]

Since Goergen was writing of the gay religious order priest, I want to insert a sidebar here. While reading Jeannine Gramick's *Homosexuality in the Priesthood and Religious Life*, I was amused to find that Matthew Kelty, the Cistercian monk and friend of Thomas Merton, wrote, "It is my conviction that gays make superb celibates, the best celibates, the more so in community. I do not think the heterosexually oriented man should try to live celibacy."[8] Contrary to the Instruction, Kelty is proposing that gays make wonderful monks and priests.

But let me get back on course. I want to tell you of a priest who did choose to take the road less traveled. He told me recently that he is happy to have me share what happened when he came to his personal crossroads.

On March 25, 2004, Father Fred Daly, a priest of the diocese of Syracuse, New York, announced to his parish that he was gay and celibate—and loved being their pastor. And his parishioners made it clear after his announcement that they loved him back.

Father Daly's announcement, to no one's surprise, made the papers. Now more than his parishioners knew of his orientation. What followed from his bishop and brother priests is interesting: silence. Just a week or so after speaking up, Daly concelebrated a funeral liturgy of a prominent layperson along with nine or ten other priests. Half of these priests, he knew, were gay themselves. Not one of them mentioned his announcement. There was not one "I wish you hadn't done that" or "That must have taken a lot of courage" or "What's it been like for you since you came out?"

A month or so later, at a communal penance service at another parish, Daly was in the sacristy with twenty other priest confessors. Again, no one said a word, save one priest who said to him privately that what he had done took real courage. Once again, Daly believed that half of the priests at the penance service were gay.

I'm convinced most U.S. priests would respond to a brother priest who came out in the same manner that the priests of Syracuse responded to Fred Daly. The plight of gay clergy is such that attention, any attention, to the reality of substantial numbers of homosexually oriented men in their ranks renders them mute. Coming out of the clerical closet reminds Catholics that there is indeed a closet. It rips tears in the curtain of denial that permits gay priests to dwell in their own world of sacred secrecy.

Along the way, Fred Daly faced some painful consequences for coming out, but he is glad he did so. He has served in a number of parishes in recent years, and, with just a few exceptions, his parishioners have been welcoming and accepting of his orientation.

No doubt there are dozens of Fred Dalys among gay American Catholic clergy. I know of only a handful. However many there are, they stand pretty much alone.

Years ago, a priest I know wanted to tell his bishop and the diocese's auxiliary bishops that he was gay. He asked if I would facilitate a meeting with his bishop and he asked me to accompany him. At that meeting, the priest spoke simply and directly, and it went something like this. "Bishops, I want you to know something about me, something that I think is important." To the diocesan bishop, he said, "I think of you as my spiritual father and because of that relationship I want you to know that I'm committed to celibacy, but that I'm gay." The bishops really didn't know what to say. It came down to something like, "Well, we'll be praying for you." The meeting was over. By telling the truth about himself, this gay priest had broken the code of silence. And in doing so he had put his bishop and the auxiliaries in an awkward situation. The bishops, it seems clear, didn't want to know this man's orientation!

I earlier proposed that the denial or closeting of a core component of one's identity is bad for the soul and that it inhibits the joy of spiritual freedom that is at the heart of the Gospel and that is meant to be at the heart of each person's vocation. If this is true—and the psychological, sociological, pastoral, and experiential evidence strongly suggests that it is—then the sooner gay clergy who wish to come out do come out—at least to their friends, family, and brother priests—the healthier the priesthood will be, the healthier our church will be.

Some Final Thoughts

Mark Jordan and Ellis Hanson have asked the obvious but often unaddressed question: Why would a gay Catholic, aware of the church's insistence that homosexually oriented people are "disordered," seek admission to seminary formation and then, at the moment of ordination, kneel in submission to a bishop who embodies the very authority that insists there is something not right with him?[9] There is no one single answer or response to the question. Perhaps, for some, it's because there is a subtle, seductive energy to the esoteric and elitist culture of Catholic clergy. Declare the erotic off-limits—especially in a milieu of divine selection and sacred dignity—and you at once make the celibate priesthood a secure haven ripe with a romantic aura.

For others, perhaps, it's because a sincere Catholic gay man may choose to live celibately, as the writer Eve Tushnet has acknowledged she has done.[10] From a theological perspective, the gay candidate might sense that God's Spirit has awakened in his own spirit the charism of celibacy, which I've argued in my book *Freeing Celibacy* remains a valid, healthy, and holy way of life for those men and women, gay or straight, whose "truth" is the committed single life for the sake of the Gospel.[11] The subtitle of this chapter is "the plight of gay clergy in the Catholic Church." But I suspect being gay is not a plight for all gay priests. From their perspective, we might change the subtitle to "the delight of gay clergy in the Catholic Church."

Taking another tack on this question, Hanson, in his book *Decadence and Catholicism*, offers the following dangerous comment. (I say "dangerous" because here Hanson links the potential for pederasty with the homosexual orientation.) I leave it to the reader to judge its merit.

> I have often been asked . . . why a gay man . . . would become a priest. The motives are so numerous . . . that the real question ought to be why straight men become priests. . . . The feminized or effeminate pastoral persona, the pleasures of ritual, public trust and respect, freedom from the social pressure to marry, opportunities for intimacy with boys, passionate friendship and cohabitation with likeminded men, and a discipline for coping with sexual shame and guilt.[12]

And Mark Jordan, drawing on the work of John Shekleton, gives this response to the question, "why do so many gay boys grow up to be priests?"

> Because they are promised an exchange of their anguished identity as outsiders for a respected and powerful identity as an insider. Because they want to remain in the beautiful, queer space of the liturgy. Because they are drawn to public celebration of suffering that redeems. Because they want to live in as gay a world as the Catholic church offers.[13]

Bear with me as I turn now to the church's canon law. Canon 277 reads: "Clerics are obliged to observe perfect and perpetual continence of the sake of the kingdom of heaven and therefore are obliged to observe celibacy, which is a special gift of God, by which sacred ministers can adhere more easily to Christ with an undivided heart and can more freely dedicate themselves to the service of God and humankind."[14] Priests, the canon says, "are obliged to observe . . . celibacy, which is a special gift of God." Church authorities have never, to my satisfaction anyway, been able to explain how they can legislate a "special gift from God," that is, celibacy. If the gift of celibacy is imposed, regardless of one's orientation, can it also be healthy, liberating, and holy?

When celibacy is healthy, liberating, and holy, it is freely embraced as one's "truth," as, in this sense, a gift. But not all priests are gifted with the charism of celibacy. And so it is with the majority of persons who find themselves attracted sexually, romantically, and emotionally to people of their same sex. In effect, by its current teaching, the church is applying

Canon 277 to the LGBTQ community. To paraphrase: "Gay and lesbians are obliged to observe perfect and perpetual continence, which is a special gift of God, by which they can adhere more easily to Christ for the salvation of their souls."

Gay or straight, the celibate lifestyle works when it is an individual's truth. When it is undertaken only because it is imposed by legislation, moral or canonical, it easily leads to truncated human development, eccentricities of all kinds, intense loneliness, moral anguish, and, in some cases, tragically, a propensity to sexual abuse of adults and minors.

Most priests have learned, both from their own sexual histories and from their pastoral experience, that sex is good. And like most good things in life, it is dangerous. It can extol and expand the human spirit, assuage the deepest of human longings, tease us with a taste of divine ecstasy. At the same time, philosophers of every age confirm our commonsense awareness that sex can also restrict the human spirit, compound our human loneliness, and lead to the violent abuse of bodies and souls.

Whether clergy or laity, we all would be wise, we know in our hearts, to be wary of sex. At the same time, we know we would be wise to be grateful for and respectful of this mysterious gift of God. I take some comfort from the theologian Lisa Sowle Cahill, who notes, "All people at least some of the time are unsure how to understand their sexuality and how to behave sexually in ways that are morally praiseworthy rather than reprehensible."[15]

It is fair to criticize the church when it comes to sex. It has consistently demonstrated an almost paranoid fear of sex—a fear and suspicion that has scarred untold thousands of believers. It is also fair to acknowledge the church as bearer of considerable wisdom in matters of human sexuality. Among the treasures it offers, the Catholic Church will not let us forget that "sex makes promises." Sheer absurdity to many. A saving wisdom to others.

8　The Experience of a Pastoral Advocate and Implications for the Church

BRYAN N. MASSINGALE

Marquette University

This reflection on Catholicism and LGBT realities flows from my multiple and overlapping identities as a priest and pastor, professor and scholar, and man of color. In it, I wish to consider the experience that attends being an advocate for justice for LGBT persons within the Catholic Church and what attentive listening to that experience may reveal about this faith community.

One of the defining experiences that shapes my perspective on LGBT issues occurred when I co-facilitated a session several years ago for students at Marquette University on "Culture and Sexual Identity." Over the course of the evening, we examined how various cultural groups construe human sexuality in general and homosexuality in particular. About thirty students attended; twenty identified themselves as gay/lesbian and also stated that they had some form of Catholic religious formation. None of these twenty, however, currently identified as belonging to the Catholic Church. I asked them why. Their reasons varied, but one young man expressed a common sentiment. He said, "It's hard enough to figure out who I am and how to live my sexuality without having to take on the Catholic Church as well." He shared this view with neither rancor nor sadness but simply as a self-evident fact.

I was no stranger to difficult conversations with LGBT persons about Catholic faith and ethics, yet for some reason these young adults' matter-of-fact dismissal of the church deeply affected me. Indeed, it broke my heart. I thought, "Surely our faith must have something more affirming and life giving to offer them." My heartbreak fueled a resolve to develop and offer a course on "Homosexuality and Christian Ethics," which explores the full range of complex positions that Christians have on LGBT issues.

Today, I continue to maintain a deep and abiding conviction that—at its core—Catholic faith can and should be more affirming of the diversity of gender identity and expression. In all honesty, however, my experiences in trying to create spaces for a more positive and life-affirming message have sorely tried and tested this conviction.

Let me describe two of these experiences. First, in the fall of 2006, I published a reflection in my local diocesan newspaper on a proposed amendment to my state's constitution that would not only further prohibit same-sex marriages—which were already illegal—but also foreclose any legal recognition of same-sex committed relationships. I argued against that measure on the grounds that it went beyond mere support for "traditional marriage" and in fact endangered the human rights of many individuals and families. Without endorsing same-sex marriage, I used very traditional Catholic moral reasoning, as well as arguments employed in similar circumstances by then–Archbishop Levada of San Francisco and then–Bishop Niederauer of Salt Lake City, to argue that a "no" vote on this amendment was the best way to safeguard all of the Catholic values at stake. The stance I took on this question, however, was contrary to the guidance being given by Wisconsin's bishops.

To say that the article was noticed would be an understatement.[1] Internet bloggers fervently denounced me as a "renegade priest" who "misleads the faithful" and "encourages immoral conduct." One even opined that I was "spreading Satan's fumes" throughout the archdiocese. Other writers offered commentaries that are too vile and hateful for public sharing. Even five years later, when we meet at various gatherings, some church leaders make it a point to tell me that they believe that my ethical analysis of this legislation was flawed. It is safe to say that writing this now dated and very modest article has cast a pall over my relationships with many Catholic bishops.

These experiences have been replicated with increasing intensity in the years that have followed. To offer a second example: In March 2011, I was part of a briefing for members of Congress and their staffs that discussed a Catholic justice perspective on LGBT-related legislation pending before Congress. As my students would say, "major drama" ensued over my presence at this event. Church officials attempted to curtail or curb my participation on the grounds that it was sponsored by groups who dissented from authentic church teaching on same-sex acts. My local bishop made an unprecedented request that I submit the text of my remarks to him prior to delivering them. And the Internet firestorm that erupted in the briefing's wake made the 2006 experience seem like a dress rehearsal. Fanned by conservative Catholic websites, I was assailed with letters that accused me of having "a spirit of sexual perversion," denounced me for holding "duplicitous views" that are "absolutely inexcusable for a Catholic priest," and encouraged me to "do the honorable thing" by leaving the Catholic Church and joining the Episcopalians—a refuge for "clergy of your ilk." Some letters were so worrisome that I was advised to inform law enforcement, and I did turn them over to my university's Public Safety office.

These two events are representative of the range of experiences that I and many others, particularly priests, typically endure when we attempt to affirm LGBT persons in the church: intimidation, appeals to loyalty, a summons to obedience, and, when these fail, being denounced as "bad priests," "traitors," "suspect," "disloyal," and—perhaps the most ecclesiastical of opprobria—"imprudent."

I do not relate these experiences in an appeal for special sympathy. Other advocates and allies have had experiences similar to or worse than mine. I share these because I want to go underneath them and examine what they signify and reveal about the Catholic faith community's relationship to and understanding of its LGBT members. I contend that such experiences signal *a pervasive climate of fear*, one that borders on hysteria.[2]

Discussing the diversity of sexual identities and gender expressions among us arouses deep and, sadly, well-founded fears for many supportive pastoral ministers, scholars, and even some bishops: fears of investigation, intimidation, letter-writing campaigns, and silencing; fears of loss of preferment, livelihood, church membership, and/or a cherished vocation; fears of hassle and harassment; fears over the denial of tenure and/or promotion; and most pointedly, fear for one's very safety—even from fellow believers. Catholicism's relationship with LGBT persons is such that even modest attempts at discussing issues such as gay bullying and gay teen suicide—on which there should be little controversy—regularly generate such wariness and anxiety that enormous sums of energy must be spent to "keep peace" in the community and to assure potential critics of one's loyalty to the church. Just as regularly, this climate of fear leads, at best, to silence, avoidance, and coded speak (that is, where an audience has to read between the lines to hear what the speaker is really intending to say). At worst, this climate entails duplicity, complicity, and double-speak (that is, where the speaker or author says one thing in public and another in private). Fear is costly. The cost of silence, duplicity, and complicity is betrayal: the betrayal of one's convictions, one's values, one's beliefs, one's very self.

But—and I want to emphasize this point—this climate of fear is costly not only for LGBT persons and their allies. *This fear has deep implications for Catholicism itself.* Such pervasive fear signals a faith community that is deeply anxious about its identity. One can only conclude that dialogue on LGBT issues arouses such anxiety and hostility because, in real ways, it threatens—or at least is experienced as threatening to—an ecclesial self-understanding so fundamental that such discussions must be stopped, controlled, and silenced even at great cost. This self-understanding functionally declares that "Catholic" = "straight."[3] That is, at the heart of the story that Catholicism has told about humanity, and integral to the way that the Catholic faith community officially identifies itself, is the belief that heterosexual persons, heterosexual love, heterosexual intimacy, and heterosexual friendship—and *only* these—can *unambiguously* and without qualification mirror holiness and mediate the Divine.[4] This operative self-understanding of Catholicism functions despite rhetorical appeals to universality. Its overriding influence helps explains Catholic allies' many adverse experiences with faith-based LGBT advocacy, no matter how modest these attempts may be. Moreover, the power of this self-understanding is such that it exists regardless of and serves to undermine the church's official and perhaps even sincere affirmations of personal respect and pastoral concern for LGBT persons.[5]

Why, then, is this climate of fear so significant for the nature of Catholicism? Why does it call for serious reflection and concerted response, not only for the sake of LGBT persons and their allies but for the sake of our very identity as church? Because such profound fear and deep anxiety, I contend, are profoundly contrary to the Gospel and compromise the integrity of the church itself.

This challenge to the church's integrity as a vehicle of and for God can be expressed in the following troubling yet fundamental questions: *Why, and how, have issues of gender and sexual expression become so defining of Catholic identity that contrary voices must be so proactively policed and silenced and dialogue of any sort is so deeply to be feared? Further, what are the deep theological, moral, and practical implications that follow from the conviction that the infinite love of God can never be found in loving same-sex relation-*

ships? For example, wouldn't this conviction be a kind of idolatry, given the Christian faith commitment that "God is love" and abides in all loving persons (1 John 4:16)? What, then, are the existential and pastoral challenges of belonging to a faith community that publicly espouses such an idolatrous, or at least severely deficient, belief?

I know that such questions are too complicated for this specific contribution, which focuses not on theological matters but rather lived experiences. They are, however, among the pressing questions that my experiences as a pastor, scholar, educator, and member of the Catholic community bring to the surface. I believe that conversation on such probing questions is at the heart of what must happen if the church is to proclaim effectively the life-giving message that all are truly radically equal in dignity in the sight of God—a conviction that I still hold, despite its being sorely tried and tested.[6]

9   Lord, I Am (Not) Worthy to Receive You

WINNIE S. VARGHESE

St. Mark's Church-in the-Bowery, New York City

Dignus est.

I am an Episcopalian, a chaplain, and priest.

A few years ago, I attended a meeting in Detroit, Michigan, about our church's response to a proposal for a "covenant" for the global Anglican Communion. The Episcopal Church is a member of the Anglican Communion, a worldwide fellowship of Christians, predominantly the legacy of the British Empire. There were a lot of us around the table considering what The Episcopal Church could do in response to the proposal for a covenant, which many understood to have the potential to establish a single authoritative magisterium for the Anglican Communion. As you can imagine, this was a troubling idea for many. At one point in our deliberations, a representative of the Virgin Islands lightened the mood and made a point by telling us a joke. The joke, which our colleague attributed to the bishop of Honduras, clarified something about who we are as Episcopalians and how we approach the topic of sexual diversity within and around the church. There was a hurricane in Honduras. It was a terrible disaster, and more was coming. A member of the media asks an evangelical pastor: "What does it mean, what is God saying to us?" The evangelical pastor replies, "The people should return to God, confess their sins, and return to God." He asks the Roman Catholic bishop: "What is God saying to us?" The Roman Catholic bishop responds, "The people should return to the church, confess their sins, and return to God." Finally, he asks the Episcopal bishop: "What is God saying to us?" And the Episcopal bishop says, "It is hurricane season."

The discernible realm of nature is a space we live comfortably within as Episcopalians. In seeking truth we, like Roman Catholics, are comfortable engaging the sciences and society's best tools of discernment in order to discover more about the truths or principles that define creation and thereby reveal to us more of the Creator.

Yet, despite our receptivity and commitment to acknowledging God's truth in all of creation, we—Roman Catholics and Anglican/Episcopalians alike—have somewhere along the way been misled into what I think is a heretical norm, an understanding of human nature that has caused us to believe that most of us, by nature of the bodies we occupy, are not worthy to hold our heads high and to share fully at the table of the Bread of Life or even to gather the crumbs. The entrenchment of this false norm was not the work of the church alone, although the church was a partner in this oppression. Historically, it was primarily the work of power, specifically the dynamics of empire, which first defined the poor and the weak as not worthy, or worthy only of domination. Then it designated great swaths of humanity as in some way "less than," in order to justify allowing their basic humanity to be undermined en masse by slavery and economic exploitation by Christian people and Christian nations. Worth thereby became a commodity.

Democracy, on the one hand, and contemporary understandings of the worth of all people, on the other, both defy this dehumanizing power dynamic. Yet to this day, the church continues to hold, in its practice and teaching, that worth or dignity requires or can be conferred by acts of affiliation with certain institutions and by conformity to sexual norms declared legitimate by a celibate clergy. This state of affairs appears absurd to outsiders because, I think, its persistence is very much like a vestigial flap, which by its survival invites explanation, possibly affection, or unfounded awe while in fact signifying only that something used to be there.

Dignus est is the phrase used in ancient liturgies to proclaim the worthiness of a candidate for ordination—"s/he is worthy." It might be the most significant change I have encountered in our regular worship in my lifetime, that the notion of being unworthy before God, previously reinforced at each Mass as all pronounced the *"Domine non sum dignus"* ("Lord, I am not worthy") prayer before communion, is gone from our regular Eucharistic practice. The Episcopal Church has made significant changes in the last thirty years, though the work to affirm the dignity and worth of all has proceeded slowly. Only after decades of educating and organizing did we get to the point of electing and ordaining our first openly gay bishop. The first resolution by the General Convention of The Episcopal Church that stated something positive about homosexuality was made when I was a toddler. Now I am forty.

Yet, in the last twenty years, over the course of my adult life in the church, we have gone from a church deeply conflicted about the status of our closeted and out gay clergy, bishops, and lay persons to a church that has learned to love and respect gay people and to put that into practice in most areas, at least in some manner. We remain conflicted about our degree of inclusivity, and we still have among us the remnants of generations for whom being closeted is a permanent way of being, but we have created space for emerging generations to re-form us into the church we know we must be. Bishop Gene Robinson's ordination in 2003 was a catalyst for many other bold decisions in The Episcopal Church, but it was not the beginning.

Our current prayer book (the *Book of Common Prayer*, 1979) was also put into regular use when I was a toddler. It is at once modern, ancient, and traditional, with a deep bow to a regular Eucharistic practice that had not been the norm for most of our church for at least a century. This was a significant liturgical change, and because it was a change, it was considered by some to be "liberal." But the changes our new *Book of Common Prayer* comprised could also be understood as promoting a church polity that was more catholic and liturgical, by invoking a new urgency and space for transformation, a seriousness about "real presence" and the in-breaking of God into our highly rational practice. And in the new liturgy, the language of unworthiness before God is gone.

I understand that what is traditionally meant by unworthiness, "*non sum dignus*," in the church is subtle, referring to scripture (Matt. 8:8) and expressing a position that, it could be argued, is true insofar as our lives as fallen humans are replete with sin. But I do not believe that our negative modern sense of our selves, as failed consumers, spouses, children, and wage earners, is the intention of either the liturgical language or the Gospel text. And *that* kind of failure is where I believe most of us go in our prayerful imaginations when we hear the language of worth.

To take this a step further in relation to the topic at hand: I do not believe we approach the altar hoping that God will hear us if we are worthy. I believe we approach the altar hoping to hear God, and we frame that listening by the words we say. Jesus shows us that those whom society names unworthy are the ones to whom Jesus goes to show the power of God. In the encounter between Jesus and the "unworthy," the tables are turned, healing is received, conversations initiated, and salvation proclaimed. But the unworthiness proclaimed by society and perpetuated by the macro- and microdynamics of empire is not a title to take on for ourselves or for the church to apply. Nor is accepting this kind of designation an act of humility. Rather, this imposition of unworthiness is an act of degradation perpetuated by those with power over those who have none. It is a tool of empire. And amid this distorted cultural context, we had previously been trained to impose unworthiness upon ourselves in prayer, as though those very powers that Jesus decries had become for us the voice of God. The Episcopal Church decided to change that in our current prayer book. Thank God.

We are also returning to ancient modes of prayer that predate the British Empire: we often stand, following the practice of the ancient church, instead of kneeling, as was done in the presence of a sitting monarch; some of the language of kingship is muted; we are invited to imagine the reign of God as something quite different than the power structures of our society and even quite different from the seemingly benign, antiquated power structures of Britain. It can feel to some like a lack of discipline or seriousness, but I think it is a return to imagining, as in the garden, that we are responsible for ourselves; a return to desiring fellowship with God; and a return to working against the shame and pride that keep us from that fellowship.

The theology now reembedded in our liturgy and presented for our reflection and action on a weekly basis is that we, as individuals, in our essence, are worthy. The liturgy emphasizes that we who read or sing together have been created and more wonderfully restored in the image of God. Now that might sound like a light thing, and critics say it does not take seriously enough the power of sin in our lives. But I think it does something different. It clarifies the action of sin—the sins we commit, those committed against us, and those structural sins that are beyond our individual power—as actions distinct from our core being. Our true selves are formed in the image of God and seek to recover the clarity of that image. It is evil that is foreign to us, not good. Of course it is more complicated than that, but I think the formative theological impact of the renewed liturgy has made an enormous difference in how The Episcopal Church has perceived the changes in society toward LGBT people. This, combined with our tradition of continual openness to discovering new facets of God's truth everywhere in our world, has given us space to imagine that a person's experience of a basic drive in terms of desire or gender expression, when it is not in conformity to social expectations, might nonetheless be a good or neutral value and not an eruption of an ever-present potential to sin.

When I was very newly a chaplain at UCLA, a young man whom I encountered on campus one day asked if he could meet with me because he was going to be engaged. He was eighteen. We walked together, and I began mentally preparing my "why we don't get married at eighteen" speech and hoping, as a twenty-seven-year-old, to try to figure out how to deliver it with authority. We were crossing a street, me preoccupied, and him continuing to talk about his betrothed, marriage, and how exciting this relationship was, when I realized that he was talking about another man.

In my opinion, this young man is a child of our 1979 prayer book. He was from a conservative part of the church, but he had not been taught by the church to be suspect of himself. He was the first of many who have proven to me that the culture of our church has radically shifted, not least because of the possibilities for flexibility in our individual self-understandings that have been formed in us as people who pray this prayer book.

In one generation of local practice of prayer, the deeply held self-understandings of individuals have been transformed by our intentionality in language and ritual. Of course I don't want to imply that using the liturgical formulae simply or magically provided this young man with wholeness and self-acceptance. He did the work for himself, or perhaps it is better said that the language of prayer, experienced in this community, allowed God to work in him. And it is important for us, as church community, to see that through our faithful, renewed practice, we can play a real part in making that kind of change happen.

Most members of the congregations and chaplaincies I have worked within cannot tell you what the difference is between the theology of the new Eucharistic prayers and of the old Eucharistic prayers. They don't need to be articulate about it to be influenced by it. They pray it. This young man had never heard anything else.

To give you a little more perspective on the kind of transformation that can happen and how quickly it can happen, let me share with you a little more about my own story. I was twenty-seven at the time I encountered that young man at UCLA. I had come out ten years before, when I was seventeen years old, to myself. I come from a liberal Christian family that does not talk about sex. I never heard anything negative about homosexuality except from one teacher, and nothing from a religious authority. Yet I was a suicidal teenager, not able to imagine how I could live through adulthood as I was—though at the time, I could not have told you what my internal conflict actually was. This is a story told by many queer people. My brain kept me alive by not letting me know what could not be tolerated in my parents' house.

When I was seventeen, I went away to college, and in a "Women in Hebrew Scripture" class, I began to learn about reading the Bible as an ancient text, stripping away my assumptions of what the text was and was not allowed to say. In contesting my filter—which had been put in place to enable me to see in the text only what I was supposed to see—I did the same for myself. I remember reading for class one day, just reading the texts assigned for homework, and *getting it*. Getting the story of salvation. Getting the Gospel, like old-school evangelicals get it. It felt like being saved. Maybe that's what it was, except that I don't use that language. I got that I was a part of that story, and I got that I was gay.

I remember in that moment feeling free. I had grown up in an environment that was actually quite open in many ways. But I knew enough to not consider the possibility that I was gay, because it was not safe even to think it. I remember that moment well, and I remember then thinking, "I've got to call my parents—they will be so excited that I figured this out." And then thinking, "Well, maybe I should talk to somebody else first—but who?"

As you can probably imagine, my parents were not excited to find out. My life fell apart when they found out, but I was old enough and had enough resources to survive, and the resource most important for my survival was some skill in reading the Bible.

I know that we all have within us the capacity to survive, and our primary resource as Christians is in knowing what is of God in us. In struggles for freedom it is not simply that God is on our side. It is that what is held against us or called out as evil or lesser, and what is suppressed in our communities, is, on the contrary, something we *can* know, we can teach, we can believe is good—a part of our creation in the image of God. This knowledge, this recognition of our truth and our *worth*, is the source of our power to struggle and survive. When we deny it or it is denied us, and when we believe that denial to be true, we are as good as dead. We imagine ourselves as dead; we carry death with us.

———————

I have buried far too many young people—as has every pastor. Trying to say some word of comfort to a family, when often I don't know if it is the family that really drove that child to this end, and not knowing who else in the room might be struggling with the same weight. I think that all I as a pastor—or any of us—have to offer is some small word of hope to those like us whom we pray will simply survive to a place or time where there might be a little more freedom or a few more resources to start again.

I want you to hear "*Dignus est*" and pray it for yourselves. We hear that we are not worthy, everywhere, all the time. The smartest among us, the bravest, and often the most joyful still carry that burden. As a pastor I regularly meet in church people in their fifties who have been out for a year or even less. Often these are people who are advocates for peace and justice for everyone else on the planet yet who have not been able to face themselves or to be public about who they are until a year ago, or six months ago, or two years ago—because of what society or the culture of our churches has taught them.

A little glimmer of hope is all that so many people have needed. In my church we just married a man, a brilliant advocate for working people around the world, fearless. He's called the "Cobra" by the AFL-CIO: he's that fearless. He's not afraid of Wal-Mart. He came out at his workplace while watching the inauguration of President Obama. That was the first time he had had the courage to speak this truth about himself. He is one of the most joyous people you will ever meet, but the church had done a number on him. He had never heard a good word from Christianity until he came to The Episcopal Church. I'm not telling you to leave your church; often change comes because we remain where we are, if we can. But the church is not the end; your salvation is.

———————

I will end where I started. The way we seek truth as mainline, liturgical Christians will lead us to inclusion. I find this resonating in the words of the gay Catholic theologian James Alison. What he foresees for the

Roman Catholic Church is illustrated, I think, by the actions The Episcopal Church has taken. So I close with James Alison's words, from a letter to a young, gay Roman Catholic. He writes:

> Do not be surprised, then, that they will be considered loyal and trustworthy who pursue every conceivable psychological false lead with a view to finding scientific backing for the claim that being gay is a pathology. They will receive approval as a sign of contradiction, of not yielding to the spirit of the age, while you will be considered a bad Catholic, if a Catholic at all. For long after the evangelical groups—which gave birth to reparative therapy, and the ex-gay movement have moved on and their leaders apologized for leading people astray, such ideas will find Catholic backers and supporters, since they flatter current Church teaching. But don't be afraid of these ideas. And don't hate their propagators. They are our brothers. The very fact that these brothers understand that if the Church's teaching is true, it must have some basis in the discoverable realm of nature, means that ultimately, it is the evidence of what is true in that realm which will set us free. It will be bigger than what either you, or I, or they, can guess right now and it will set us all free.

Dignus est.

Part III: Practicing Education

Listening to Voices of Students and Teachers

This section begins with an essay by Teresa Delgado, a professor of Christian ethics at a Roman Catholic liberal arts college, who describes the ways in which her campus community responded to a transgender colleague who had undergone genital reassignment surgery and to a group of students who had advocated for a public event on safer sex practices. Both situations, Delgado writes, represented opportunities for participants to engage in the "subtle, complex, and poignant interpersonal, institutional, and moral 'dance'" that characterizes discussions of LGBTQ concerns in Catholic institutions of higher education. Naming this dance prompts Delgado to discuss a series of questions about heterosexual privilege, conscience, institutional identity, and her own identity as a Catholic, heterosexual, feminist scholar.

Next, John Falcone describes what he calls "Rainbow Ministry" and "Queer Ritual Practice," two sets of practices that have marked his career in Catholic secondary education and social justice ministry, his present role as a doctoral student in a Catholic theological institution, and his personal relationship with Catholicism. Drawing upon his experiences as a student leader and upon his partner's practice of wearing a rainbow pin to Catholic liturgies, Falcone highlights the ways in which these and kindred practices create space for what he names the work of the Holy Spirit.

In the final essay here, Jeanine Viau presents findings from her in-depth interviews with more than a dozen LGBTQ men and women who attend Catholic universities in the greater Chicago area. Viau puts at the center of her text the voices of these individuals, who recount in their own words what it has been like to learn about Catholic teachings on homosexuality, or to be bullied by both teachers and students, or to encounter silencing among family members and peers, or, most poignantly, to experience the suicide of a friend and lover. Viau movingly captures these young people's descriptions of their experiences and the ways in which many of them have employed resources from the Christian and Catholic traditions to empower themselves and others. Her essay situates these intensely personal testimonies against the background of Catholic social ethics, laying the groundwork for further practical-theological explorations of their narratives. Her findings recall both Delgado's notion of the "dance" undertaken by LGBTQ and ally members of Catholic institutions and Falcone's sense of the practices through which LGBTQ individuals and communities can carve out personal and theological space for their fuller flourishing.

10 A Delicate Dance

*Utilizing and Challenging the Sexual Doctrine of
the Catholic Church in Support of LGBTIQ Persons*

TERESA DELGADO

Iona College

When asked to consider how the Catholic Church's response to
LGBTIQ persons and issues affects my work life, particularly as a person
who works at a Catholic institution, my thoughts were drawn to two distinct experiences, the first in relation to a colleague at the college where
I teach who underwent genital reassignment surgery and the second in
relation to the student group on our campus that advocates on behalf of
the LGBTIQ community.

Let me first speak of my faculty colleague whom, for our purposes, I
will call Mary. When I met Mary, she was in the latter stages of her genital reassignment. In our brief conversations, she was candid with me
about her experience, the physical hurdles that still awaited her, and the
concerns she had about returning to the college once most of the final
series of surgeries was complete. In this final stage, I believe she took
about a year off. When she returned, she was beaming; she looked wonderful, simply beautiful, and seemed genuinely happy to be back. Yet I
worried for her. In her absence, there was chatter about "that professor
who was trans"; even the first-year students I was advising asked about
her with a sense of trepidation. More importantly, I was concerned about
the "official" response from the college—an institution founded in the
Catholic tradition of higher education by the Christian Brothers—and
whether she would be welcomed or, in spite of her tenured status, alienated and isolated.

In an open conversation during that year's "Coming Out Week" (and
the fact that we had a Coming Out Week is a testament to our students,
whom I'll get to in a minute), Mary spoke about her experience: how she
knew at an early age that the person she was inside didn't coalesce with
her biology, how she has developed a "new family" since her biological
family has rejected her, and how in her work and professional life at a

Catholic college she has found the most welcoming and affirming space of all. She mentioned with gratitude the support she has received from everyone, from former students with whom she has maintained contact to current students and colleagues. This was the best-attended noontime event I had witnessed in my six years on the faculty. And here is what surprised me the most: For all the church's outward and official talk about the "disordered" nature of those persons who do not fit the heterosexual norm, our Catholic institution didn't treat her as such. Instead, Mary was treated with respect and dignity in everything from the more administrative aspects of changing the name on her identification card to her full inclusion back into the life and work of the college.

The second experience I would like to relate is centered on the students at the college who are involved in advocacy with and for LGBTIQ persons on campus. Their group is called the GSA, which stands not for Gay Students' Association but instead for Gay/Straight Alliance—a compromise made with administrators in order for them to allow such a group to meet on a Catholic campus. It seems it was less of an offense against Catholic teaching to speak of solidarity with homosexual persons than to affirm their very existence. Interesting.

For "Coming Out Week" in April 2011, GSA students wanted to hold a conversation with an outside speaker regarding safer sex practices, but they needed a faculty person to moderate the event. As the faculty director of the Peace and Justice Studies Program, I was more than willing to take on this role. The students hoped for an open forum that would frame the dialogue in the context of Catholic moral teaching around sexuality yet still allow for discussion about specific sexual practices (including condom use in varied situations). Challenged by this potentially polarizing moment, I decided to introduce the event (again, well attended) with a brief overview of the Catholic Church's official stance regarding sexual activity expressed outside of a heterosexual marital norm. After some lively discussion where students reflected upon the church's teaching, including a refreshing acknowledgment of its wisdom in some areas, the general consensus among students in attendance leaned in the direction of critique and challenge. They were not willing to concede that healthy sexual exploration must be limited to those in married heterosexual relationships. Then we spent the majority of the time discussing condoms, dental dams, and water-based lubricants.

Reflecting on these two experiences, it strikes me that all the participants found themselves engaged in a sort of subtle, complex, and poignant
interpersonal, institutional, and moral "dance." As with any dance, there
are spoken and unspoken rules of engagement as well as a need to participate in reciprocal give and take, push and pull, teach and learn. Those of
us working in Catholic settings who affirm LGBTIQ persons and experience, I believe, must learn to do various versions of this delicate dance in
our work lives, work places, and in our professional scholarship. In my
case, as a theologian and ethicist, I must be more than attentive to and
aware of the church's official doctrinal stance regarding sexuality and
the sources from our tradition that inform that stance. As a constructive
theologian/ethicist, I am also called to challenge that doctrine when it is
death dealing instead of life affirming, when it breaks rather than builds
up the spirit, and when it leads to attitudes and actions that can cause one
of God's children to jump from a bridge or slit his wrists or inject poison
into her veins. I know with whom I want to dance.

Dancing for and with my LGBTIQ students and colleagues, as well as
dancing with the Catholic Church's doctrine, means that I have had to
deal with other colleagues who ask, "Do you think you should sponsor that
program since it may lead to a removal of institutional funding?" I can
understand the anxiety at the center of this question; in times of financial
uncertainty, when it is increasingly difficult to attract sources of institutional advancement and development, everyone at the college is expected
to keep our financial well-being at the forefront, without introducing programming that may undermine this goal. However, if a Peace and Justice
Studies Program at a Catholic college doesn't advocate for the least of these,
who will?

Others have told me, "Maybe you should wait to get tenure before align-
ing yourself so boldly with controversial persons and issues." Comments
like these suggest a whole new meaning to "coming out": for those of us who
can claim heterosexual privilege, choosing to remain in that privileged
space for our own benefit, which is to say not advocating for our LGBTIQ
brothers and sisters until it is safe for us, becomes yet another example of
a silence that equates not with life but with death.

My stance as one who is open to and affirming of LGBTIQ persons and
experiences means that as a Catholic theologian and ethicist, I am unwilling to assert the absolute primacy of current Catholic moral teaching or

to make it the exclusive and definitive norm on matters of sexuality. My theologically grounded preferential option for and with my LGBTIQ neighbors means that, in my work life as a scholar and professor, I put my relationships with my LGBTIQ colleagues and students before my relationship with the hierarchy of the church, come what may.

My particular work space—in an institution that claims its Catholic heritage but does not answer directly to the hierarchy of the church[1]— allows me to push against some of the doctrinal boundaries around sexuality. I don't think I could work in any other type of environment. The uniqueness of working at an institution that is grounded in its Catholic heritage *and* willing to engage in robust dialogue within the contours and margins of that tradition has allowed me the intellectual freedom to be theologically and ethically constructive. I am blessed by the opportunity to incorporate the best of my tradition without the fear of being silenced, expelled, or banished for offering a different perspective on the landscape of Catholic moral theology.[2] Being in this environment means that I cannot be dismissive of the heritage of which I claim to be a part. Nor do I wish to be.

In my professional life, as a scholar trained under the mentorship of the womanist theologian Delores Williams at Union Theological Seminary, I take Alice Walker's definition of a womanist very seriously, and it inspires my affirmation of LGBTIQ persons in my scholarship and my life: "a woman who loves other women, sexually and/or nonsexually. . . . [who is] committed to survival and wholeness of entire people, male and female."[3] The primary norm in my scholarship as a Catholic heterosexual woman is that of love: loving others for who they are in all their being. Again, Alice Walker's definition of womanist is guiding wisdom: "Loves music. Loves dance. Loves the moon. Loves the Spirit. Loves love and food and roundness. Loves struggle. Loves the Folk. Loves herself. Regardless." Love is at the heart of our relationality with others and the world around us. It's very simple, really. It reminds me of a song I was taught at the Church of the Nativity on Dyre Avenue in the Bronx: "And they'll know we are Christians by our love, by our love; yes, they'll know we are Christians by our love." The norm of love seems so simple, yet we know it is far from it.

We have tremendous resources for promoting authentic love within our Roman Catholic tradition, and we must avail ourselves of these. These resources can allow us to dance the delicate dance of moral and spiritual integrity within a tradition that remains so full of ambiguity and contradiction in the midst of its proclaimed certainty. At its best, our Catholic tradition encompasses the affirmation of the senses, the sensual, the erotic and ecstatic in ways that allow us to rejoice and delight in the body as a locus for revelation and the movement of the Holy Spirit. Our Catholic tradition of embodied love—love present in physical form in the person of Jesus Christ and through our celebration of the Eucharist—is one that affirms the giving and receiving of love through our bodies. As such, we can use this embodied theology and ethic as a guide to discerning the presence of love embodied in the lives of LGBTIQ persons. To be sure, heterosexual persons do not have a monopoly on what authentic love looks like.

We have the legacy of those within our church who have spoken prophetic words at the risk of their own lives and careers, speaking out in solidarity with those who live among the shadows. In our own time, I am grateful for the work of Sr. Margaret Farley, whose book *Just Love: A Framework for Christian Sexual Ethics* has been profoundly influential for my work in particular, and for Roman Catholics in general, by emphasizing the norm of justice as a starting point for sexual ethics.[4] Not surprisingly, Dr. Farley's book was presented with a "Notification" by the Congregation for the Doctrine of the Faith (published June 4, 2012) that stated that it did not conform to the teaching of the magisterium of the church, particularly in relation to moral theology. Mary Hunt has continued to inspire my work, from her visiting professorship at Colgate University in the 1980s to her unyielding dedication to the rights of women and the call to serve the church. Her vocational passion is embodied in the work of WATER (Women's Alliance for Theology, Ethics, and Ritual), which she co-founded and co-directs, enfleshing the commitment to women-church and affirming the calling of all persons to serve the church we love. Ivone Gebara, a Brazilian Sister of Notre Dame, continues to teach the hierarchy about what it means to listen to the voices of the church. As one of the theologians cited in Matthew Fox's text, *The Pope's War*, Gebara has described herself as "a naughty bee accused of producing honey of a different flavor"; she has been a staunch advocate for justice on behalf of poor women in Latin America and across the globe, challenging the patriarchal framing of evil and salvation as death dealing to the most vulnerable in society.[5] I am grateful for those who work and minister within other denominations and traditions, particularly those, like Marvin Ellison, Ellen Armour, and Emilie Townes, who are working toward full affirmation of LGBTIQ persons and whose work continues to inspire my own. These are examples of faithful voices within the Roman Catholic tradition, as well as in dialogue with the Roman Catholic tradition, who have been doing this delicate dance within the discourse of Christian sexual ethics and moral theology, to demonstrate the ways our LGBTIQ neighbors embody the authentic love of God in their very being, in their love for one another, and in their witness to the world.

I am also grateful for the courage of so many LGBTIQ Latinos and Latinas who are coming out to share their struggles and stories in the midst of a community, both religious and cultural, that is so incredibly hostile to them and their experience. My own scholarship is informed and inspired—in fact propelled—by women and men who have been wounded by a culture and faith tradition—Catholic at its core even if now, in many sectors, moving toward Pentecostal or mainstream Protestant expression—that has been reliant on a belief in a literal interpretation of an inerrant biblical text. All too often, we in the Latino/a community don't question the intent of the interpretation, we don't question doctrines espoused by clerical authority, and we don't question the hierarchy of family structure. When those of us within the Latino/a community with the power and privilege to speak refuse to do so, our silence further conspires against our Latino/a LGBTIQ neighbors who dare not come out of the closet. This makes my public affirmation of LGBTIQ persons and experiences doubly challenging because not only does it potentially alienate me from my faith community, but it alienates me from my own Latino/a community of accountability. Yet I can't help but think of those within the community whose family, church, and culture have rejected them. As a Latina Catholic theologian, they are the reason for my work life, my work space, and my scholarship. Springing from my love of God, a God of love and justice, I take these words to heart: "Whatsoever you do to the least of these, you do this to me."

So the delicate dance continues. I will continue the uneasy task of utilizing the rich tapestry of my Roman Catholic tradition, centered on the one who has been made flesh and embodies the eternal love of God, while challenging the ways in which that love has been usurped as the exclusive

property of a select few, to be expressed only in select ways and for specific and particular goals. I believe, as a Roman Catholic, that God's authentic love can be witnessed in far more spaces and places than we've been
taught to see; I have witnessed this love in my LGBTIQ neighbors, and I
have been moved profoundly by it. We must train our eyes to see differently,
tune our ears to listen intently, and then move our feet and dance together,
so delicately.

11   Do Not Quench the Spirit

Rainbow Ministry and Queer Ritual Practice in Catholic Education and Life

JOHN P. FALCONE

Boston College

When colleagues at Fordham invited me to speak about the intersection of professional life and LGBT (lesbian, gay, bisexual, transgender) identity, I was excited! After I graduated from Fordham, I spent a year in the Jesuit Volunteer Corps (working with St. Louis Effort for AIDS) and almost three years as a social worker. I then earned my Masters of Divinity from Union Theological Seminary and worked for almost a decade as a Catholic high school teacher and campus minister, often in inner-city settings. I've spent most of my professional life as an out gay man within Catholic institutions, living in the often difficult tension between frankness and prudence, between tradition and change. A practice of constant discernment, of continual negotiation and "coming out," can be a source of personal and professional strength. I have come to see this practice as a "Rainbow Ministry"—a vocation, a school for discipleship, and a form of service to others.

For the past five years, I have been a doctoral student in Theology and Education at the Boston College School of Theology and Ministry (STM). I've been involved with a group of LGB and allied/straight students also studying at the STM. (No one there has yet publicly identified as "T"ransgender.) Over time, what started as a monthly brunch meeting has turned into a leadership venue for ministers and ministers-in-training. Our group has expressed itself publicly mainly through the medium of *ritual*. We have created, and have invited the entire STM community to share in, a number of original and powerful prayer services that combine word, image, movement, and art. At these services, many queer and straight students have preached and presided at worship for the very first time. Administrators, faculty, and students have prayed for social justice and ecclesial healing. We have called for the dawn of queer liberation and for the intercession of queer and straight saints. I describe this as "Queer Ritual Practice."

In this essay, I illustrate my experiences of Rainbow Ministry and of Queer Ritual Practice. I describe how these experiences have led me to deeper integrity and to deeper freedom at worship and at work. Since I am a theologian-in-training, I end with a theological reflection on the ways that the Holy Spirit moves through these queer Catholic practices. I've never thought of myself as a "Holy Spirit" type of Catholic. I was raised as a middle-class Italian American by immigrant parents in the Bronx. I feel at home with processions and statues, and more latterly with academics and with ancient texts—not so much with speaking in tongues and messages from the realm of the Spirit. But I've become convinced that the Holy Spirit has a palpable impact on our lives. The Spirit both disturbs and upholds us. She invites us to unleash our creativity and to unshackle our witness and our prayer. In the midst of our decisions and dynamics, the Holy Spirit nudges us toward fidelity to God's revelation and opens us to God's desires for positive change.

Experiences of Rainbow Ministry

My partner Matias lives in London, because until recently American law prevented us from living as a married couple in the United States. Matias is Indonesian, firmly Catholic, and by trade an engineer. Two Sundays a month, he goes to the local Anglican church, where the preaching is insightful, the theology is progressive, and the communion is open. Every other Sunday, he puts on his rainbow cross lapel pin and wears it to Mass at his local Catholic parish.

Matias considers this his "rainbow cross ministry." He knows that his ministry has been successful when, as he walks up to Communion or shakes hands at the Sign of Peace, the other person's gaze is transfixed by that cross. He can see the thoughts begin to form: "What does this mean? Is he gay? Isn't he Catholic? How can he be both? Should I have shaken his hand? Should I have refused him Communion? How am I supposed to react?"

Matias's fortnightly ministry models one way that LGBT Catholics can develop their faithfulness, courage, and skill, and it evokes similar virtues in the people he confronts. His witness is subtle yet risky, especially in cultures where discretion and conformity are prized. Because he jams together two seemingly incompatible identities—that of being openly gay and that of being a devout and bona fide Catholic—he courts marginalization. He also generates teachable moments for both himself and the Catholics around him. How can we foster more powerful practices of truth telling and more skillful practices for living in the inevitable tension that results? Matias's version of witness creates difficult but Spirit-filled spaces where Christians with different identities can develop real competence for living together.

Borrowing Matias's language, I use "Rainbow Ministry" to describe any faith-filled, well-calibrated practice that employs courage, witness, and teachable moments to build skills for inclusive community. Rainbow Ministry offers both graces and challenges, especially in professional settings. I share three of those challenges here.

The first concerns getting a job. Queer people continually ask ourselves how out we want and need to be in our lives and our work. A résumé is a tool for job hunting, but it can also be a political and educational tool. My résumé contains a record of my work in AIDS services and of my leadership in LGBT Catholic organizations. It challenges potential employers to think about gay people in Catholic ministry. It gives me the opportunity to have open and forthright discussions both during the hiring process and over the course of my employment. It allows me to be very upfront. Potential employers know they will be hiring someone who is willing to be out on the job, and I'm making it clear from the outset that, if you can't handle that reality, I don't want to work in your organization.

The second challenge concerns the tensions between keeping my job and telling the truth. When I worked in poor and working-class schools, I told the principal that I would be out to adult staff and faculty but that I would avoid coming out to the students. If a student, or a class, or the school community really *wanted* to know, or if there were some crisis and I decided that they *needed* to know, I would make my sexuality public. With that moment, the focus of instruction would shift from Bible, liturgy, or social analysis to my own identity in the classroom. I would also become a liability to the school's fundraising and diocesan support—a liability poor kids can't afford. I must be prepared to resign and to turn my own resignation into a teachable moment for everyone concerned. For me, that moment never came. Sometimes my bosses and I were able to work around such dilemmas. Sometimes they were too anxious about finding a replacement (or perhaps too nervous and conflicted about their own closeted identities) to push me over the edge.

The third challenge concerns life at the margins. As a gay religious professional, I work and live at the margins of my own denomination. I've had the grace of working with unchurched teenagers, with gay targets of spiritual abuse, with people with AIDS who are deeply spiritual but can only be religious with caution. When I first came out, I stopped attending Catholic Mass and became involved in an Episcopal parish. I needed a faith community where I didn't feel compelled to police my own conversations and thoughts. On retreat a year later, I had a realization: "As a card-carrying Roman Catholic, I have the right to enter any Catholic church around the world . . . and to feel *un*-welcome, because I am gay." At that moment, I began to embrace my Catholic identity in a more mature and critical way, with a kind of unattached joy. I did not end up converting to Episcopalianism, but I still take communion regularly at Episcopal churches. My parish home is now Dignity—a community of LGBT believers who consider ourselves Roman Catholics in exile from the hierarchical church.[1] Like so many other marginalized Catholics, we persevere in our faith despite leaders who label us "dissidents" or who insist that we have been excommunicated. We partake of a peculiar grace: we serve as a living contradiction to the politics of dominance and submission that has so burdened the Body of Christ. Marginalized Catholics are called to share this grace with those who depend on a rigid identity, with those who cling to a sense of God's love and God's plan that is far too narrow and stingy.

As a Catholic religious educator who is gay, I have a duty to use my professional religious clout, a duty to open up spaces where believers and seekers can discover and develop their own voices of faith. Framing my work as a Rainbow Ministry helps me practice this calling in truth telling and sustainable ways.

Experiences of Queer Ritual Practice

Ministry depends on support and renewal—from fellow believers and from the Spirit of God. I have often found spiritual sustenance in the rituals and prayers of the underrated, where God's power is made perfect in weakness (2 Cor 12:9). I have felt God's Spirit at work at Dignity, at Spirit-filled Protestant and interfaith services, in faith-filled Catholic communities, and at the rituals of people with AIDS. Certainly, these have been "queer" prayer experiences because they welcomed LGBT people. But they were also "queer" (odd, eyebrow-raising, transgressive) because they spoke uncomfortable insights, because they innovated with traditions and images, because they united all the "wrong" kinds of people.

When inspired by God's Word and Spirit, Queer Ritual Practice becomes a form of Rainbow Ministry. At the School of Theology and Ministry, my experience of this prayerful practice began in the fall of 2010, with a monthly Saturday brunch meeting of gay and bisexual men. The STM is a fairly new project, created in 2008 by the merger of Weston Jesuit School of Theology and Boston College's Institute of Religious Education and Pastoral Ministry. As I came to realize, small groups of lesbian and gay friends had already found one another within the student body, but we rarely identified ourselves publicly. This made it difficult to gather and organize in more than twos and threes. The Saturday morning brunch group became the first explicitly LGB caucus at this new Catholic graduate school of theology.

Between January 2011 and May 2012, the group and its members became more active, productive, and prophetic. We called ourselves GIFTS: "GLB Inclusive Fellowship of Theology Students." Our first project was an April 2011 all-school prayer service titled "Knit Us Into One." Inspired by liberation and feminist theologies and by examples of creative liturgy, we designed the service to address multiple tensions at the STM, including those between "Weston" and "IREPM"; "liberals" and "conservatives"; first-years and second-years; and queers, allies, and skeptical straights. In September 2011, the administration invited GIFTS to become an "official" student organization; we appeared on the STM website and were welcomed into student government. That fall, we produced another prayer service to mark the feast of Sts. Sergius and Bacchus (popularly regarded as an early Christian same-sex couple). We also received funds to attend the More than a Monologue symposia at Yale and Fairfield Universities.

The backlash came in November 2011, when I published an article that described our visit to the Fairfield Monologue gathering.[2] In the wake of that article's appearance, the STM administration revoked our official status, reprimanded our leaders, and laid out strict guidelines for future activities.[3] To regain official recognition, we would have to foreswear any more "advocacy" work. We must eliminate the words "lesbian," "gay," and "bisexual" from our group description, and I personally must be banned from group leadership. The result among our members was anger, confusion, frustration, and infighting, as any shrewd administrator might have predicted. Less predictable was the eventual upshot: another prayer service, in April 2012, entitled "From Silence to Song."

I want to focus on two of our prayer services as examples of Spirit-filled Queer Ritual Practice. The first is the "Knit Us Into One" service, which I mentioned earlier. In January 2011, our brunch group decided to host a prayer service for and with the STM community. We assembled over a dozen student writers, researchers, and artists (including the same-sex partners of several student planners). We asked ourselves: "What does our community need right now?" and "What particular gifts as LGB students and queer-supportive allies can we share to meet those needs?" Our greatest wish was to foster a unity in which we could celebrate our rich diversity. This was our statement of purpose: "As LGB students and their allies, we invite all to recognize and share their gifts, for the building up of the Body of Christ."

Our service reflected this openness. It also expressed our anger toward homophobic oppression. It reflected our frustration over the "don't ask, don't tell" attitude toward sexuality in general that pervades so many classrooms and churches. It celebrated the power of "coming out" as queer, or as an ally, or as whatever is not fully "appropriate" ("I'm a survivor of childhood abuse," ". . . an alcoholic," ". . . pro-choice," ". . . a traditionalist"). It celebrated the power of integrity: of being at one within oneself, embracing one's own gifts, and embracing the gifts of others. And it turned us toward God as the author, the source, of creativity and change.

The center of the service was a litany: LGBT saints and heroes, allies to the LGBT movement, straight heroes who struggled for justice in society and inside the church. As the litany progressed, we bound small cardboard icons of each "saint" into a braided felt-strip fabric. Then we invited each member of the congregation to sign his or her own name on a pendant and to bring it forward for binding as well. The main reading reflected the purpose to which this community of witness was called:

We must no longer be children, tossed to and fro and blown about by
every wind of doctrine, by people's trickery, by their craftiness in de-
ceitful scheming. But speaking the truth in love, we must grow up in
every way into him who is the head, into Christ, from whom the whole
body, joined and knitted together by every ligament with which it is
equipped, as each part is working properly, promotes the body's growth
in building itself up in love (Eph 4:14–16).[4]

In this space of reflection and action, God's Spirit could invite us to a new
kind of living: a living out loud and as one.

The second significant ritual was developed in the spring of 2012 under
much more painful circumstances. When GIFTS was shut down and dis-
rupted, many members were in the midst of exploring their own relationships to sexuality, to spirituality, and to the hierarchy of the Church. The
experience was particularly damaging for these students, and the process
of recovery was slow. Some members never came back. Those with the
strength to continue worked together to create "From Silence to Song."

The arc of this service stretched from singing, to silence, and back to
song. We began our prayer in the round, singing a lively Black spiritual.
Between the second and third verse, the co-presiders laid a hand on the
shoulder of the persons beside them—a signal to silence their voices. Hand
to shoulder, person to person, the silence spread until only the cantor was
left. From that point on, the assembly remained mute, through prayers,
readings, petitions, and ritual actions. "We ask this through Christ our
Lord . . . (silence)." We heard music from Godspell and the Black church
tradition. We heard a student sermon on the crippling silence that so often
leads gay teens to suicide. The turning point was our Gospel reading:

"You spirit that keeps this boy from speaking and hearing, I command
you, come out of him, and never enter him again!" After crying out and
convulsing him terribly, it came out, and the boy was like a corpse, so
that most of them said, "He is dead." But Jesus took him by the hand
and lifted him up, and he was able to stand. When he had entered the
house, his disciples asked him privately, "Why could we not cast it
out?" He said to them, "This kind can come out only through prayer"
(Mk 9:25–29).

So, we prayed. Steeped in silence, we prayed for developing nations, for
the victims of sex trafficking, for the ministries that women and lay

people bring to a clericalist and male-dominated church. We prayed for the courage to interrupt bullying, violence, and oppression. We prayed for prisoners, for their families, and for prison reform. We prayed for the earth and all her people. We prayed with poems by Mary Oliver and Adrienne Rich (both award-winning lesbian writers) and by Alfred Pang (an STM student). We prayed that the Holy Spirit might seek us out in our silence, might open our minds to God's judgment, might free us with God's life-giving Word. We prayed that each person and group might be restored to a place and a voice of their own.

Then, finally, one by one, we each rose as the Spirit moved us to join in the closing anthem, "How Can I Keep from Singing?" Led back to our voices and our songs, we came together in the center of our worship space and processed out, chanting and clapping.

Experiencing the Holy Spirit

When Rainbow Ministry and Queer Ritual Practice reflect Gospel values, the Spirit of God moves within them. Describing the shape of Her movements can help us discern what is godly. Here, two theological terms may be helpful: *parrhesia* and the concept of "emergence."

Parrhesia is the ancient Greek word for "*saying everything.*" It helps us to name how the Spirit transforms us. *Parrhesia* means "freedom and frankness of speech." More and more, LGBT people and our allies have learned to embrace *parrhesia*; we have learned how to "tell it like it is." A spirit of "don't ask, don't tell" leaves people fragmented and disunited, easily manipulated and confused. A spirit to proclaim the truth with courage is the essence of prophetic witness; it is the essence of "coming out."

Parrhesia was a key virtue in both ancient philosophy[5] and early Christian practice: "for I will give you words and a wisdom that none of your opponents will be able to withstand" (Lk 21:15). In the Greek translations of the Hebrew Bible and in New Testament and early Christian writings, *parrhesia* is portrayed as a gift of God's Spirit, a boldness that comes from the Lord.[6] Modern New Testament translations call it "confidence, fearlessness, openness, courage" and the ability to speak the truth "plainly." When queer Christians employ faithful witness in the practice of wise Rainbow Ministry, they model the gift of godly *parrhesia*, and they teach others to embrace it as a virtue.[7]

"Emergence" is a concept that theologians have borrowed from the natural sciences to help understand how the Spirit does Her work.[8] Contemporary science affirms that the universe is full of intrinsic "uncertainties"; there are "gaps" that defy our power to predict—from quantum indeterminacy and chaos theory, to the patterns that emerge spontaneously within artificial intelligence, to human culture, society, and improvisation. This is not merely a failure of science; it is the nature of our cosmic reality. The universe is structured for freedom; it is looser and more flexible than some human beings might prefer! As a number of theologians have suggested, it is here that spiritual forces can do their work. Spirit exerts a kind of "top-down causality": the unpredictable but palpable influence of the whole upon the sum of its parts.[9]

The Holy Spirit is the power and the wisdom of God at work, "liberating and delivering" people "from distress, possession/obsession captivity, and disintegration."[10] She is the force field that mediates God's great vision and God's great desire for the world. She nudges forth insight and wisdom; She brings unity while maintaining diversity (just as She did on the morning of Pentecost); She makes power to blossom from weakness, at the margins and up through the cracks. She works at the points of dynamic emergence— sometimes suddenly, sometimes through obvious synergies, sometimes with imperceptible subtlety. When we create and partake in good ritual, we resonate with Her creative style. Through our research and writing, our art, insight, and song, we permit the Spirit to move us in new and more humanizing directions. By practicing godly queer ritual we invite others into Her creativity; we teach them to use ritual aright.

If we follow the prompts of the Spirit, our projects will heal and transform us, and our lives will become more whole and more holy. But, as Paul, and Loyola, and so many others attest, if we follow a differing spirit, the result is neurosis, fear, and oppression. Such dynamics can possess people and institutions; they breed lies, abuses, and cover-ups; they bring destruction unless they are cast out.

Rainbow Ministers and Queer Ritual Artists

At the crossroads of LGBT identity and of their Christian vocation in the world, many queer Catholics have discovered an invitation. They feel called to a faith-filled truth telling that combines courage, freedom, and imagination. It is a calling to be shrewd and discerning, wise as foxes and reconciling as doves. It is a calling to shape teachable moments that can lead to more inclusive communities.

We Catholics have always been a people who embrace the unity of service and sacrament. If my journey as a queer Catholic catechist has taught me anything at worship and work, it has shown me new ways to embrace that "full, conscious and active participation . . . which is demanded by the very nature" of the sacraments.[11] By adopting and adapting our rituals, by embracing frank patterns of ministry, and by making witness, prayer, and symbolic action our own in ways that are both Christian and creative, we can move with the Spirit of God.

12   Calling Out in the Wilderness

Queer Youth and American Catholicism

JEANINE E. VIAU

Loyola University Chicago

> I did just as I was commanded. I brought out my baggage by day, the baggage for exile, and in the evening I dug through the wall with my own hands; I brought it out in the dark, carrying it on my shoulder in their sight.
>
> *Ezekiel* 12:7 NRSV

Eve Kosofsky Sedgwick articulates an apt starting point for this reflection: "Seemingly, this society wants its children to know nothing; wants its queer children to conform or (and this is not a figure of speech) die; and wants not to know that it is getting what it wants."[1] Sedgwick's diagnoses take on flesh in the stories of LGBTQ student activists from two urban Catholic universities, whose stories I collected through open-ended interviews focusing on the connections between gender, sexuality, religion, and activism.[2] The recruitment phase of my project coincided with the surge in media and activist attention to the deaths of several gay youth in the early weeks of the fall of 2010.[3] In each case, the suicide was connected to reports of antigay bullying. This surge in public attention helped spotlight more than three decades of research regarding the particular vulnerability of gender and sexual minority youth to bullying, violence, suicide, and other life-threatening forms of social alienation.[4] But despite sustained documentation in clinical, sociological, and educational circles, the social dimensions of these problems have gone largely unaddressed. Even today, as in decades past, queer youth continue to face widespread and unrelenting hostility within their primary social institutions.[5]

The term "queer" originated as a derogatory term in the early twentieth century. The term is reclaimed and appropriated in productive ways by gender and sexual diversity theorists, activists, individuals, and communities. However, its history and ongoing negative use raise problems for many researchers and activists.[6] I use the term "queer" with particular intention and for its fecundity of meaning. The majority of my collaborators, the LGBTQ student activists whom I interviewed, share this intention as they reclaim this term and use it positively and inclusively to describe their communities and their personal identities.

As reclaimed language, this term has the power to acknowledge the historical and continuing demoralization of queer persons while simultaneously playfully giving voice to hope for a just future. It reminds those who claim it and those who hear it to remain vigilant about resisting heteronormativity and attending to those who are still in the wilderness. In fact, queer space and time is always present on the margins of history, and there will always be queer(ed) identities that need recognition and advocacy. This marker also helps supply a liberating standpoint from which to see, judge, and act: namely, "a preferential option for the queer." The voices of queer youth are often ignored or compromised both on account of their perceived immaturity as youth and on account of their particular vulnerability to social violence as queer youth. As doubly queered folk, the work of these courageous young people is prophetic and compelling for Christian communities seeking renewed approaches to gender and sexual justice.

These commitments connect my ethnographic work to a larger movement, a movement that aims to recognize the experiences of marginalized persons and communities as primary sources for theology and ethics.[7] In that spirit, each section of this essay begins with the experiences of the LGBTQ student activists who generously shared their time and stories with me. The narratives I present here are only a sampling of the stories I collected in the larger study, and even those I bring forward here are incomplete. Clearly, these narratives cannot represent all of the experiences and perspectives of LGBTQ youth in the United States or even in Catholic institutional settings, especially considering the demographic similarities among my collaborators. However, I do propose that the stories of these young people provide some generalizable insights for theological ethics and for shaping future studies of LGBTQ youth experience in social institutions. Prioritizing their voices is a needed first step toward fashioning effective methodological and theological interventions within an institutional church that is in denial about the queer bodies hanging from its rafters.[8]

Mapping an Institutional Terrain

Alan was a college senior at the time of our interview and a leader in his school's LGBTQ student activist group as well as in the larger network of university organizations in Chicago. He identifies as a white, cisgender gay male.[9] Regarding the relationship between religion and gender and sexual minority issues in the public forum, he expressed his view plainly: "[If] you take religion out of the equation, there's no justification for what anyone does, you know, against the LGBTQ community." Alan's assessment is the result of his sustained engagement with a wide range of news media sources and his participation in counterprotests and activism in response to the activities of antigay Christian groups such as Westboro Baptist Church. It has also been shaped by his direct experiences with the Catholic community.

Alan is a confirmed Catholic who taught CCD through high school.[10] He is no longer practicing, although he maintains a relationship with God and Jesus and still finds some of Catholicism's core teachings influential in his life. Like the majority of my collaborators who grew up attending church, Alan recalls hearing the condemnation of homosexuality preached from the pulpit in his home parish. The only other time Alan can recall that sexual diversity, much less gender diversity, was mentioned within his faith community was in the context of abuse prevention training for CCD instructors. Alan remembers a statement in a true-or-false exercise meant to dispel the misconception that homosexuality is synonymous with pedophilia. Alan has a somewhat nebulous understanding of Catholic teachings regarding gender and sexuality, which he has extracted mostly from news media coverage of the hierarchy's statements regarding contraception and same-sex marriage. The message has been received, nevertheless: not married, not procreative—not permissible.

Recalling the beginning of his first year in college, Alan remembers with gratitude his Catholic university's opening Mass and the intentional welcoming of gender and sexual minorities at the liturgy. But as his commitments within the LGBTQ activist community continued to expand and church authorities continued to condemn publicly, he found it increasingly difficult to reconcile the two. For Alan, this institutional posturing results, at least for now, in the loss of a faith community. For other gender and sexual minority youth, however, religious condemnation contributes to life-endangering situations, as I bring forward below. First, however, let's notice how Alan's experience helps us transpose particular experience into something larger and more revealing, what Dorothy Smith describes as a "territory to be discovered." Such "territory to be discovered" emerges from people's experience, and exploring it "opens up an institutional complex."[11] Alan's thoughts and experiences open a window onto broader dynamics within American Catholicism, dynamics that characterize the religiosocial terrain that my collaborators are actively navigating.

A first dynamic is the alignment of Christian values, often called traditional family values, with political opposition to the interests of gender and sexual minorities. For example, in response to the recent "surge" of suicides, conservative Christian interest groups and leaders lobbied publicly against the use of gender and sexual minority language in antibullying policies and legislation. The U.S. Catholic bishops were among the most outspoken in this matter.[12] Afraid that these laws could eventually be used to support marriage equality, the bishops abandoned the cause of the victims for the sake of preserving church teaching and authority.[13] This brings forward a second dynamic indicated in Alan's experience, namely, his confusion and dissonance with official church teaching about gender and sexuality.

The U.S. public and many Catholics are confused, even infuriated, by the magisterium's handling of issues related to gender and sexual justice. The most glaring example is the sexual abuse scandal, the local effects of which surface in Alan's story.[14] Rather than take responsibility for silencing victims and continuing to allow offending clergy access to children, the Vatican issued an instruction linking the sexual abuse crisis with homosexuality in the priesthood and launched an investigation to weed out seminary candidates and priests who "present deep-seated homosexual tendencies."[15] Despite what may have been *said* officially, the effect of these official *actions* was to treat homosexuality as essentially synonymous with pedophilia in official church teaching. Magisterial authorities have yet to correct this error. As is evident in Alan's experiences, parish communities must, in turn, take it upon themselves to dispel these misconceptions. Local communities also bear disproportionately the burden of education and abuse prevention, as well as the aftermath of healing and reconciliation for victims, their families, and the communities where violations occurred.

Alienation is the third dynamic that I wish to highlight through Alan's story. Negligence concerning clerical abuses, as well as the seeming disconnect with the realities of members' lives and their related vocational and pastoral needs, are significant contributing factors to the crisis of attrition facing the Catholic Church in the United States. Recent studies reveal that many Catholics are dissatisfied with church leadership and/or fundamentally disagree with magisterial teaching regarding gender and sexuality. In a 2010 poll, the Public Religion Research Institute (PRRI), in partnership with Religion News Service (RNS), found that "Catholics were most likely to give their churches negative marks [for their handling of the issue of homosexuality], with nearly one-third giving their churches a 'D' (15%) or an 'F' (16%)."[16] The Catholic public intellectual Peter Steinfels cites the 2008 U.S. Religious Landscape Survey to talk about "American Catholicism's crumbling condition."[17] This study found that one in three adult Americans who were raised Catholic have left the church, an attrition rate far greater than that of any other religious group in the United States. The statistics given for still-affiliated Catholics are also illuminating. Despite the hard line held by church officials, 48 percent of American Catholics interviewed said that abortion should be legal in all or most cases, as opposed to 45 percent saying illegal in all or most cases. Regarding homosexuality, 58 percent said that homosexuality should be accepted by society, as opposed to 30 percent saying that it should be discouraged.[18] These statistics reveal that *even among faithful* Catholics, there is no consensus with regard to church teachings about gender and sexuality.

Perhaps the most disconcerting news from these studies is that young people are among the most dissatisfied and, thus, the most likely to leave the church. The Pew Forum found that a majority of former Catholics reported having left the church before the age of twenty-four. The PRRI/RNS poll findings indicate a significant generational gap in respondents' assessments of their faith communities: "Nearly half (47%) of young adults (age 18 to 34) say that messages from places of worship are contributing 'a lot' to negative views of gay and lesbian people."[19] The figure is less than one third for Americans sixty-five and older. One wonders how the prophetic mission of the church will survive when, like Alan, so many young people are choosing to invest their creative energies and talents elsewhere.

Yet, despite an ecclesial culture widely characterized by hostility and apathy, there are emerging efforts to energize Catholic communities' sympathies for the struggles of gender and sexual minorities. As my research indicates, many Catholic universities and even some high schools are now home to LGBTQ student activist groups and programming. Diversity and ministry offices on these campuses are attuning to the needs and concerns of gender and sexual minority students. Faith sharing and interest groups are going strong at the parish and diocesan levels. Theologians, clergy and religious, lay ministers, and individuals have been working for some time to reconcile faith and gender and sexual diversity through creative practice and reflection. In the next section, I turn to specific experiences with institutional homophobia in the lives of my collaborators. I emphasize the resilience with which they respond to deeply challenging circumstances. In the last section, I reflect on how their commitments could be used to reorient Christian vocation and, subsequently, inspire hope for a more just church.

Callings Out in the Wilderness

Baruch—"The teacher ignored it"

Baruch identifies as a cisgender, gay male. He was a first-year student at the time of our interview. Of his racial and/or ethnic background, he says, "I'm mixed. I'm German, Mexican, and Puerto Rican." Baruch routinely attended church growing up and experienced a multidenominational upbringing, including exposure to Baptist, Nazarene, and mainline Protestant traditions through multiple family members. From preschool through eighth grade, Baruch attended a nondenominational Christian school. He remembers having attractions to men from a very young age, so in fifth grade, when his Bible teacher taught that "people like you are just absolutely disgusting, like an abomination, scum of the earth," he was aware that she meant him—hence his use of the second person. Baruch reflects, "I have always been raised in a church, and I had always gone through religious schooling. So to hear your Bible teacher say that people like you burn in hell, it crushes your world because then you think, 'Something's wrong with me. I don't know what to do. I don't know how to change it. What did I do wrong?'" These lessons coincided with frequent homophobic bullying from his peers. The power his teacher represented as an authority figure, combined with the abuse of his classmates, led to an attempted suicide. Baruch tried to hang himself in fifth grade.

Baruch tells me that this experience led him to a critical engagement with his tradition. He has made it a priority to read the biblical passages that are often cited in discussions about homosexuality, to understand them in their biblical and historical contexts, and to form his own opinion about their relevancy to his life, a life that he identifies as a Christian life. Another episode from Baruch's story sheds light on his commitment to survival and self-affirmation. Baruch told me about another experience with bullying that began in his sophomore year at a Catholic high school:

> It was in my geometry class, and Lord knows I'm not good at math, so I had to ask a lot of questions or whatever. Well, there was a boy who sat next to me, and then his little minion, as I like to say it, was behind me. And every time I would raise my hand or even just do the motion, I'd hear "faggot" or "cocksucker" or "butt pirate," everything that you can think of. And he would say it loud enough so you knew the whole class heard it.
>
> The teacher ignored it. I don't wanna say that she acknowledged it, but you knew—you could see that she had heard what these guys were saying. And nobody would say a thing, and they would just all titter to themselves or whatever. It never ended. Literally, every time I saw him, even in the hallways or whatever, he would say something. He would shout something at me or push me or whatever. And it got to a point where even just hearing his name made me physically sick to my stomach, and I would go to the bathroom and vomit. It never ended until senior year, when I just—I completely owned it. I was like, "Okay, fine, you're gonna call me a faggot? Do it to my face, 'cause I am one. What, are you scared?" It stopped.

Finn—"Like everyone's just people"

Finn identifies as "transgender—slash—genderqueer—slash—gender variant" and claims a queer sexual orientation.[20] He often identifies simply as a lesbian or gay in order to avoid confusion. At the time of our interview, he was a junior in college and a leader in his university's LGBTQ student activist group. Finn grew up in a white Irish Catholic family, which he describes as "conservative" and "religious." He connects this religious conservatism to the homophobia that he experiences in his family life. When Finn originally came out to his mom as "gay," she expressed unconditional love for him and minimized the issue: "She was like, 'I'm always gonna love you. I really don't care. And like that's just part of who you are. You're a good person. That's the main part of what I want for you.'" However, she requested that Finn not talk about it around his dad. "She was like, 'Just don't bring it up with your dad because your dad knows, but your dad is having a way harder time than I am dealing with it. And like it shouldn't be talked about, and like he's just like not happy with it. And like he has to deal with like his super conservative family. So like just like don't bring it up.' And I was like, 'Okay.'"

She also asked that Finn not tell his younger siblings. Similar to the rationale regarding his father, Finn attributes this restriction to his mom's concerns about the religious communities to which his family belongs: "I'm not supposed to say anything because they both go to religious schools where like my family knows people, and they don't want like their like religious community to know that like they have a gay daughter and things like that, but they all know. Like I wear suits and shit. And I'm pretty sure they caught on." Finn notes that his siblings already know, that in fact, he says, "They actually like are super supportive and like encourage me to be as gay as possible."

His mom is less encouraging, especially when Finn subverts gender expectations in his outward appearance or uses terminology that makes his mom uncomfortable:

> Like I haven't come out as like gender variant just because like I really just don't ever foresee wanting to deal with that with them.
>
> But I like constantly have to like say stuff to my mom, and I feel like a lot of it is like a continual coming out process because I have to like continuously say like, "well, no, I identify as queer," and then she'll be like "well, why do you say that?" . . . She says, "why do you stereotype yourself? Like everyone's just people."
>
> And then—but then I use that for like my gender argument when I'm like "okay, well, if I'm just like Finn and I'm not like—if I'm not [just] gay, then I'm not just female mom, so I'm gonna like wear a suit, and you can't say anything about it." And then she gets pissy, and she's

like "fine, fine, that's fine. Do it. I don't care. I don't know why you'd want to wear a suit." I'm like, "okay. Fine. Whatever."

This recollection and the ones that precede it reveal the incredible burden that queer youth bear in coming out to family, friends, and institutional authorities. Coming out is not a one-off experience. It is a commitment to educate. It is a calling. With regard to his parents' homophobia, Finn describes the resolution he made before coming out: "because one of my primary identities is that I'm queer, I think I might have to like cut them out of my life at some point. And like, I don't know why, like at eighteen I was like I'm gonna make this jump, like be prepared mentally for like having to like not have a family anymore." Queer persons have to face this reality over and over again, always preparing for the possibility that they and/or their relationships with parents, siblings, best friends, mentors, employers, churches, and strangers will not survive if they break the silence. Finn recalls "crying out of happiness" when his mom accepted his initial coming out. This was enough for them to begin the process of coming out together, a process that Finn has generously committed himself to, even with homophobic discouragement and silencing at every turn.

John—"It's when you can feel like closest to God"

John's story speaks to the desire to reconcile nonconforming love with love for one's faith tradition. Queer persons of faith often find themselves in this kind of love triangle. John was a college sophomore at the time of our interview. He identifies as a white, cisgender gay male. He was raised Catholic and still identifies strongly with his tradition. Both of John's parents teach theology at the college level. He attributes to them a deep love and appreciation for Catholicism and a commitment to inquiry and interpretive agency, especially regarding issues of sexual ethics in church teaching. John reflects: "[my dad] sort of showed me that you can be Catholic and not agree with everything that the magisterium says."

John believes that a pro-love emphasis for human sexuality, rather than one grounded in procreative potential, could change the church and enable it to welcome many who are currently alienated. In a fifty-page transcript of my conversation with John, the word "love" occurs fifty-eight times. John uses the language of love to speak about his parents, the Catholic Church, the tradition, sexuality (generally and personally), his beloved, and Jesus. For John, all of these loves are connected: "Like I was told by like my parents how sex is supposed to be like a beautiful thing. And when it's with the right person, it can be like your closest—your most perfect expression of love, and it's when you can feel like closest to God." These connections are most pronounced in John's reflections about the suicide of his beloved, Jude. This event occurred in January of John's first year of college. When they started dating, Jude had recently come out to an extremely hostile family and religious community. Two weeks prior to his death, Jude was violently assaulted by members of his church community who had found out about his relationship with John.

John recalled that about one to two months into the relationship, Jude became depressed. This coincided with Jude's disclosing to John that his father had been sexually abusive toward him. John was the first person whom Jude had told about the abuse. John was also the one who reported Jude's father to the police. Although Jude was receiving counseling at his college during this time, he was relying heavily on John for support. John recollected, "And so for me, I was the carrier of all of this pain that he had to go through. . . . it was almost like I experienced [the abuse] too, because it was so real for me, like how he described it. And so my first semester here was just a mess trying to handle like transitioning to a new school and all these academics, and then dealing with him." At the time, John was not out to his friends or family, so he was limited in seeking his own support. When he finally told his friends what was going on, he initially referred to Jude as his best friend, not his lover. John reflected on the circumstances leading up to and surrounding Jude's death:

> [the hate crime] was about a week or two before his suicide. So I think that was sort of like the last straw and . . . he was just so depressed. And I think that's what led to it. I mean, it's sort of hard to know because, you know, he called me and just said like I'm sorry, and hung up. And that's how I knew like it was happening, so I called the police.
>
> But, you know, it was—like [he stabbed himself] right in his heart. So it was—like he went to the OR, but it was sort of just too late. And . . . I mean, for a while, like I blamed myself because, you know, I thought— like I tried to handle all this on my own.

And while other people knew, like people at his school knew, and he was seeing counselors and stuff, like I was the one who really sort of knew like how bad it was. And I just tried to take care of it on my own, and now I sort of wish I wouldn't have done that.

John's story is tragic and fraught with complications. There is much to observe in it about the evils of religious condemnation and silence regarding non-hetero-conforming love. In addition to the tragedy of Jude's deterioration and death, John felt alone and unable to disclose fully his own struggle to potentially supportive friends and family members. Also, not having appropriate experience or resources for coping with such trauma, John made some questionable decisions. For example, reporting Jude's father to the police may have further compromised Jude's emotional and psychological health and possibly endangered him physically. Another questionable practice was John's continuing to allow Jude to use him as his primary source of support when John was not equipped to help. Reflecting on John's experience, it is easy to become overwhelmed by this young man's entanglement in the quagmire of finitude and sin.

John, however, wrests himself free. He turns to his tradition to grieve the death of his beloved and to fashion a vocational response to Jude's life. John locates Jude in the "Community of Saints," as an ever-present intercessor alongside other martyrs for social justice whose sacrifices he admires. He honors Jude's courage as exemplary: "He was from, you know, such a non-accepting family . . . and his church was not accepting of him at all, and yet he had the strength to come out to them regardless. . . . So once he committed suicide, that was sort of, for me, like a— you know, like what am I doing? Like how selfish is this, to be hiding while other people are in pain because they can't come out?" John did come out to his friends and family. What's more, he interprets Jude's death vocationally, asking, "What purpose can this play in my life?" John has discerned Jude's death as a summons to activism: "[God] wants me to be an activist about these issues because, you know, this is such a personal story for me that I can really make a difference. And if this wouldn't have happened to me, then my voice wouldn't, you know, really reach as many people, I guess." John's thought brings me to some closing reflections.

Reorienting the Vocational Compass

Dawn is Methodist and grew up very active in her faith community. She was skeptical about attending a Catholic university, because she experienced bullying and marginalization growing up in a primarily Catholic Midwestern suburb, and because she has strong feelings about certain justice issues, especially women's ordination. Dawn was a senior at the time of our interview and very active with multiple activist groups at her university. She identifies as bisexual and sometimes queer, depending on the day and how she's feeling, or perhaps with whom she is interacting. She thinks that bisexual is a better way to express her sexual preferences. However, this identification often elicits criticism and/or hostility from certain groups within the LGBTQ community. Some accuse her of "buying into the gender binary," the idea that there are two, distinct gender identities that correspond to two, distinct biological sexes.

As Dawn reflects on her desire to become a minister, she recalls one of the only times she can remember that her faith community addressed gender and/or sexual diversity. People at her church, including the pastor, were talking about a Methodist minister who had been defrocked for being a lesbian. When I asked Dawn about their response to the incident, she said, "Indifference, and disconnect. They were like, 'Oh, that's like not here. That's not our problem,' kind of thing, which really upset me." This upset Dawn not only because she is queer. It upset her because she is Christian.

Dawn is very clear about the importance of social activism for the Christian life. When I ask her about resources from the tradition that support this commitment, she immediately invokes the parable of the Good Samaritan. Dawn tells me the story. "A regular guy gets beat up by robbers. A priest walks past and doesn't help him. And then like a local figure walks past him, doesn't help him. Then the guy that comes and helps him is a Samaritan who is looked down on by society, and he helps the man and dresses his wounds, and puts him on the back of his donkey, and takes him to a town and pays the innkeeper to take care of him. And says that he'll return and pay for whatever else is needed."

Dawn's experience and her invocation of this parable are helpful for summarizing themes that can be traced across the stories of my collaborators. First, "the teacher ignored it": queer youth find themselves abused and abandoned by the people and communities responsible for protecting them, including teachers, parents, friends, and church. Second, "everyone's just people": Well, perhaps, but not when one considers the institutional configurations that support hierarchies organized across differences. What I mean is that power is often ordered, either in rule and/or in social practice across differences, including differences of sex, gender, race, class, age, ability, education, marital status, sexual orientation, and institutional ordination. The clergy-lay distinction in the Roman Catholic Church is a clear example. If "everyone's just people," then why is it that queer youth have to come out or that Finn has to justify his desire to wear a suit? Why is it that lesbians cannot be Methodist ministers or, in the Catholic Church, that men "presenting deep seated homosexual tendencies," or women, or married people, cannot be ordained to the ministerial priesthood?

Latent within the parable of the Samaritan and within the stories of my collaborators is the systemic disenfranchisement of queer folks from the fullness of human vocation and, for those who are Christian oriented, their baptismal call.[21] They are always burdened with the first vocation of coming out, and this "calling" defines and limits their participation in human society and the broader mission of the church. Heterosexual and gender-conforming folks, even some members of the queer community, often, maybe without knowing it, veil their privilege behind the idea that "everyone's just people." This formula speaks to persons' desire for identity recognition beyond singular, hyperpoliticized, and stereotyped markers and represents a powerful rhetorical position in arguing for human rights and social equality: I am just like everyone else, just gay. However, this stance can also impede the questioning of deeper or subtler forms of heterosexism and of the institutional practices that sustain heteropatriarchy. In order to root out institutional sin, communities must be willing to listen to the voices of marginalized members and then to question the norms that maintain marginalization and the relational hierarchies that manufacture and are manufactured by those norms.

A final theme, "it's when you can feel like closest to God": these youth have been called out of comfort into queerness, called into sackcloth to grieve the deaths of their beloveds, called to testify through word and action to their apostolic inheritance. Finding themselves in the wilderness— ostracized by peers, school authorities, family, and church—they struggle, and they emerge to educate, to love, to speak. They speak despite the threat of death, of loss of family, of faith. They are doing just what their experiences of struggle and desire and loss command them do. They are surviving. They are paying attention to one another's brokenness and to the brokenness of their communities. They are investing their resources in healing without the expectation of repayment. Isn't it time that their communities stopped to help, to listen, to love?

Part IV: Practicing Belonging

Voices Within, Beyond, and Contesting Ecclesial Borders

The opening essay of this section, by Kate Averett, reflects on stories—those that we are told about life and those that our lives actually tell. Tracing her own story, Averett recalls a family, childhood, education, and youth suffused and indelibly marked by Catholicism. She describes being burdened, as a young adult Catholic, by the mounting sense of tension between what her church taught and how its leaders behaved, on the one hand (for instance, the clergy sexual abuse scandal was a moment of felt betrayal for her), and her own sense of queer identity, integrity, and vocation to marriage, on the other. These tensions led to a dramatic internal struggle that culminated during Holy Week, 2010. At an existential crossroads, Averett made a painful choice. Reprinting the metaphorical "breakup letter" that she wrote at that time, she expresses the reasons for her decision, not without pain or regret, to end her relationship with the institutional church.

Witnessing to a different path taken, Jamie Manson's "Tainted Love" describes the unsettling, wearying, and heart-rending mixture of belonging and marginalization, acknowledgment and invisibility that shapes her experiences as an active Catholic who is young, out, lesbian, and in a committed relationship. Echoing themes sounded by Cozzens and Massingale, Manson dwells on the special harm and hurt that result when clergy (many of whom are themselves gay) and other Catholics, fearing exposure or shrinking from risks, fail to stand up for or fully stand with their LGBT brothers and sisters as they themselves face personal risk, exposure, and cost in the struggle for acceptance and participation in church and society.

The next essay, by the psychiatrist and professor Michael Norko, offers an example of the solidarity Manson finds too often lacking among her fellow Catholics, lay or clergy. Detailing the events and actions taken by Connecticut's Catholic bishops following that state's Supreme Court decision allowing gay marriage (see Chapter 3), Norko recounts a story of awakening to his responsibility and calling, as a lay Catholic professional, to enact solidarity with his LGBTQ neighbors by engaging with church leaders. Though his attempts to open avenues of communication and collaboration with the bishops of his state were not met with success, Norko's embrace of his baptismal calling as a lay person energized efforts that contributed significantly to making the More than a Monologue conference series a reality.

The author and columnist Dan Savage recounts the story of his strongly Catholic Chicago childhood and of his complex journey from a pious, seminary-aspiring altar boy to an adult "agnostatheist." Both his identities as a gay man, husband, and father and his perduring, deeply harbored responses to his familial Catholicism and the Catholic Church play central roles. He writes with special poignancy about his mother, whose unshakeable love for her son and critical but unflagging faith made her a living link between Savage and Catholicism, both in her life and in her death. While harshly denouncing the harms inflicted by the church through its treatment of sexuality and sexual diversity, Savage also speaks about the ache of loss that he feels not only at his mother's death but also at his inability to feel wanted or welcomed in the faith community of his childhood and family.

The concluding piece is a quiet, concise, but powerful essay by Mark A. Clark. The product of a deeply Catholic upbringing, Clark speaks of the love of God, the lively sacramental sensibilities, and the profound values that the church nurtured in him. Animated by love for God and desiring to serve, Clark entered minor seminary as a college student. But when, after falling in love, he confronted his gay identity, Clark found himself unmoored, disoriented, and virtually abandoned by the church he had so loved. Today, as a physician and medical school professor, Clark cherishes his Catholic faith and has found a welcoming parish community. But he struggles with, laments, and questions the disjuncture between what his scientific training and faithful life experience have taught him about being a gay man in relation to God and neighbor and the present state of church teaching on these matters.

13   The Stories We Tell

KATE HENLEY AVERETT

University of Texas at Austin

> Before, we all learned the stories of great men as truth; this was the
> way the world was, and we were just born unlucky, in the wrong body
> in the wrong place at the time. This kind of widespread belief, among
> both us and them, affected how we all lived and dreamed. The stories
> which we thought were truth delimited our imagined possibilities.
>
> This is the argument which says that some stories are downright
> dangerous. They hurt our sense of self when we hear them and remem-
> ber them, and opportunities to revamp and rebuild ourselves are dam-
> aged by the wide circulation of these stories.
>
> *Gargi Bhattacharyya*[1]

As children, we're told stories to teach us about the world. Through
fables, fantasies, and fairy tales, we're taught to listen for "the moral of the
story," trained to understand that stories can be true and that they can also
contain Truths. We learn to look for the metaphor in the stories we're told,
metaphors that teach us about what is True and Good and Right.

These stories help us imagine the possibilities for our lives. But in
providing us with a range of possibilities, they also limit what we imagine
for our future. We learn through the silences in the stories that there are
things we were never supposed to imagine possible. When, in making
those futures into reality, we bump up against experiences that don't
make sense, we turn to the stories of our childhoods, searching for a moment of recognition, something to help us make sense of things again. If
we don't find what we're looking for—when we fail to see ourselves reflected in our stories or begin to realize the silences are about us—it can
make us feel invisible or even impossible.

I would like to tell you a story about the power of stories. It is a story about
my growing up Catholic and growing away from and out of Catholicism. It

is a story about how the stories of my childhood almost made my adult-hood impossible, about how I learned that I needed to find, and even invent, new stories in order to make myself a possibility.

Dangerous Stories

The Story of Girls

We were told: Jesus had followers, apostles—friends, really. They learned from him, and then, when the time came, they became the teachers. They became the leaders. They became the priests, just like us, they said. Standing at the front of the church on Sunday mornings, they told us the story of the priesthood. And then after the story, we prayed that some of the children in the room would become part of this lineage, some day. *Lord, hear our prayer.*

I don't know why it didn't sink in right away, until that day when my mom had to spell it out for me. Girls can't be priests. Only boys. Sorry, sweetie. I had to go back to the story and make it make sense. Jesus had followers—friends, really—and they were only boys. I knew there were girls there—we heard about them, too—but I guess they hadn't been friends, really. They hadn't been picked by Jesus to be the teachers, the leaders, the priests. There must have been something special about the boys—and something less than special about the girls. What's the moral of the story? Boys are better, girls are less. Jesus loves you, but not like that, really.

The Story of Heterosexuality

What is a sacrament? It's a visible sign of God's grace. It's a special moment, a special occasion, when we can best see and know God's love. There are seven, but you don't get them all, they taught us; the ones you get depend on your calling. And we all have a calling: the priests, the nuns—and wouldn't it be wonderful for some of you to be priests and nuns?—but also your parents. Their calling was matrimony. When they got married, that was a sacrament, too. Their calling was to be husbands and wives, and to be mommies and daddies. God wants you to have that kind of love, they said, and really, what a noble calling, to be a mommy.

Look at Mary, they said. She's so beautiful, so holy, so beloved. We knew her story—it was part of the rhythm of our year. Every December, we heard about her faith, her calling, her "yes" to being the Mother of God. Every spring, we heard about her pain, losing her son. Her job wasn't just to give birth but to be there to support her child. What a noble calling, to be a mommy.

What's the moral of the story? That girls *are* special, because they can be called to be wives and mothers, that God probably had a husband already picked out for me, a plan to fulfill this destiny. Why would I have looked to anyone other than a boy, then, to find the person God had picked for me? None of the stories hinted that I might want to look elsewhere.

The Story of Betrayal

This was the saddest story of them all but maybe the story that I needed most to hear—the story that called into question all the other stories. I wasn't quite a child anymore when I began hearing this story. I still hear it frequently.

The story goes like this—a man, a priest, one of the men in that great lineage going back to Jesus' friends, did a bad thing. And then he did it again, and when the priest in charge heard about it, he moved the priest to another place so nobody would find out. And when he did it again, he got moved again.

The power in this story was in how it was repeated. It had some different characters, in each iteration—and some the same—but the story sounded familiar, more and more painfully familiar, each time it was told.

Sense of Self

The third story shook me to the core. It made me look back to all the other stories I had been given to make sense of the world. It made me, finally, look at the stories a little bit critically. I looked for Truths to help make this betrayal make more sense. Some of the morals of the stories helped—people are fragile. They betray, but Jesus forgives betrayal.

Every time I doubted my faith (and there were many such times), I found a story to help with that. When I felt betrayed, I found a story for that. But when I fell in love with a woman, there was no story for that. I searched, and I searched, but what I was feeling wasn't anywhere in the stories. *I* wasn't in the stories. All of those stories were about what was True and Good and Right, and I couldn't see myself anywhere. Perhaps I wasn't good? Perhaps I wasn't . . . true? Real? Possible?

Revamp and Rebuild?

As I searched for myself in the stories of my faith, I found others who were also searching. We searched together for stories about us, stories that helped us figure out what was True and Good and Right. We found a few, like Ruth and Naomi and Jesus and the Beloved Disciple. We worked to rebuild our sense of self through these stories and through stories of love and justice that helped combat the stinging sensation that some of the other stories—and lack of stories—still left us with.

But as much as I tried to fortify myself with these other stories, the old stories were never replaced. The story of girls, the story of heterosexuality, and the story of betrayal were still being told over, and over, and over again, and every time I heard them they put another crack—small enough to be almost imperceptible—in my sense of self. I didn't notice it happening at first—each crack was so tiny—until it was too late and the cracks so many that they had done irreparable damage. My sense of self was shattered.

Break

The night it shattered was during Holy Week, 2010. I don't even remember now what happened that day, although I recall that the day started with my clock radio playing NPR, with yet another report about clergy sexual abuse and cover-up. Hours later—I think it was around two in the morning—I couldn't sleep. I couldn't breathe. I couldn't do anything, because the stories were failing me. And that's when I realized that the only way out was a new story. I picked up my laptop and I wrote:

> My heart is so heavy right now, I'd swear it was causing serious damage to my other internal organs. I feel like I can't quite catch my breath. It's not quite that I can't breathe, but that I can't seem to be able to breathe

deeply enough, like if I could just get one giant gulp of air in my body would feel better, normal, not so tight, not so heavy.

Do Catholics who leave the Church always feel like this? Like they can't breathe, like their heart is simultaneously going to burst and turn to lead in their chest? I confess I envy people who speak of being an ex-Catholic with an air of lightness in their voice. I wish it were so easy. Is it really easy for them? Was it easy when it happened? Did it really just "happen," like one moment they were Catholic and the next, nope, they'd made up their mind, they were done? Because it's not working like that for me. Several times these last weeks I've pronounced that I'm done—actually said those words, to my wife, to my mom, to my sister—and yet I don't feel done. I feel like I'm still trying to make some decision, standing at the edge of the pool trying to work up the nerve to jump in, not being able to decide which is more terrifying, jumping in or chickening out.

You'll have to forgive my overuse and overlap of metaphors here, but I'm having a hard time thinking in linear, straightforward terms. But I'm feeling these days like I'm in the midst of a breakup, you know, the really horrible kind where you know it isn't going to work but you want it to so badly that every fifteen minutes you manage to get yourself entirely convinced that it actually can work, only to remember five minutes later why it can't, only to repeat the cycle over and over and over until it makes you crazy and you can barely remember who you are let alone the reasons why you're breaking up. And all the while you feel like you can't catch your breath, because even while you're certain you can't keep living like this, you're almost equally as certain that you'll suffocate without them. Almost.

I wake up in the morning to the sounds of radio news reports, new reports every day, of the abuse perpetrated by priests and covered up by the hierarchy (in order to save the Church from embarrassment?!) and I just want to cry and go back to sleep and forget it's happening, in part because I feel complicit—this is my Church, we're all one body, when the eye suffers does not the hand suffer too, and when the hand reaches out and abuses another does not the whole body participate in that abuse?—and in part because it reminds me that this is the end for us, that the gulf between me and the institutional Church has widened too much and has reached the point of irreparable damage, and that sooner rather than later I'm going to have to deal with it. This is what the term "irreconcilable differences" means, I guess. I no longer look to the Church and see any of my values, my priorities, my convictions reflected back at me. Sure, it's in the teachings, oh the teachings that I love so much, the social encyclicals, the preferential option for the poor, the stuff that has inspired those who have inspired me, the liberation theologians and Dorothy Day and well, if the Church was good enough for them perhaps I can still make it work? But I'm deluding myself if I think that the teachings of the Church are the Church, for there is nothing, nothing, NOTHING of the preferential option for the poor in this scandal, there's not justice in the hierarchy's response, there isn't even the slightest display of concern for the powerless and I just can't find Jesus anywhere in all of it, not anywhere at all. And I'm actually crying as I write these words because there is so much about this tradition that I hold so dear, and I feel like I'm abandoning the real Church, the people of God, my fellow sisters and brothers, but at the same time I've had enough. Enough. ENOUGH.

I'm just too worn down. I'm tired of explaining how one can't ever stop being Catholic and of talking of my formed conscience and the terrible beauty of holding in tension one's love for the Church and one's distaste for certain teachings because it's getting harder and harder to convince myself, let alone others. I'm sure I believed it once, that I could remain a Catholic despite the institutional Church, but my ever-tenuous conviction has faded fast these last few weeks. This place has become too foreign to me, and I can no longer call it home. And I'm so, so sad about that. My heart is so heavy it feels like it's crushing me. I can't catch my breath. But I won't be able to catch it if I stay. And I might be able to, if I go. So, standing at the edge of the pool, I jump.

I'm done.[2]

New Stories

Looking back, I wonder if the day I wrote this truly was a turning point in my relationship with the church. On the one hand, I've remained "done" since that day. I've experimented with different ways of labeling my religious identity—former Catholic, ex-Catholic, "I was raised Catholic"—no longer identifying as a Catholic but usually with some reference to my Catholic upbringing. But on the other hand, when I'm really honest with myself, I admit that not a lot really changed that day. I can see that I had been in the process of moving away from the church for some time before that. At times I felt like I was drifting away, not sure whether or not to fight the drift—not regularly going to Mass, not feeling like I was missing it, not fully present when I did go. At other times I felt like I was being pushed away, like the times I went to Mass and heard antigay (or "promarriage") messages in the homily or the prayers of the faithful and wondered why I bothered to try when it seemed I wasn't wanted there. And still other times, I felt like I was actively distancing myself—when planning my own wedding, for example, and rejoicing at the freedom my partner and I had to make the ceremony what we wanted it to be and feeling thankful not to be constrained by the language of the Catholic liturgy.

To use yet another metaphor, the morning news the day I wrote myself out of the church may have been the straw the broke the camel's back, but it wasn't the clergy sexual abuse scandal that caused me to leave; rather, it was the total weight of all of the dangerous stories. When I wrote what I now refer to as "my breakup letter to the Catholic Church," I wasn't so much ending things as acknowledging that it had been over for quite some time. In writing it, I gave myself permission to acknowledge, and continue to do, what I had already been doing: no longer looking to the stories of my childhood as the primary sites of meaning making, opening myself up to many new places to seek stories—as well as giving myself permission to make my own.

Afterword

This is a story about the power of stories: their power to shape us, to limit us, to crush us and nearly kill us. But also, it is a story about the power of new stories to dig us out from under the weight of the dangerous stories. The power of new stories to save us, to make us remember that we are possible. If the old stories have power, then the new stories must have power, too.

14 Tainted Love

The LGBTQ Experience of Church

JAMIE L. MANSON

National Catholic Reporter

My reflection on the experience of gays and lesbians in the Catholic Church comes from my own story as an outspoken Catholic lesbian and also from my years of sharing in the stories of the countless gay, lesbian, bisexual, transgender, and queer Catholics whom I encountered as a church minister over the past six years.

For me, all of these experiences and stories boil down to this truth: All that LGBTQ Catholics really want is to go to church—and, in some cases, to serve the church—without being made to feel that our sexual orientations and/or gender identities taint our faithfulness to the church and to God.

My partner and I share a deep passion for serving the church, especially by working with the poor, the hungry, and the homeless. Our commitment to this work does not come simply from a desire for the common good but from the yearnings of our spirits. I'm a Catholic with a Master of Divinity degree, and my partner grew up Evangelical and attended a Midwestern Bible college. Part of what brought us together as a couple is our mutual conviction that the margins are a sacred place where we have some of our deepest experiences of "church," the way Jesus envisions and incarnates it in the Gospels. It is in the face of the broken and desolate that we most clearly see the face of Christ.

Yet, because we're in a same-sex relationship—as opposed to remaining celibate, as Catholic and Evangelical beliefs would have it—we walk into most churches and church-related activities with deep trepidation. We look around the room to see if we can locate any congregants who appear to be gay and not out of place. We know to avoid holding hands during prayers unless we feel confident that it is a safe space. We know not to be immediately forthcoming about our relationship if someone talks to us after the service.

Of course, we are blessed to live in the New York City area, where there are a number of LGBTQ-friendly churches from which to choose. But we live in a bubble. And a visit to my partner's family in western Michigan is enough to make that bubble burst. Because of their Evangelical beliefs, it wasn't until two years into our relationship that my partner's family was even willing to meet me. When we were finally introduced, I was blessed that their desire to show good, old-fashioned Midwestern hospitality seemed to supersede their religious convictions about our "lifestyle choice."

But the Midwestern welcome often screeches to a halt when we attend Sunday services with them, where I am typically introduced as my partner's roommate. After every service we attend with her family, we often breathe a sigh of relief that no antigay remarks were made at any point during worship.

Our luck ran out, unfortunately, during one Father's Day weekend. The preacher decided to dedicate his forty-five-minute sermon to Galatians 5, where Paul offers his litany of sins that can keep a Christian from "inheriting the kingdom." Paul mentions fifteen kinds of transgressions, ranging from witchcraft and rage to idolatry and drunkenness. Yet this pastor decided to spend more than half of his sermon fixated on Paul's mention of the sin of "sexual immorality." And he zeroed in on one particular form of sexual immorality: homosexuality. He explained to the congregation that, in the original Greek, Paul used the word *porneia* to describe sexual immorality. Then he explained that while *porneia* covered a multitude of sexual sins and sounded more a lot like "pornography," it most aptly described homosexuality. Why? Because, like pornographers who objectify those they film, homosexuals objectify their lovers by going against "the laws of nature." Therefore all of those who give into this kind of sexual immorality have "written off Christ" and "would never inherit the kingdom."

Near the end of the sermon, the pastor mentioned briefly that Paul follows his list of sins in Galatians with a list of what he calls the "fruits of the Spirit." Here Paul tells us that love, joy, peace, forbearance, kindness, goodness, faithfulness, gentleness, and self-control are all the manifestations of those who "belong to Christ Jesus." According to this pastor, these gifts are only available to those in a married relationship between one man and one woman.

Like good Evangelicals with deep Dutch Calvinist roots, my partner's parents never brought up the sermon to either of us. But my partner and I were, in a strange way, glad that we were present in that church for that particular sermon. It forced her parents, for the first time in their lives, to listen to an antigay sermon while sitting next to a loving same-sex couple deeply committed to doing the work of the church.

What we wish we could have told them and this pastor, however, is about the ways in which our relationship has brought the fruits of the Spirit more fully into our lives. Rather than separating us from Jesus, the joy and peace that we bring to each other's life has actually helped us participate more fully in the very life of God. And, in fact, those fruits have also made us much more fruitful within our own community by helping us grow in generosity and in our willingness to take greater risks in loving others.

The experience drove home for us once again this painful truth: regardless of what good work we do for the church, we know that many church people will see our efforts as tainted because of our same-sex relationship. The members of my partner's home church, for instance, are extremely proud of the work that she is doing with the poor in New York City. However, if they knew she was in a relationship with a woman, they would cease to talk about her so proudly. (They might gossip, of course!) All of her good work would be somehow less valid in their eyes.

Like my partner, I have had similar experiences of feeling that my sexual orientation taints my work in the church. As a columnist, I do sometimes write about gay and lesbian issues. But more often I write about the spiritual hunger of young adult Catholics in the church. My essays on this theme have led several editors from religious presses to invite me to write books on this topic. Unfortunately, once these editors learned that I am openly lesbian, they rescinded their invitations. I have been disinvited from many speaking engagements for the same reason. Though my insights into non-LGBT religious issues are appreciated, my voice somehow loses credibility or becomes less desirable by my being openly lesbian.

Of course, my story and my partner's stories are just a few of the countless narratives of suffering, shame, and isolation caused by the anti-LGBTQ rhetoric of Evangelical pastors, or archconservatives like Bill Donohue, or the U.S. Conference of Catholic Bishops. But, in my experience, it is another group of religious leaders who cause me the greatest pain. For me, even more troubling than the faith-based culture warriors who work against justice for LGBTQ persons are the liberal and progressive religious leaders who will not take a public stance on affirming the goodness of gay and lesbian people, including those gay and lesbian people who are in loving, committed relationships.

Many religious leaders are very well aware that there are countless gays and lesbians doing the work of justice, feeding the hungry, giving shelter to the homeless, ministering in refugee camps, protecting victims of all kinds of violence. They know these LGBTQ people, they love them, and they *privately* support them. However, I'm not sure they realize the spiritually damaging results of their unwillingness to be more forthright and prophetic about their support of gays and lesbians. I have been told many stories by those engaged in Catholic ministry to LGBTQ persons about priests and bishops who agree with and, in some cases, even donate to their cause but refuse to help them publicly with their work. "This is almost my daily experience of church leaders and workers," one prominent, longtime activist in the Catholic LGBTQ community told me recently.

Perhaps most painful of all are those priests, nuns, and lay ministers who *are* gay or lesbian, who are out to themselves and perhaps even to members of their communities, but who will not risk their own positions of authority by being open about what they know in their minds and hearts about themselves and about LGBT people. So many gays and lesbians in religious positions feel that they have to operate "under the radar" and keep silent about their identities in order to answer God's calling. But by doing so, they reinforce the idea that one needs to hide in a closet for the sake of serving the kingdom of God.

I know a Catholic gay couple who have been together forty years. Throughout that time they have attended Mass every Sunday, they have had longstanding friendships with the priests from their parish, they were even friends with their former bishop. When the time came that they could get legally married, they had a small wedding in a neighborhood restaurant. They invited a few of their priest friends, many of whom they have known for decades, to come to the wedding and dinner. Not one of them accepted the invitation for fear of being "caught" by diocesan officials.

One priest friend did agree to stop by for a drink but refused to stay for dinner. But when the day of the wedding came, the priest did not show up. I can still see the look of pain and disappointment on the face of one of the grooms. When I spoke with him later in the evening, he was still hoping that his priest friend would put in an appearance. And then he said something about the priest that stunned me. "I'm not sure why he didn't show. At least his lover of thirty years is here."

I'm not suggesting that these folks take out a full-page ad in the *New York Times* declaring their sexual orientations. But, in even these small ways, gay and lesbian religious leaders and ministers who stay silent are acting in collusion with the aching shame and outright bigotry that many in the hierarchy perpetuate about LGBTQ persons.

As much as I want to understand their need for self-protection and their desire to hold on to their positions in ministry, I wonder if these religious leaders understand how much shame this creates. By not accepting their friends' invitation, what they are ultimately communicating is, "Honoring your love is not worth risking my clerical status." I wonder if they can comprehend the soul-shattering repercussions of such decisions. By refusing invitations like this, they perpetuate the religiously based myth that same-sex relationships do not have the same potential for goodness and holiness as heterosexual ones. They know this is a myth but will not take a risk to shatter it.

Perhaps by making these claims I am buying too much into our therapeutic culture's need for self-disclosure. For previous generations, one's sexuality was more of a private matter. Today, though, I believe that many in the new generation of Catholics and Christians will not trust religious leaders who are not honest about their identities. To create trust and be a spiritual leader of integrity, one must exhibit the courage of one's convictions. People both young and old, gay and straight, are starving for religious leadership that is grounded in authenticity and courage. Given the hierarchical nature of the Catholic Church and other denominations, any real transformation of minds and hearts about the goodness of LGBTQ persons will have to come from our religious leadership.

Many argue that it is too risky for religious and spiritual leaders to speak out. But not to speak out only creates shame and reinforces the culture of denial mandated by the institutional church. Some try to rationalize their staying in the closet by professing how much they love their ministry and how painful it would be to lose it. Most out ministers understand this pain well, myself included. Many have lost their jobs and their spiritual communities because they dared to live authentically. By taking this risk they made a sacrifice in the true sense of the word: they let go of something precious for the sake of greater holiness. In this case, the holiness lies in shining a light on the extraordinary work that is done in the church and for the church by LGBTQ people. The priests and ministers that I know who have come out speak honestly about how challenging the journey is. But not one that I have met has ever said that she or he regrets the decision.

Some say that religious leaders should not have to come out because sexual orientation shouldn't matter. Unfortunately, we are far from the day in our church when sexual orientation and gender identity are nonissues. As long as LGBTQ persons who long to serve their church are viewed as tainting their communities, and as long as LGBTQ couples are told that their love is intrinsically disordered or a sin against God, sexual orientation and gender identity matter. Not only do they matter, but these differences and diversities are gifts that help all of God's people understand that they are God's beloved children.

And that, ultimately, is the desire of all LGBTQ persons who want to be a part of a church or serve the church: to have our relationship with our loving creator affirmed and to experience the love of God through the welcome and support of our faith communities. When LGBTQ persons are made to believe that their sexual orientations and/or gender identities taint their relationship to God, all that the church accomplishes is estranging God from God's beloved creation.

If the story of the incarnation teaches us anything, it is that God longs to be in deep communion with all of humanity. By alienating LGBTQ persons from God, the church actually stands in the way of doing the work that God hopes to do through the church. Rather than allowing God to reach out to us, the church and its leaders often fracture our relationships with God or stunt them before they even have a chance to grow.

If the story of Jesus' life and death teaches us anything, it is that those who wish to follow the Gospel must risk our status, if not our very lives, to uphold the dignity of all of those marginalized by religious authority. Ministers who support the cause of the full inclusion of LGBTQ persons in the church must take the risk of bringing the love of God more fully into the lives of LGBTQ persons. This will help closeted LGBTQ ministers find a safe, supportive community in which to come out. Only then can all LGBTQ people have the opportunity to share in Jesus' promise of a new, more abundant life and have the chance to bring that life more fully into the church.

15 A Voice from the Pews

Same-Sex Marriage and Connecticut's
Kerrigan Decision

MICHAEL A. NORKO

Yale University School of Medicine

On October 10, 2008, the Connecticut Supreme Court announced its decision in *Kerrigan v. Commissioner of Public Health*.[1] The court concluded that the state impermissibly discriminated against individuals on the basis of sexual orientation by not permitting same-sex couples to be married, thus legalizing marriage for same-sex couples. (See Chapter 3 in this volume for the personal narratives of one of the eight couples who were parties to that lawsuit.)

In responding to what it called the "severe and sustained discrimination" against gay persons and to the "long-standing intolerance" of intimate homosexual conduct in our culture, the court was, in my view, making a statement about social justice.[2] This perspective resonated with my understanding and appreciation of Catholic social teaching as a lifelong Catholic and later-life divinity student. This was a deep resonance, with roots in the domestic church of my upbringing, in service in Appalachia required as part of my Catholic high school training, in a married life blessed with children, in a career of public sector psychiatry, in years of annual retreats, and in communion with fellow Catholics devoted to serving others. My studies of Catholic social ethics and ecclesiology in divinity school added a dimension of intellectual understanding and historical tradition to these decades of experiential learning. I was truly gratified to learn of the *Kerrigan* decision through the media.

That same day, the Connecticut Catholic Conference (CCC), the public policy and advocacy office of the Catholic Bishops in Connecticut, posted its response to the *Kerrigan* decision on its website.[3] The heading declared, in bold letters, "Connecticut Catholic Conference, on behalf of the Catholic bishops, clergy, religious, and laity of the State of Connecticut, condemns today's Connecticut Supreme Court decision on same-sex 'marriage'; calls for a 'Yes' vote on a Constitutional Convention."

Before going any further, I must note that the language of *condemnation* is not unleashed without powerful emotional effect. It is a language of anger and judgment, affectively connected to death dealing. It is the language (spoken or not) with which I have seen many patients painfully rejected by their parents, their families—from whom they longed for expressions of love. I was stunned, perhaps naïvely, by the deliberate use of that language by Mother Church.

After several paragraphs decrying the "terribly regrettable exercise in judicial activism" and the intriguing criticism that the Supreme Court had "chosen to ignore the . . . will of the people" by "imposing a social experiment upon the people of our state," the statement concludes with this argument: "The real battle in this court case was not about rights . . . but about conferring and enforcing social acceptance of a particular lifestyle; a lifestyle many people of faith and advocates of the natural law refuse to accept. This ruling creates an inevitable conflict between people of faith, the natural law and the authority of the State." Finally, the statement called upon Catholic people to vote in favor of a Constitutional convention, expressing the clear hope that a public referendum would overturn the decision.

Let me try to unpack my reaction to this statement from the bishops. First, as the official representatives of the Catholic community, the bishops made their statement, condemning a civil judicial decision characterized by inclusion and acceptance of my neighbors, on *my* behalf. For me, this statement amounts to a message of exclusion and intolerance. I do not recall being consulted on the condemnation that was to be made in my name; there were no deliberations, no opportunities for comment or the exchange of ideas. Had there been such an opportunity, I most certainly would not have approved this message. I know many other members of the laity, religious, and clergy who also would not have approved this message, yet the statement was made with the implication of universal Catholic solidarity on the matter.

In fact, if we are considering the "will of the people," the evidence shows that U.S. Catholics have been out in front of every other religious group in their support of same-sex marriage and civil unions, with a clear majority of Catholics now favoring civil marriage for same-sex couples.[4] Many observers relate this to the abiding reception among Catholics of the church's teachings on social justice.[5] This is, indeed, precisely the context in which I view these matters.

At its heart, the *Kerrigan* decision acknowledged the reality that gay and lesbian couples fall in love and want to live in committed relationships in which they will be treated like other people are treated. It is hard for me to understand how that amounts to a "social experiment." Every major faith tradition in the world espouses some version of the Golden Rule—that's not experimental. How can the Golden Rule possibly apply to some people *but not to others*? How could that possibly be?

Then there is the "lifestyle" argument: "The real battle in this court case was . . . about conferring and enforcing social acceptance of a particular lifestyle; a lifestyle many people of faith and advocates of the natural law refuse to accept. This ruling creates an inevitable conflict between people of faith, the natural law and the authority of the State."[6] The bishops presented their "lifestyle" claim (that is, the notion that homosexuality is merely a way that some people choose to live, which other people are free to judge, criticize, and reject) as a bald stereotype, thereby giving "people of faith" permission to engage in acts of intolerance and exclusion of those who are "other" while declaring such attitudes "*inevitable*" as a matter of adherence to faith and natural law. There are, of course, no data in the social and behavioral sciences to support the "lifestyle" claim and no basis in Christian scripture for the rejection of "the other." It is shocking to me that the church would, by asserting this baseless argument, implicitly legitimize the refusal to accept others *as a matter of faith*.

In the weeks that followed the *Kerrigan* decision, leading up to the November elections, the Connecticut Catholic Conference aired nightly television ads that featured a woman standing in front of the State Capitol building, urging us to vote for a Constitutional Convention. By taking that action, the bishops were going beyond issuing a statement that troubled me; they were now committing significant financial resources to broadcasting this troubling statement, instead of using those resources to meet real human needs. Things had gone, in my opinion, from quite bad to quite a bit worse.

So I started talking to people in the church. Was I missing something? Was I the only one so upset? I talked to priests, nuns, lay ministers, a Catholic scholar, and a canon lawyer. No one had anything to say that helped me make any more sense of this response from the hierarchical church. No one disabused me of my reactions, though I was grateful for the opportunities to talk about them with thoughtful and learned Catholic people. (In retrospect, I think I spoke to so many fellow Catholics, in part, because I was surprised by the strength of my reaction to this sequence of events. Yes, my formal study of Catholic social teaching and ecclesiology had better equipped me to examine critically this message from the bishops rendered on behalf of all the unconsulted faithful. But there was more. I felt compelled to move on this matter, in what I now appreciate as a spiritual experience.)

During my discussion with the Catholic scholar, the suggestion was made that perhaps we ought to hold a conference to explore these issues and ask those questions. Three years later, that seed became manifest as the More than a Monologue series of conferences—the product of the dedicated work of many collaborators who came to the table.

Many of the people I talked with encouraged me to continue to seek answers to my concerns. So, some weeks later, I wrote to the CCC to ask where the funds were coming from to support their extensive media campaign aimed at reversing marriage for same-sex couples. I received no response. At that I wasn't particularly surprised.

Months went by, and my discussions continued. By the spring of 2009, I had come to realize that I needed to take seriously the messages from Vatican II about my responsibilities as a member of the laity, particularly those found in *Lumen Gentium* (LG),[7] *Gaudium et Spes*, (GS),[8] and *Apostolicam Actuositatem* (AA).[9]

In the Dogmatic Constitution on the Church (*Lumen Gentium*), the entire laity (the "People of God") are established by Christ as his witnesses, to whom he provides an "appreciation of the faith (*sensus fidei*)."[10] They are to communicate that appreciation to church leaders: "the laity are entitled, and indeed sometimes duty-bound, to express their opinion on matters which concern the good of the church."[11] All people, "according to their own gifts and duties must steadfastly advance along the way of a living faith, which arouses hope and works through love."[12] Indeed, the laity are to be encouraged "to take on work of their own initiative."[13]

In the Pastoral Constitution of the Church in the Modern World (*Gaudium et Spes*), the Council proclaimed, "The laity are called to participate actively in the entire life of the church; . . . they are to be witnesses to Christ in all circumstances and at the very heart of the human community."[14] The "whole People of God" are advised to "listen to and distinguish the many voices of our times" in order to grasp the depth of revealed truth.[15] This endeavor requires use not only of theology but also of psychology and sociology in order to develop a "purer and more mature living of the faith."[16] The faithful are to keep abreast of developments in science and technology, as well as culture and morality, in attending to this mission. They are also to be "accorded a lawful freedom of inquiry, of thought, and of expression, tempered by humility and courage in whatever branch of study they have specialized."[17]

The Decree on the Apostolate of the Laity (*Apostolicam Actuositatem*) obliges all members of the faithful to assume active roles in promoting the growth of the church, lest they "be considered unhelpful both to the church and to themselves."[18] They are to bring "before the ecclesial community their own problems, world problems, and questions regarding humanity's salvation, to examine them together and solve them by general discussion."[19]

I therefore decided to raise more formally my concerns with church leaders. I sent letters to the Conference and to each of its five bishops individually. I share here relevant portions of that letter, which represented my reaction to the bishops' response to the *Kerrigan* decision.[20]

> I am writing to express my concerns about a number of issues related to the legislative agenda of the Connecticut Catholic Conference.
>
> First, I object to the October 10, 2008, statement of the CCC in response to the *Kerrigan* decision being made in my name. This is clearly an issue about which Connecticut citizens differ, including Catholics, and such a statement of intolerance and exclusion should not be made as if it represented the unambiguous view of all the clergy, religious, and laity. Perhaps the five Bishops are unanimous in this view, but I doubt all the clergy are, and I know that the religious and laity are not.
>
> Jesus never preached intolerance or exclusion, and he opened his table and his mission to all who would follow him. His criticisms were instead aimed at those who cloaked themselves in the righteousness of their laws while forgetting to love their neighbor.
>
> I offer this concern in the spirit of disclosing my desires to my pastors with "liberty and confidence" (*Lumen Gentium* 37), noting that it is the laity's "special task" to engage in the temporal affairs of the world (*LG* 37). The body of civil rights enjoyed by groups of citizens is clearly such a temporal affair. As a husband, father, and psychiatrist, my place in the world brings me to see this matter from a far different perspective than

that offered by the CCC. I accept the statement of the CCC that its views on this issue are not expressed in hatred, but . . . [t]hese views illustrate a prejudice against gay and lesbian people. . . .

In *Apostolicam Actuositatem*, the laity are instructed to foster the "art of living fraternally and cooperating with others" and to recognize the work of the Spirit in all people of God (*AA* 29). I cannot live fraternally with my gay and lesbian neighbors as a member of the Church while the Church promotes my neighbors' exclusion from a common good in civic life. The Council Fathers acknowledged that this role of the apostolate "*in the social milieu* . . . is so much the duty and responsibility of the laity that it *can never be performed properly by others*" (*AA* 13, emphasis added). I would, therefore, urge the CCC to refrain from such future statements, and to seek instead ways in which the entire apostolate might work to examine this issue, and hopefully to resolve it more adequately by our common deliberation (*AA* 10). That such inquiry should be informed by psychology, sociology, and other sciences, of which the laity have special expertise, is an important recognition formulated in *Gaudium et Spes* (44, 62).

I have written to share my voice on these subjects in confidence and hope, as I am guided to do by Vatican II's important statements on the significant role of the laity in the Church. I also write to offer to engage in future deliberations of these important civil matters within a fuller representation of the lay apostolate. I write hoping that the Church will do more to educate the apostolate about its responsibilities under Vatican II and to manifest that teaching in the example of inviting true deliberations, professing the Church's belief that the Spirit enlivens the thoughts and actions of the entire apostolate, the full assembly of the baptized.

I would gladly serve toward these ends, bringing to the table my special expertise of more than 25 years as a physician, psychiatrist, and forensic psychiatrist as well as my general expertise as a lay person engaged in the demands of family and fraternal life in the temporal world and my modest experience as a student of the sacred sciences.[21]

I received no response to this letter from any of its recipients.

Also based on discussions with my Catholic colleagues, I had decided to send letters to the editor to two of our diocesan newspapers, offering a much-abbreviated version of these ideas. One newspaper acknowledged receipt of my letter. Neither published it.

Shortly thereafter, after much contemplation, prayer, and discussion, my wife and I decided to become what I will call "post-Diocesan" Catholics. This is at least one step short of being "post-Catholic," a term gaining currency, which I see as referring to disaffected Catholics who have left the church but not without some continued reference back to it. I think the term "post-Catholic" expresses not only separation but also sadness and loss. It is this same sadness and significant loss with which my wife and I wrestled, as we clung to the potential of parish life, in which we had experienced fellowship, service, and a sense of belonging and purpose in multiple Catholic communities over the years. But that potential had faded substantially in our recent parishes through the attrition of active, caring members and the waning of liturgical energy. A concerned episcopacy interested in listening might well have mitigated those effects, but instead we experienced unresponsive authority, regressive clericalism, and the callous waste of precious resources to purchase intolerance. It became emotionally and spiritually impossible for us to continue as we had.

In part, our being post-Diocesan means no longer contributing to the Annual Bishops' Appeal. It means no longer belonging to a parish, from which a portion of our donations would go to the diocese for divisive expenditures that bring pain to our neighbors. Thankfully, our current status also includes the ability to enjoy worship and communion in non-diocesan Catholic communities. It also means continuing to support financially the social justice work of the church through a variety of wonderful Catholic institutions.

In becoming "post-Diocesan" Catholics, we have voted with our feet and with our wallets. But we are not without hope. If there were no room for hope about the church, there would be no reason to engage this conversation, no reason to work from within the institution or to contribute to its mission, and no reason to join, or persevere, in Catholic communion.

The church still possesses and declares a powerful vision for humanity. In canon law, among the "Obligations and Rights of All the Christian Faithful"[22] is this message: "From their rebirth in Christ, there exists among all the Christian faithful a true equality regarding dignity and action by which they all cooperate in the building up of the Body of Christ according to each one's own condition and function."[23] It is the work of the entire Body of Christ to see that the church leads to the Kingdom of God that Jesus preached. To this end, Canon 212.3 tells us that it is the right and at times the *duty* of all the faithful to manifest their opinions to their pastors on matters of the common good, the dignity of persons, and the good of the church.[24]

If we truly believe that the Spirit works through all of us, then the laity must accept that we are designed by the Creator as vessels for manifestations of the Spirit. The Council observed the reality of this contemporary "sign" of the "manifest action of the holy Spirit making lay people nowadays increasingly aware of their responsibility and encouraging them everywhere to serve Christ and the church."[25] Thus it is our responsibility to be open to the inspiration and calling of the Spirit and respond according to our gifts.

It was a sincere effort to exercise this responsibility that motivated many of us to gather at the 2011 More than a Monologue conference series, in faith, in hope, in conversation, and in action. Those are the hallmarks of a church embracing its calling and deliberating and marveling at its potential. That church is at hand today, awaiting its fulfillment in liberation from the human fears that inhibit it.

As the Body of Christ, we must recall that Jesus had nothing good to say about people of faith who viewed Samaritans as "other." How can we, in faith, participate in the "othering" of our LGBTQ neighbors, whom we are commanded to love? How can we fail to stand up and speak out and ask for more from our church and for our church?

16   At a Loss

DAN SAVAGE

My dad was in the first class of the ordained permanent diacon-ate. This sentence may require some unpacking for my non-Catholic read-ers. So here you go, heathens: Before a man could become a Catholic priest, he would typically spend a year serving as a Catholic deacon. Dea-cons are to priests as novices are to nuns—or they used to be. In the 1980s, to address a growing shortage of Catholic priests (a shortage that has since gotten worse), the church created the permanent deaconate. Ordained deacons could do almost everything priests do—pass out wa-fers, preach sermons, baptize babies—and so my dad was up on the altar of our church every Sunday when I was growing up. Which makes me something of a rarity among Catholics: I am a preacher's kid. (Techni-cally I'm the kid of *two* preachers, as my mother was a Catholic lay minister.)

As the son of a Catholic preacher man—just one of his four children—I attended Catholic grade schools, and yes, I was an altar boy. But, this isn't a story about being sexually abused by a priest. Because I wasn't sexually abused by a priest. Looking back at my childhood, I can identify a couple of close calls—a priest from our parish once took me and another boy skinny-dipping at a Catholic school's indoor pool after hours—but the experiences were creepy, not abusive. In addition to being a Catholic dea-con, my father was also a Chicago cop—a cop who loved his children and wore his service revolver wherever he went—and that fact may have given pause to any rapey priests who crossed paths with his children.

I am no longer a practicing Catholic. If I had to apply a religious label to myself, it would be "agnostatheist," an awkward hybrid of agnostic and atheist. I don't believe in a higher power, but I do cross myself on airplanes. I once blew up at a friend who thought he was being funny when he in-verted one of the crucifixes in my "ironic" collection of Catholic kitsch. And when I take the Lord's name in vain—when I mutter "Jesus Christ" through clenched teeth as my lead-footed husband passes someone going ninety miles an hour—I am seeking the protection of a higher power.

But I go right back to not believing once my plane safely lands or once Jesus or Joseph Smith or Xenu safely delivers us back to the right-hand lane. Which makes me a hypocrite and an ingrate, I suppose, but not quite an atheist or a believer. Not quite.

I wasn't supposed to turn out this way. I went to the same Catholic grade school my mother and grandmother did; I had the same fourth-grade homeroom teacher—Sister Mary Amadeus—at St. Ignatius as my mother. I was baptized as an infant; I had my first communion at age seven; I was confirmed at age thirteen.

But even at age seven—the age of reason, according to the Catholic Church—I was having trouble reconciling this "loving father in heaven" I'd heard so much about with this "eternal damnation" thing the nuns were constantly threatening us with. But the fatal blow was the realization that I was gay. This realization came at roughly the same time I entered a Catholic high school for boys who were thinking about becoming priests. It was a bit like realizing you're an alcoholic on the first day of work at the Budweiser bottling plant.

Despite all those years of Catholic schooling, my first reaction to the realization that I was gay wasn't, "Holy shit, looks like I'm going to find out what that eternal damnation thing is all about." Instead I thought, "What the church says about homosexuality—that can't be right. They must be wrong." This intuitive sense that the church was wrong about homosexuality—this unshakable conviction that the church was wrong about *me*—led me to wonder what else the church might be wrong about. Virgin births, maybe? Transubstantiation? Resurrection? Masturbation? It didn't take long to arrive at the biggest doubt of all: the existence of God.

I transferred to a public high school and stopped going to church—except for the odd family wedding, baptism or funeral. (And they are all odd, aren't they?) For most of my adult life I was likelier to walk into a Planned Parenthood clinic for a Pap smear than to walk into a church.

Then my mother died.

A virus can lie dormant in your body for so long that you can forget you were ever infected. Then something happens that weakens your immune system and the virus seizes its opportunity. For more than two decades the Catholicism I'd contracted at St. Ignatius had lain dormant, manifesting itself only in airplanes and passing lanes. But the seeming immunity I'd long enjoyed was weakened by my mother's death. Because after that sunny, awful day in Tucson, Arizona, when my mother's life ended, I started slipping into Catholic churches.

Not for weddings or funerals, but on totally random days of non-holy non-obligation. Tuesday afternoons, Friday mornings. And I wasn't just going to church. I was going out of my way to go to church. There's a Modernist Catholic chapel near my office in Seattle. The Chapel of St. Ignatius at Seattle University—I think St. Ignatius is stalking me—won a big architectural award (the New York chapter of the American Institute of Architects honored it; a scale model of the chapel is now part of the permanent collection of the Museum of Modern Art in New York), but I think it's ugly. All Modernist Catholic churches look the same to me—like someone slapped a crucifix on the living room wall at the *Brady Bunch* house.

St. James Cathedral in downtown Seattle, which is a much longer walk from my office, looks like a Catholic church should. It looks like St. Ignatius, actually, the parish church attended by four generations of my family. Acres of stained glass, rows of marble columns, crowds of plaster saints. St. James is open for "private contemplation" seven days a week. In the months after my mother's death, I found myself slipping into St. James on more weekdays than I care to recall. The church was usually empty, aside from one or two volunteers straightening up the hymnals and offering envelopes in the backs of the pews—or that's what they were pretending to do. I think they were really there to keep an eye on the homeless people that sometimes come in to get out of the rain. Every once in a while the priest would hurry through, taking care to avoid making eye contact with me or any of the other bums.

When my mother used to call with bad news—a relative I hadn't seen in years diagnosed with cancer, an old friend with a desperately ill grandchild—she would always say, "I know you don't pray, Daniel. Just keep them in your thoughts." My mom knew that thoughts were the best I could do. And for months after my mother's death, sitting in the pews at St. James Cathedral, I stared at a marble statue of the Virgin Mother, trying to keep my mother in my thoughts.

We were close in that cliché way that so many gay men and their mothers are. Today anti-gay bigots argue that being gay is a sinful choice that gay people make because our parades look like so much fun. Psychologists and psychiatrists used to argue that being gay was a choice your mother made for you. Mothers who were too close to their sons, mothers who "smothered" their sons, risked turning them gay. The shrinks got it backward, mistaking one of the consequences of being gay—one of the perks of being gay—for the cause. The kind of relationship I had with my mother didn't make me gay. I had that kind of relationship with my mother because I was gay.

By her own estimation my mother was a good Catholic. She believed that Jesus was her savior and that He died for her sins; she believed in the Resurrection, the Trinity, the Sacraments, the Virgin Birth, the Immaculate Conception. (Don't make the mistake of confusing those last two: Jesus was born to a virgin; his mother Mary was conceived without original sin—those are totes different paranormal phenomena, people.) My mother also believed that sex was sacred, and that people, particularly people who had children, should be married. To each other. But she didn't believe that being a good Catholic meant blind obedience to the old men who ran her church.

You could say that my mother was a good American Catholic. She believed that women should be priests and that priests, male or female, should be allowed to marry. Even each other. And after four pregnancies in four years—and a heart-to-heart with a parish priest who told her that the pope *might* be wrong about birth control and *definitely* wouldn't be paying her children's Catholic school tuition—my mother concluded that birth control was not a sin.

"Catholics have long realized that their own grasp of certain things, especially sex, has a validity that is lost on the celibate male hierarchy,"[1] the Roman Catholic author and historian Garry Wills wrote in an essay in *The New York Review of Books*. My mother was one of those American Catholics—a woman with a better grasp of sex than the elderly celibates.

My mother prayed that the leaders of her church would come around during her lifetime, particularly on the issues of celibacy and the ordination of women. Unfortunately, the church, under the last two popes, moved further away from her. Whenever the current pope, "Benny," as she called him, or the previous pope, "JP2," condemned birth control, attacked gay people, or insisted that women could never be priests, my mother would call me, sigh audibly, and say, "It's like they're trying to make Lutherans of us all."

But she refused to leave the church. It was her church, too, she insisted, just as much as it was Benny's or JP2's. And popes had been wrong in the past, she'd say. If previous popes were wrong about the movement of the planets, then, by God, the current pope could be wrong about contraception. The little voice in her head said the same thing the little voice in mind did: "That can't be right; they must be wrong." But that voice, a voice that destroyed my faith, somehow strengthened hers.

And my mother's faith was tested.

When I was in high school, the Catholic television network in Chicago featured my family in a special—my dad the deacon, my mom the lay minister, and all four of their confirmed children. (Confirmation is like a bar mitzvah for Catholic kids, only with fewer presents and more modest parties.) One of their sons was even a high school seminarian. We were the perfect Catholic family. We used to joke—just a few years later—about the Catholic television network returning to do a "Where Are They Now?" special. We were still a Catholic family, of course, but we were no longer perfect. My dad had divorced my mother, resigned from the deaconate, remarried, and moved to California. My mother was dating and having sex outside of wedlock. My brother Billy had gotten a vasectomy. A couple of pregnancies were terminated. And I had come out of the closet.

While my mother was a liberal, pill-popping, ordination-of-women-backing Catholic, she nevertheless took it hard when I told her I was gay. Her first impulse was to call a priest. Father Tom, whose last name I won't disclose for reasons that will become clear in a moment, rushed over. Sitting on the front porch, my mother broke down in tears and told Father Tom why she was so upset: "Danny says he's gay."

Father Tom put his hand on my mother's knee and said, "So am I, Judy."

Father Tom told my mother that it was better this way. He knew I had thought about becoming a priest and worried that I might be doing it for the same reason he did: to hide from my sexuality. He had tried that, and it didn't work. Then he had tried to drown his homosexuality in alcohol, as so many Catholic priests of his generation did, and that didn't work either. He assured my mother that it was better for me to live this way—it was better for me to come out, even to her, *especially to her*—than to live the life he had lived.

Whenever someone asks if I was abused by a Catholic priest—and you would be surprised how often gay Catholic adults are asked that question—I always say no, I was never abused by a priest. I was saved by one.

Thanks to Father Tom and my mother's own moral sense, the same moral sense that prompted her to trust her own judgment about contraception, my mother came around on the my-son-is-gay issue pretty fast. And she came out swinging. A rainbow bumper sticker on her car, a PFLAG[2] membership card in her purse, and an ultimatum delivered to the entire extended family: I was still her son; and anyone who had a problem with me had a much bigger problem with her.

The Catholic Church still has a problem with me.

One of the cards in the back of the pews at St. James, tucked in with the hymnals, is addressed to nonpracticing Catholics. WELCOME BACK it reads in large letters at the top.

> Are you a Catholic who's been away from the church? Welcome Back classes are designed to help you return to the sacraments and regular church attendance.

A return to the sacraments. I sometimes fantasize about "returning" to the sacraments, particularly the sacrament of confession. "Forgive me, father, for I have sinned. It's been twenty-nine years since my last confession. I hope you packed a lunch."

I sit in the pews at St. James because part of me—the part that had me slipping away from work and into church—wishes what I was taught at St. Ignatius was true. I want there to be heaven. I want my mother to be looking down on me. Though, and I say this both as a gay man and a professional sex-advice columnist, *not all the time.* There are things a mother has a right not to know, my mom used to say, and I did my best to keep those things from her while she was alive.

My mother's death, somehow and unexpectedly, drew me back—not to the faith or to sacraments, but to *church,* to a church, to the pews of St. James Cathedral. I am tempted. I wouldn't have wasted so much time sitting in St. James in the months after my mother's death if I weren't. My husband wouldn't have found numerous WELCOME BACK cards in the back pocket of my jeans that awful spring if I weren't tempted.

But when I feel tempted, when I feel like, maybe I could go through the motions, maybe I could return to the sacraments, maybe I could take what comfort I could from the church and its rituals, the pope goes to Africa and says that condoms spread AIDS, or an archbishop in Brazil excommunicates a Catholic mother for getting her nine-year-old daughter a life-saving abortion but not the Catholic man who raped and impregnated that woman's nine-year-old daughter.

Or I contemplate how the church views me and the two people I love most in the world, my husband of eighteen years and our fifteen-year-old son, and I think, no, I can't even go through the motions.

The church doesn't want me back—not as I am. Every other week there's a story in the news about a Catholic grade school expelling a child who has gay parents or a Catholic parish firing a gay employee—someone they knew to be gay or lesbian when they hired them—for marrying their same-sex partner. When it comes to homosexuality, church leaders are growing ever more, er, rigid.

Gay Catholics are being targeted in ways that straight Catholics are not. While the church still opposes birth control and abortion, divorce and remarriage, and all non-procreative sex acts (even within marriage), and has become more aggressively political over the last two decades, it can't identify and persecute heterosexual Catholics who trust "their own grasp of certain things." Catholic women have abortions at the same rate as non-Catholic women. Ninety-eight percent of Catholic women use birth control[3]—presumably with Catholic men. Ninety-three percent of Catholics support the use of condoms to prevent disease and HIV transmission.[4] Seventy percent of American Catholics think abortion should be legal.[5] Sixty-seven percent of Catholics believe premarital sex is morally acceptable.[6]

When it comes to the issues of sexual morality, straight Catholics—Catholics like my mother—are telling the celibates that while they may run their church, they may not run, or ruin, their lives.

When a Catholic priest stands on the altar on Sunday and looks out over his congregation—like my father once did—he sees Catholic mothers and fathers sitting with one or two children. He can't see the birth control pills and the abortions that prevented those couples from having more children than they wanted or could provide for. He can't tell just by looking who among his flock has been divorced and remarried—or who, for that matter, masturbates. The church condemns homosexuality as "intrinsically and gravely disordered." The church uses the exact same language to condemn masturbation: "Masturbation is an intrinsically and gravely disordered action,"[7] reads the Catholic catechism. But there is no effort to turn away the children of divorced and remarried Catholics, or the children of Catholic families that by some miracle only have two children, or to seek out and fire heterosexual church employees who use birth control or masturbate.

The pope, cardinals, archbishops, bishops, and priests know that straight Catholics are using birth control, obtaining abortions, having premarital sex, having sex for pleasure, and masturbating. But they can pretend not to know it because they can't actually see it. All straight Catholics automatically get rounded up to "good Catholics" because their sexual sins can only be guessed at or inferred.

Priests can't do the same when a gay couple walks into a church. A priest can refuse to see—or refuse to do the math on—all the masturbating, birth controlling, divorcing, and remarrying that he knows straight parishioners are getting up to, but he can't *not* see homosexuality. So long as we insist on coming out, so long as we insist on living and loving openly, our "sin" is visible to the naked eye. And church leaders can't see past our homosexuality; they can barely see our *humanity*, which is hugely ironic, considering how many of those priests in the pulpits of Catholic churches are gay themselves. Father Tom was one of them. I was almost one of them.

Of course I don't think homosexuality is a sin at all. But for the Catholic Church it all comes down to the nature and purpose of sex. Back to the Catholic catechism: "The deliberate use of the sexual faculty, for whatever reason, outside of marriage is essentially contrary to its purpose,"[8] as human sexual expression must open to the "gift of life." Birth control, masturbation, homosexuality—any sex act that isn't open to the "gift of life" is wrong. Some well-meaning "liberal" Catholics claim that the church isn't singling out gay people since all non-procreative sexual activity is wrong regardless of whether it's gay or straight. But only gay people are expected to live lives devoid of intimacy and romantic love. (And, I'm sorry, but you can't claim that supernatural phenomena—miracles—routinely take place and then insist that homosexual acts are closed to the "gift of life." Either God can do anything or he can't, AMIRITE?)

"The natural purpose of sex is procreation,"[9] Wills writes, summing up the church's position, and any use of it for other purposes is "unnatural." But a primary natural purpose does not of necessity exclude ancillary advantages. The purpose of eating is to sustain life, but that does not make all eating that is not necessary to subsistence "unnatural." One can eat, beyond the bare minimum to exist, to express fellowship, as one can have sex, beyond the begetting of a child with each act, to express love.

The Catholic Church would like human sexuality to be about one thing—reproduction—but biology tells us differently.

"For *Homo sapiens*, sex is primarily about establishing and maintaining relationships, relationships often characterized by love, or at least affection,"[10] writes Christopher Ryan, in *Psychology Today*. "Reproduction is a by-product of human sexual behavior, not its primary purpose."

"The vast majority of species have sex only to reproduce—a function reflected in a very low ratio of sex-acts-to-births,"[11] Ryan continues. "Gorillas, for example, have intercourse at most a dozen times per birth." Humans are different. "We and our chimp and bonobo cousins typically have sex hundreds—if not thousands—of times per birth."

The church got sex wrong. It is confused about what sex is for, confused about what sex does, confused about why we have it and why we have so much of it—shocking, I realize, considering that the church is run by people who don't have sex. (Or aren't supposed to have sex.)

Fact is, straight people have more sex—a lot more sex—than they do babies. And gay people have sex for the same reasons straight people do . . . *most of the time*. Gay or straight, we're all having sex for pleasure, for release, and to cement bonds of intimacy. And every once in a while, some of us—even some of us who are gay—have sex in order to make a baby.

The church has backed itself into a familiar corner. One day the church will have to admit that it made a mistake. And one day the church will have to admit that scores of popes, hundreds of theologians, and countless princes of the church were wrong. Wrong about sex. Wrong about birth control. Wrong about masturbation. Wrong about pleasure. Wrong about homosexuality. One day the church will have to admit that it got human sexuality wrong, just as it got the movement of the planets wrong.

I'm not holding my breath.

This is typically where Catholics and non-Catholics alike jump in and ask why someone who isn't a Catholic—or isn't a Catholic anymore—cares so much about the church's teachings on human sexuality. Why concern yourself with the teachings of the Catholic Church when you're not a believer? I could claim that the Catholic Church's teachings concern me only inasmuch as they impact my life. I could point out that the Catholic Church is a political player in the United States, and it backs anti-gay legislation and supports efforts to ban my marriage, adoptions by same-sex couples, and civil rights protections for sexual minorities. I could insist that I don't have the luxury of ignoring the church.

But I would be lying.

Oh, the church's teachings do impact my life and the church actively persecutes gay people and I don't have the luxury of ignoring the church—all of that is true.

But while I can't see myself going back to the church—I can't see myself going through the motions of the sacraments, despite their comforting familiarity—some part of me wants the church to want me back. I want the option of going back. Not because I *believe*—I don't—but because I ache. I ache for my loss.

There are very few tangible remains of my childhood and of my connection to my mother. I have photographs, yes, and I have my memories, and I have some mementoes. But the family home is gone, my mother's possessions dispersed. There's nowhere I can go to feel my mother's presence, no space I can enter that we once physically shared, other than church.

That's why I wound up spending so many afternoons at St. James, the church that reminded me so much of St. Ignatius—St. Ignatius, the church where my mother was baptized, where she took her first communion, where she married, and where her funeral was held. In church I feel her presence, not God's presence, and I can almost feel her looking down on me from the heaven she believed in so passionately.

And if she was right—if there is a heaven and she is looking down on me—I hope she remembers to look away now and then.

Because there are things a mother has a right not to know.

17 "Church, Heal Thyself"

Reflections of a Catholic Physician

MARK ANDREW CLARK

Columbia University

I grew up in a working-class family in Rockland County, New York, the fifth of six children, one of two boys, and the only gay child of my parents. I was fortunate to have very loving parents whose primary focus was on their family and on their faith.

From my earliest memories, being Catholic was not peripheral but really central in our family's life. We children were diligently schooled and received the sacraments, prayed the family rosary, and absorbed the rhythm of the liturgical calendar as part of the flow of daily life. When it came time for my first confession and communion, and later my confirmation, I remember being drawn in by the sacredness of the mystery of faith. My CCD teacher and my parents communicated that mystery to me, and somehow it struck me that these sacraments were in fact encounters with God, who, I was told, had a personal interest in me. That early period began for me the process of deepening my knowledge of the reality of God's presence in my life. I was utterly convinced that God is real, present, and interested.

At about the same time, I began to know that I was different in a way that I could never speak about to anyone. I didn't know what it was to be gay; I didn't know that such a thing existed. But, somehow, I knew that I had a shameful secret that I had better keep to myself. And I did. I buried it so deeply that it didn't resurface until my second year of college. Like many gay and lesbian people, I managed to keep myself compartmentalized in such a way that would allow me to function in this world of contradictions.

My love for God was real. I attended Fordham University as an undergraduate at the Rose Hill campus in the Bronx, where I studied philosophy. I was thinking about becoming a priest, and I spent the first year and a half of college in the newly minted Neumann Residence, a pre-seminary house of formation for the archdiocese of New York. I was blissful. I loved school, I loved community life, I loved God, I loved the brothers I lived and prayed with, and I loved the rhythm of morning prayer, classes, apostolic work, evening mass, communal meals, study, and sleep.

Then, in my second year of college, I met someone in class and had my first gay romantic encounter. The experience initiated a relationship that was, for me, revolutionary, revealing, frightening, and amazing. I was in love. I was discovering my sexuality. I was in shock. And I was horrified. I had no one to talk to. When I told my confessor that I was gay, he looked at me with very kind eyes and said, "No, you're not." Which wasn't very helpful.

I left the Neumann Residence within a month of all these events and moved into off-campus housing. Looking back at that time, now with professional medical training, I can say with a fair degree of certainty that I experienced a major depression that lasted months. The best way I can describe it now is that my personality and everything I had understood about my life up to that point had been torn into fragments. I had no way, no concept, to unite my sexuality and my need for human love with that other great love in my life, my love of God. And there seemed to be no one on the horizon—anywhere—who could give me the life-saving message that being gay and loving someone do not, in any way, invalidate me, my faith, my love of God, or God's desire to have a relationship with me. Unconsciously, I felt forced to make a false choice between my identity as a gay man and my relationship with God. The fracture took a huge toll. I look back on it as the darkest period of my life, a time from which it did in fact take years for me to recover.

As an adult, I have gradually learned that God does not ask me to choose between being who I am and encountering God's love. Rather, now I know that the closer I come to God, the more I will experience the joy and acceptance of living as my true self, and the more I will have quiet confidence in God's delight in me exactly as he created me.

For me, like many of us, the interface between Catholicity, sexual identity, and professional life is complex. In the best-case scenario, these factors would each inform one another and comprise an integrated whole. I'm grateful for the many elements of my Catholic perspective and faith that enrich my care of patients and my participation in the education of residents and medical students. These include Catholicism's emphasis on the value and dignity of each person, its commitment to service, and its proclamation of the necessity for justice in how we meet the healthcare needs of our community, among countless others.

However, in the context of my professional life as an emergency medicine physician, a residency director, and a medical student educator, Catholic teaching about homosexuality is problematic. The medical, psychiatric, and scientific communities in which I've been trained have all, for quite some time now, abandoned the notion that homosexuality is a kind of pathology in need of correction. Instead, homosexuality is now generally understood as part of the brilliant spectrum of normal biological variability in nature. Additionally, medical, scientific, and psychiatric opinion today, as far as I've been trained and as far as I can see, would evaluate the health, the vitality, the life—the goodness, if you will—of an intimate relationship based on its ability to engender productive, creative, and fulfilling lives for its partners, not on whether or not the partners are able to procreate. For me, the lag between church teaching, on the one hand, and scientific understanding as well as personal experience about sexual identity in our time, on the other, is disturbing. This disconnect is reminiscent of the same medieval closed-mindedness that demanded that Galileo recant his findings that the sun does not in fact revolve around the Earth, even when we knew better.

How do I live my professional life, my gay identity, and my faith? Put simply, my faith informs my professional work. I quietly invite my students and residents to go within and look for deeper meaning, taking care not to impose my point of view on any of them. On a daily basis I invite God into the decisions I make, and I try to listen for direction in whatever I do, professionally and personally. I believe that it is only through a deep, ongoing personal relationship with God that I am transformed and am able to be a channel for change around me, whether in my professional life or in the church.

At the same time, I, with many other people of faith, experience deep pain and frustration at the conflict between official church teaching about homosexuality and my personal experience. I am troubled by the fact that I find greater acceptance of myself as a whole person in my professional community as a physician than I do from the official hierarchy of the church of my family, my childhood, and my life. I find the "love the sinner" line particularly offensive in its condescension and its uninformed and uncharitable lack of understanding with regard to homosexual relationships and persons. I am troubled by the denials of science, psychology, and the personal experience of countless people of faith that are all inherent in the church's refusal to budge from its official historical teaching on this topic. Yet in the face of this pain and frustration, I strive to remember that the church is in fact you and me and the whole community of believers and that she is a pilgrim church moving ever so slowly toward greater understanding and perfection, if only we allow her to do so.

Afterword: Reflections from Ecclesiology and Practical Theology

TOM BEAUDOIN AND BRADFORD E. HINZE

Fordham University

Why would "More than a Monologue" be chosen as the title of a project devoted to sexual diversity and the Roman Catholic Church? It is often perceived that in the Catholic Church, only one voice "counts" and only one voice is being heard—the collective voice of the bishops in union with the pope. In the Catholic tradition, the bishops and pope are recognized as the official spokesmen for and teachers of church members; they comprise the so-called magisterium or official teaching authority, whether in regard to sexual diversity or any other topic. The bishops of the United States fulfill this mandate for members of the church in the United States locally, regionally, and nationally by presenting and defending official church teachings on sexual morality, including those pertaining to birth control, abortion, and homosexuality. As apologists for and defenders of official teachings, the U.S. bishops, joined by some other members of their church, have over the past twenty-five years become particularly outspoken in public discourse and policy debates on the topic of homosexuality.

Not every Catholic agrees with this official voice. This volume was designed to provide an opportunity for a reading audience to listen to a variety of personal testimonies on the subject of sexual diversity, in the interest of promoting more open discussion in the church and, by extension, in the wider society. This effort is consistent with the promotion of a dialogical, or what is technically described as synodal or conciliar, view of the church, one based on the belief that all the faithful have a role to play in collaborating with bishops and priests in the teaching mission of the church, a view advanced at the Second Vatican Council (1962–1965). As the Dogmatic Constitution on the Church states: "the laity are entitled, and indeed sometimes duty-bound, to express their opinions on matters which concern the good of the Church."[1]

In this Afterword, following an introductory overview, the first part (primarily written by Bradford Hinze) treats these personal testimonies from the perspective of ecclesiology, the scholarly study of the church. The second part (primarily written by Tom Beaudoin) considers these same contributions in light of the emerging field of practical theology, which focuses on the theological meanings of practice and experience in church and society.

The Testimony Before Us

Before delving specifically into the issues raised by the voices collected in this volume, it is worth considering the following questions: Who are the speakers? What is it that they have to say? Who is being addressed? What is the hoped-for response?

Who are the speakers? As the Introduction by Christine Firer Hinze and Patrick Hornbeck has indicated, the speakers are lesbian, gay, bisexual, and transgender (LGBT) individuals and their parents, friends, teachers, lay ecclesial ministers, and pastors. Most are currently practicing Catholics, although some have left the church because of its official positions on homosexuality and/or its advocacy of these positions in the public realm.

What is it that they have to say? The most prevalent theme that emerges from these heartfelt statements is that LGBT individuals have felt personally discriminated against, abused, and deeply wounded (1) by the church's teaching that homosexuality is an objective disorder, (2) by the church's public rhetorical campaign in favor of the Defense of Marriage Act and against gay marriage and anti-discrimination legislation, and (3) by the fact that in the aftermath of the most egregious crime of our age in the church, the clergy sex abuse crisis, official church documents have diverted attention from the bishops' mishandling of the crisis by wrongly implicating homosexuality as the root cause of pedophilia and sex abuse crimes. Although the Catholic Church's most recent statements indicate that people with homosexual orientations are to be respected, their human dignity defended, and their place in the church—and even in official positions in the church—to be guaranteed, many LGBT individuals, whether they be sexually active or celibate, have felt condemned. Many have been made to feel unwelcomed in, or excluded, banished, and exiled from their church. Some are refused the sacraments—Eucharist and baptism have been denied to the children of gay and lesbian couples.[2] Others have not been allowed to serve in lay ecclesial ministry positions if they are open about their sexual orientation and relationships.[3] Based on the recent 2005 policy of a Vatican congregation, young men who believe they are homosexual are being rejected as candidates for priesthood.[4]

A second major theme articulated in these testimonies is that, influenced by formal church teachings and prevalent social attitudes, too often family members, peers, and persons in official positions have used offensive and alienating hate speech, or in other ways have contributed to a culture of abusive behavior toward LGBT people. A particularly pernicious expression of this culture is its implicit or explicit fostering and condoning of practices of bullying among young people and of the failure to publicly repudiate such behavior in Catholic institutions. Writers' testimonies express the psychological, spiritual, and physical toll this behavior takes on individuals, to the extent that some bullied LGBT youth have committed or attempted to commit suicide.

The third dominant message is that the pain and damage experienced by these authors is at times matched by the articulation of anger toward the church, in some cases to the point of acrimony and cynicism. This anger may be directed not only at the official teachings of the church and its leaders who promulgate these but also toward members of the church. Particular frustration is expressed about how Catholic teaching has bred an ecclesiastical or clerical culture of secrecy and invisibility, one in which LGBT individuals often feel forced to keep their sexual orientations and identities locked in the closet rather than openly conveyed, explored, and developed. Those who have chosen to express their sexual identities risk derision, abuse, and exclusion. No less wounding is the frequent lack of public support, especially by progressive Catholics and by clergy and religious (including those who are themselves gay), for those who come out and choose to express their sexual identity openly.

In response to these destructive dynamics, whether officially sanctioned or indirectly authorized, it is not surprising that some leave the church. Among those who depart are not only LGBT persons and their families and friends but also a significant number of young people who are not persuaded by official teaching and are, in fact, deeply offended by it.

A fourth theme meriting attention is voiced by LGBT individuals who have chosen to remain active Catholics and who want to be recognized and appreciated for the ways the God-given gift of their sexuality informs genuine manifestations of love in their lives, authentic spirituality, and fruitful ministries. What is abundantly clear from the testimonies in this volume is that many LGBT Catholics cherish their Catholic faith, and some of them have found parishes and small communities where they can worship and grow spiritually in environments where people are supportive of them, their sexual orientation, and their relationships, whether sexually active or celibate. Ministry to LGBT Catholics takes on many forms in numerous parishes and dioceses. Moreover, there are many Catholic institutions of higher learning where LGBT students, faculty, and staff find peers, colleagues, and networks that provide genuine support as they discover and embrace their sexual identities and form relationships conducive to their mature human development.

Who is being addressed? These essays are undoubtedly written with a Catholic audience in mind—ordained clergy, religious women and men, and lay people—but they are also directed to other religious and nonreligious readers. This is particularly important in the midst of the polarized discussion in the United States surrounding gay marriage and discrimination against LGBT individuals.

What is the authors' hoped-for response? Ultimately, the vast majority of these essays are offered in the hope that there will someday be reform of the Catholic Church's teaching and public stance on issues related to sexual diversity.

An Ecclesiological View

The contributions to this volume offer a poignant example of, and a challenge to, the call issued by the Second Vatican Council for reform of the church through the development of a more dialogical model of being church. The Council taught that every baptized individual is called to become an active contributor to the life and mission of the church. Central to this reform agenda have been efforts, in the decades since the Council, to foster renewed practices of synodality and collegiality at various levels within the church.[5] There have likewise been wide-ranging efforts to foster the involvement of Catholics in ecumenical and interfaith dialogue and collaboration and in open discussions with people of diverse worldviews. The Council underscored the call to holiness of every baptized Catholic as well as the vocation of all Catholics to participate fully as equal members before God in the life and worship of the church. While acknowledging different ministries in the church, including the office of bishops and of the bishop of Rome, the Council repudiated a paternalistic exercise of those offices and invited all church members, while seeking to honor and adhere to the faith of the church, to speak up and to exercise their freedom of conscience, all in order to build up the body of Christ as a living witness of faith. In this way, recent church teachings provide theological justification for the necessity of open discussion in the church about subjects such as sexual diversity. Conversely, these teachings repudiate a monological stance as one that actually undermines the authority and credibility of the church's teachings and of the episcopal office. Genuine continuity and reform in the church are advanced by the realization of this fuller, dialogical ecclesiology.

Yves Congar, a French Dominican theologian who was among the most important theological experts at Vatican II, wrote a book before the Council that he entitled *True and False Reform in the Church*. This landmark study, originally published in 1950, examined how the church is constantly reforming itself and argued that there must be a space for self-criticism within the church. In particular, Congar delineated four conditions for advancing authentic reform without schism. In light of these four conditions, let us consider the calls for reform of the church's teaching on sexual diversity that have been voiced by many authors in this volume.

Congar's first condition is that *genuine reforms must be advanced on the basis of charity and be motivated by pastoral concerns.*[6] The calls for reform articulated in this volume undoubtedly meet this condition. Second, *advocates for reform must "remain in communion with the whole church."*[7] This condition can be problematic for LGBT individuals who perceive their God-given sexual identity and human and spiritual development to be threatened by church teachings or who conscientiously judge the church's position on LGBT persons to be in opposition to reality and the truth. In the face of such conflict, many conclude that they must leave the church for the sake of their own spiritual and human flourishing. Yet, as a significant number of essayists here attest, many LGBT people and supporters have remained in communion with the church, working for reform by promoting open discussion of these issues in the interest of changing minds and hearts, even though they often suffer as a result.

Congar's third condition is that individuals and groups should *"have patience with delays," stand firm when there seems to be no movement, and avoid ultimatums.*[8] We encounter in this collection many examples of people who adhere to this condition. For others, many of whom have discerned their sexual identities and life paths amidst much suffering, prejudice, and defamation, this condition has proven untenable.

The fourth and final condition is that *"genuine reform takes place through a return to the principle of tradition* [and] *not through the forced introduction of some 'novelty' "*[9] Herein lies an apparent stumbling block. Whether argued on the basis of biblical witnesses, traditional beliefs, or arguments from natural law, the church's teachings on "homosexuality"— and more widely on the range of issues associated with sexual diversity— make the call for a change in the official position to seem to be based on novelty. However, manifestations of homosexuality and sexual diversity are not new. The repudiation of homosexual behavior by the church has no doubt been consistent, yet there is historical and textual evidence of the undeniable reality of such sexual diversity among humans, including members of the church throughout its history, which merits a thorough reassessment and judicious evaluation. Without denying the goods associated with hctcroscxual marriage and behavior, is there not sufficient historical, biological, and psychological evidence to warrant a reconsideration of the moral framework used to assess homosexuality and sexual diversity?

The official teaching office of the bishops, the magisterium, conceded a major point when it acknowledged the genuine possibility that a person's sexual orientation may be discovered in life and not chosen.[10] However, particularly on this subject, the bishops have been unwilling to entertain discussion of the limited and historically conditioned views of sexual reality handed on in the living tradition of the church. Catholics in the modern era have had no trouble conceding that not all statements contained in the scriptures convey the saving knowledge of the gospel, or that errors have been combined with the truth in the church's teachings over the course of its history. But there has been resistance to extending this insight into matters of sexuality. Here there is need for further resources beyond those provided by Congar.

In his contribution, Bishop Thomas Gumbleton has offered a guiding principle for proceeding: "We need," he proposes, "to face the reality that there is a basic incoherence in the church's teaching on homosexuality."[11] While Christians share the conviction that the definitive revelation of God made manifest in Jesus Christ is witnessed to in the scriptures and the confession of faith, Catholics recognize that the ongoing reception of this gospel must include openness to genuine insights provided by the "sense of the faithful" into the saving truth of the gospel. This *sensus fidelium* is not based on opinion polls but rather on the witness of holy men and women who convey the truth of the gospel in their lives through acts of love and justice. Especially in matters concerning sexuality, the doctrine of the sense of the faithful provides theological justification and impetus for open discussion in the Catholic Church among all the faithful about what the living tradition of faith teaches. Based on the belief in the goodness of the gift of God's creation as well as on Catholicism's traditional respect for the contribution of reason to faith, this discussion must entail openness to the wisdom concerning human sexuality that has been offered by the natural and social sciences. Recognizing the ongoing historical development of doctrine in light of the signs of the times, in the face of growing acknowledgment of the genuineness and holiness of the lives of LGBT persons, and in light of the findings of science, Catholics are challenged not to stifle the Spirit of life at work in the church and in the world.

One additional set of issues raised by these essays should be acknowledged and merits further consideration. Mark D. Jordan has advanced the argument that the church's repudiation of homosexual behavior is deeply interconnected through symbolic discourse and institutions of power with a gender dualism that combines a staunch defense of its all-male celibate clergy, a patriarchal hierarchy, and a homoerotic aesthetic with a virulent opposition to the ordination of women.[12] This argument is based on a complex theoretical framework that supports the hypothesis that there is, as Max Weber might have called it, an elective affinity between certain modes of discourse, practices of power, and particular valuations of gender differences and sexual orientations. Such a multifaceted hypothesis merits considerable scrutiny as well as an evaluation of both the theoretical frame and the range of evidence employed in support of this argument. The issues raised by this line of inquiry and the debates that will surface in the assessment of these arguments will presumably constitute a disputed question in theology and the church for quite some time, but perhaps one can hope that in the meantime, this contestation will contribute to ongoing dialogue in the interest of the promotion of reforms that are life giving for all members of the church.

Dialogue on sexual diversity provides not only an impetus for ecclesial reform but also an apt context for a call for ecclesial repentance and reconciliation.[13] Countless LGBT individuals, along with their family members and friends, have been deeply wounded, in all too many cases tragically so, by the teachings and practices of the church concerning sexual diversity. There will be no lasting peace on this subject until there are public statements and rituals in which church officials, in the name of the church universal, confess and repent for the abuse of LGBT persons and seek forgiveness and reconciliation.

A Practical Theology Perspective

Every essay in this book shows the human cost of downplaying lived experience in the formulation of church teaching on sexual identity, suggesting the importance of fresh Catholic theological thinking on sexual identity proportionate to the importance of these questions for (and beyond) LGBT persons inside and outside the church. Just as church teaching on "homosexuality" has proceeded without being troubled enough by its effect on real persons, Catholic academic theology should be able to challenge this teaching and proffer alternatives. A more robust practical theology in Catholic contexts, because it takes ordinary Catholic experience with theological seriousness, can contribute to such a project.[14]

Practical theology is not well known among Catholics in the United States. However, like modern ecclesiology, its contemporary form was shaped by the Second Vatican Council. The Council set the Catholic Church on a new way of thinking about the relationship between the church and the world, particularly through its Pastoral Constitution on the Church in the Modern World, *Gaudium et Spes*. The Council taught not only that the relationship between the church and contemporary "secular" society was of signal importance for the church's own identity but also that this relationship should be approached with the intention of being a respectful partnership, because of the deep human and historical impact that the church and the world have made and continue to make on each other. At Vatican II, the Catholic Church committed itself to a relationship with the world characterized by sympathy, curiosity, respect, responsibility, and learning.[15] The church's mission to "teach the world" does not disappear, of course, but this approach gives teaching the world a distinct cast: it becomes not an act of privileged power over persons whom the church can afford not to know but instead a service to humankind in aid of the divine vocation all persons share, insofar as everyone comes from and is invited toward the all-presiding mysterious reality that Christians call God. Recollection of God's mystery sets the church free anew for curiosity about its borders and identity; indeed, the church needs an essential curiosity about human experience to be called deeper into its very life and mission, to heed the urgings of the Spirit.

In the wake of Vatican II, when the study of theology and the training of theologians was undergoing substantial rethinking, some leading theologians, including Karl Rahner and David Tracy, argued that Catholics should widen the theological curriculum so as to include "practical theology," an area of theological study which at the time was seen largely as a preserve of Protestantism. For Rahner, securing practical theology in the Catholic world was essential to instantiating Vatican II in theological research.[16] In the Protestant world, practical theology had begun as a modern theological discipline that helped pastors translate between the particularity of their immediate ministerial experience and the generality of the expansive Christian tradition. By the 1980s, Protestant practical theology had expanded to embrace wider aspects of the study of faith in practice, especially the study, with the aid of social science, of practices of faith in modern society. These studies were understood to be undertaken for the sake of helping church leadership, and the whole faithful, better make their way in a complex and confusing world.

This was the context in which early calls for a Catholic practical theology, inspired by the Council and the ecumenical possibilities it opened up, were made. Proponents argued that Catholicism, too, needed a discipline like practical theology precisely to help church members think carefully about issues at the intersection of the church and the world, thus contributing to more effective pastoral ministry and prophetic social action. The development of a field of Catholic practical theology began to happen in some places, but for the most part did not happen in the United States. That does not mean that Catholic theological research has lacked interest in a more inductive approach to theology informed by pastoral-ministerial and ordinary lay experiences, but it is fair to say that a considerable proportion of Catholic theology that deals with the everyday, real-life issues engaged by Catholics and other persons in "the world" has frequently preferred the realm of the hortatory, the ideal, and the theoretical—just like official Catholic teaching on sexual identity.

However, in recent years, the promise of practical theology as a Vatican II–inspired theological discipline that would see practice/experience as theological phenomena, alongside theologies that privilege ideas/concepts or texts/scriptures, has begun to be redeemed. Through the outworking of the Council in the labors of various Catholic scholars committed to faithful practice in their own fields, the Protestant discourse of practical theology was engaged, the Catholic opportunity for practical theology was reengaged, and practical theology began to work its way into Catholic theology, beginning in the 1990s and continuing up to the present. The rapid intensification of lay ministry during that time was an unexpected boon to practical theologians, who, as specialists in the theory and practice of action, practice, and performance, could train lay pastoral workers—as well as students of academic theology—in ways different from the traditional and previously most influential training site for the theory and practice of church-world engagement, that of the Catholic seminary.

Practical theology serves the larger academic theological enterprise, the church, and the world by working in two modes: it connects theological theory and pastoral-cultural practice in academic contexts for the sake of enriching lived experience and conceptual clarity, and it studies the ways in which pastoral-cultural practice—especially the practices of the religiously nonelite, marginalized, or nonpersons—bears theological meaning.

In keeping with these two modes of work, from a practical-theological perspective, the essays in this book make important contributions toward generating new theological perspectives on the Catholic tradition while at the same time giving people more possibilities for understanding and negotiating an adult relationship to Catholicism in practice.

As these essays show, Catholicism must not only reckon with the fact that a range of church experiences bear theological meaning in people's lives but also acknowledge more fully the ways that everyday experience in ministry situations generates material for new insights about how practices bear theological meaning. For example, notice in this book how specific practices of ecclesial shame and Catholic self-censorship take an important place alongside traditional church practices of fellowship and prayer: the practiced actions of not holding hands with a partner at prayer, of calling to mind during prayers and readings that one does not actually exist ecclesially, or of processing the humiliation of suppressing the expression of whom one loves and the kind of life one desires. These practices of restraint on physical intimacy, recollection of nonexistence, and containment of humiliation are discreet and negative, but they are learned and patterned actions, undertaken with agency and performed amidst and because of the community, that shape the identities of Catholic LGBT persons. As such, these practices share a similar structure to more recognizable church practices and have similar consequences.

Equally important for practical theology are the shapes of everyday religious experience described in these pages. The essays show that LGBT persons sometimes make their own way in relation to the church by developing their own readings of scripture and tradition that include deeply motivating narratives: of Jesus' inclusivity and his own resistance to the "political" and "religious" powers of his day, of same-sex love, of the spiritual value of diversity, of passionate friendships, and of the fundamental goodness of creation. These authors reserve the spiritual right to name how and whether they will reside in the church: staying creatively active within Catholicism, residing on the margins, selectively participating, or leaving. Further, the question of who speaks with authority for Christ, for Catholicism, or for LGBT persons is a constant theme; hence the tensions evident in the essays between "remaining," "dissenting," becoming "post-Diocesan," and becoming "post-Catholic." In a word, these theologically laden accounts of lived LGBT religion are rich accounts of a complicated agency regarding religious affiliation. This agency is also consistently linked to the invocation of conscience: the essays speak to the harbor that LGBT persons frequently take in that inviolably personal depth that is, according to the Second Vatican Council, a person's "secret core and sanctuary," where individuals are "alone with God, whose voice echoes in [their] depths."[17]

What of church leadership and LGBT concerns? The wise formation of pastoral leaders is a traditional focus of practical theology. There are some references by essayists to the various life-affirming and sometimes life-saving LGBT ministries that too often reside on the fringes of the "mainstream" church, neither well known by nor well integrated with the larger church. And there are innovative suggestions throughout this volume regarding ways to pray, to read scripture, and to teach that have brought voice and hope—or at least have kept alive the struggle for recognition. Yet we hear too little in these pages about wise practices of official pastoral leadership concerning LGBT concerns in the Catholic Church. While we know that many Catholic pastoral workers innovate ways of counseling, educating, healing, preaching, and praying that support LGBT life, academic theology and pastoral training still count too little of that experience as important, and the forces of silence in the church too often keep such pastoral practices themselves closeted. Theologians and church workers can and should continue to develop this dimension of practice and thought. Indeed, the very act of taking this volume seriously, for ecclesiology and practical theology, can contribute to new forms of pastoral leadership better attuned to and open about LGBT realities and concerns.

Will the above catalogue of the practical-theological materials contained in these essays be judged illegitimate by Catholics? For those who would so judge, it is not enough to take refuge in the assertion that these theology-bearing practices are not sufficiently "orthodox" or "traditional." Practical theology emphasizes that it is through concrete, contextual practices—not texts, ideas, or teachings alone—that Catholicism, in all its ambiguity, is mediated to anyone, including LGBT persons. Where Catholicism goes from here will have to be worked with at the level of practice and lived experience, rather than merely retheorized apart from attention to the ways in which personal and communal spiritual identities are actually formed and maintained. These essays show that Catholicism's theology of sexual identity happens in the hearts, minds, and bodies of real human beings. Any future ecclesial and theological response will also have to proceed from hearts, minds, and bodies in order to be effective.

But it is just here that Catholicism can make a profound contribution to practical theology. Until now, practical theologians themselves have done too little research and writing on sexual identity. These essays show how Catholics stand poised to open up a new wing of practical theology, one focused on the ways in which sexual diversity matters for the spiritual life. Each of the practices above opens up a research avenue for Catholic theology and for pastoral engagement. Both ecclesiology and practical theology can do their part to ensure that monologue ends and dialogue commences.

Notes

Introduction

CHRISTINE FIRER HINZE AND J. PATRICK HORNBECK II

1. Information about the conferences, including videos of many of the events that the series comprised, may be found at http://www.morethanamonologue.org.

2. J. Patrick Hornbeck II and Michael A. Norko, eds., *Inquiry, Thought, and Expression*, vol. 2 of *More than a Monologue: Sexual Diversity and the Catholic Church* (New York: Fordham University Press, 2014).

3. Irenaeus's (c. 125–202) famous dictum *gloria Dei, vivens homo* appears in his *Adversus Haereses*, IV, 20, 7. "The glory of God is man fully alive, and the life of man is the vision of God. If the revelation of God through creation already brings life to all living beings on the earth, how much more will the manifestation of the Father by the Word bring life to those who see God." *Sources chretiénnes* 100, p. 648.

4. See, e.g., Janet E. Smith and Christopher Kaczor, *Life Issues, Medical Decisions: Questions and Answers for Catholics* (Cincinnati, Ohio: St. Anthony Messenger Press, 2007), chap. 1; Timothy E. O'Connell, *Principles for a Catholic Morality*, rev. ed. (San Francisco: HarperCollins, 1990), parts II and III; *Catechism of the Catholic Church* (Vatican City: Libreria Editrice Vaticana, 1993), nos. 1731–1738, 1776–1794.

5. This belief is essential to the Thomistic natural law theory upon which Catholic moral theology heavily relies, and it explicitly undergirds many church documents, e.g., Paul VI, *Humanae Vitae* (1968), no. 12; John Paul II, *Veritatis Splendor* (1993), nos. 12, 40; Congregation for the Doctrine of the Faith, "Considerations Regarding Proposals to Give Legal Recognition to Unions Between Homosexual Persons" (2003), nos. 2, 6. On the Catholic natural law tradition, see Clifford G. Kossel SJ, "Thomistic Moral Philosophy in the Twentieth Century," in *The Ethics of Aquinas*, ed. Stephen J. Pope (Washington, D.C.: Georgetown University Press, 2002), 385–411; Jean Porter, *Natural and Divine Law: Reclaiming the Tradition for Christian Ethics* (Ottawa: Novalis, 1999); O'Connell, *Principles for a Catholic Morality*, chaps. 13, 14; and *Catechism of the Catholic Church*, nos. 1954–1960.

6. See, e.g., John T. Noonan, *A Church That Can and Cannot Change: The Development of Catholic Moral Teaching* (Notre Dame, Ind.: University of Notre Dame Press, 2005); Charles E. Curran, ed., *Change in Official Catholic Moral Teaching*, Readings in Moral Theology 13 (Mahwah, N.J.: Paulist Press, 2003).

7. See *Gaudium et Spes* (Pastoral Constitution on the Church in the Modern World, 1965), no. 16, http://www.vatican.va/archive/hist_councils/ii_vatican _council/documents/vat-ii_const_19651207_gaudium-et-spes_en.html. In its treatment of conscience, the Catholic *Catechism* teaches that "[a] human being must always obey the certain judgment of his [or her] conscience. If he [or she] were deliberately to act against it, he [or she] would condemn him[/her]self" (*Catechism*, no. 1790). Concerning discernment, in "Ministry to Persons with a Homosexual Inclination," the U.S. bishops write that "the Catholic tradition speaks of discernment as that process by which a person uses one's own reasoning ability, the sources of divine revelation (Scripture and tradition), the Church's teaching and guidance, the wise counsel of others, and one's own individual and communal experiences of grace in a sincere effort to choose wisely and well. . . . Ultimately, each person . . . must discern his or her own moral decisions. . . . With all the input and support possible, both from individuals and communities, one must still face the future based on decisions made before God in the recesses of one's own heart." U.S. Conference of Catholic Bishops, "Ministry to Persons with a Homosexual Inclination: Guidelines for Pastoral Care" (2006), 8, citing *Catechism*, no. 2337.

8. *Lumen Gentium* (Dogmatic Constitution on the Church, 1964), no. 25, http://www.vatican.va/archive/hist_councils/ii_vatican_council/documents/vat -ii_const_19641121_lumen-gentium_en.html.

9. 2 Cor 4:7. However, this scriptural citation does not appear in *Lumen Gentium*. Cf. *Catechism*, nos. 770–773.

10. See especially *Lumen Gentium*, nos. 30–38 (on the laity) and 39–40 (on the universal call to holiness.

11. *Code of Canon Law, Latin-English Edition, New English Translation* (Washington, D.C.: Canon Law Society of America, 1999), cc. 211–212. Recent pastoral documents also underscore the importance of listening and dialogue concerning church sexual teaching: "The pervasive influence of contemporary culture creates, at times, significant difficulties for the reception of Catholic teaching on homosexuality. In this context, there is need of a special effort to help persons with a homosexual inclination understand Church teaching. At the same time, it is important that Church ministers listen to the experiences, needs, and hopes of the persons with a homosexual inclination to whom and with whom they minister. Dialogue provides an exchange of information, and also communicates a respect for the innate dignity of other persons and a respect for their consciences. 'Authentic dialogue, therefore, is aimed above all at the rebirth of indi-

viduals through interior conversion and repentance, but always with profound respect for consciences and with patience and at the step-by-step pace indispensable for modern conditions.' Such dialogue facilitates an ongoing, interior conversion for all parties truly engaged in the exchange." U.S. Conference of Catholic Bishops, "Ministry to Persons," 24, citing John Paul II, Postsynodal Apostolic Exhortation *Reconciliation and Penance (Reconciliatio et paenitentia)* (Washington, D.C.: USCCB, 1984), no. 25.

12. It is not possible, given the limitations of space, nor desirable, given this volume's focus on human experience, to provide a full account of official Catholic teachings on sexuality and sexual diversity. Some of the documents most often cited are *Catechism*, nos. 2357–2359; Congregation for the Doctrine of the Faith, "On the Pastoral Care of Homosexual Persons" (*Homosexualitatis problema*, 1986); and U.S. Conference of Catholic Bishops, "Always Our Children" (1997, revised 1998). The introduction and many of the essays in the companion volume, *Inquiry, Thought, and Expression*, engage official church teaching at length.

13. "Sexual identity," its features and parameters, its origins or causes, its stability or malleability, are hotly debated topics in contemporary social sciences, philosophy, theology, and culture. Interestingly, both contemporary Catholic church teaching, and many (though not all) of the contributors to this collection, describe or speak about the experience of "sexual identity" as something given and discovered rather than constructed or freely chosen from among a range of alternatives.

14. Genesis 1:27. *"Human sexuality is thus a good*, part of that created gift which God saw as being 'very good,' when he created the human person in his image and likeness, and 'male and female he created them'" (Gn 1:27). The complementarity of man and woman as male and female is inherent within God's creative design. . . . Jesus taught that "from the beginning of creation, 'God made them male and female. For this reason a man shall leave his father and mother [and be joined to his wife], and the two shall become one flesh' (Mk 10:6–8)." "Ministry to Persons," 2–3, emphasis in the original.

15. "Ministry to Persons," 3. Citing *Catechism*, no. 2363, and *Code of Canon Law*, can. 1055 sec. 1, the document continues: "'The spouses' union achieves the twofold end of marriage: the good of the spouses themselves and the transmission of life. This is the order of nature, an order whose source is ultimately the wisdom of God."

16. "By its very nature, the sexual act finds its proper fulfillment in the marital bond. Any sexual act that takes place outside the bond of marriage does not fulfill the proper ends of human sexuality. Such an act is not directed toward the expression of marital love with an openness to new life. It is disordered in that it is not in accord with this twofold end and is thus morally wrong. 'Sexual pleasure is

morally disordered when sought for itself, isolated from its procreative and unitive purposes.'" "Ministry to Persons," 4, citing *Catechism*, no. 2351.

17. "Ministry to Persons," 2, citing *Catechism*, no. 2358, and Congregation for the Doctrine of the Faith, "On the Pastoral Care," no. 10.

18. In the midst of many disagreements, these emphases can be found across the spectrum of contemporary Catholic theological reflection on sexuality, from authors who expound on Pope John Paul II's "theology of the body" to Catholic feminist scholarship on sexual ethics by writers such as Lisa Sowle Cahill and Margaret Farley.

19. That magisterial teachings on sexual diversity have been a source of pain and consternation was recently recognized by New York's archbishop Cardinal Timothy Dolan, who said on a national television program that "we've got to do better to see that our defense of marriage is not reduced to an attack on gay people. And I admit, we haven't been too good at that. We try our darnedest to make sure we're not anti-anybody." Quoted in Vivian Yee, "Dolan Says Church Should Be More Welcoming of Gay People," *New York Times* (March 31, 2013).

20. In their 2006 document, the U.S. bishops underscore that "the Church does not teach that the experience of homosexual attraction is in itself sinful." Church teaching does hold that "the homosexual inclination is objectively disordered, i.e., it is an inclination that predisposes one toward what is truly not good for the human person." Further, "heterosexual persons not uncommonly have disordered sexual inclinations as well. . . . For example, any tendency toward sexual pleasure that is not subordinated to the greater goods of love and marriage is disordered, in that it inclines a person towards a use of sexuality that does not accord with the divine plan for creation." "Ministry to Persons," 5–6.

21. For further discussion of these claims, see among many others Patricia Beattie Jung and Ralph F. Smith, *Heterosexism: An Ethical Challenge* (Albany, N.Y.: SUNY Press, 1993); Stephen Pope, "The Magisterium's Arguments against 'Same-Sex Marriage': An Ethical Analysis and Critique," *Theological Studies* 65 (2004): 530–565; Margaret Farley, *Just Love: A Framework for Christian Sexual Ethics* (New York: Continuum, 2006); and many essays in our companion volume.

22. Thus, the U.S. bishops write in 2006: "It is crucially important to understand that saying a person has a particular inclination that is disordered is not to say that the person as a whole is disordered. Nor does it mean that one has been rejected by God or the Church. . . . Other inclinations can likewise be disordered, such as those that lead to envy, malice, or greed. We are all damaged by the effects of sin, which causes desires to become disordered. Simply possessing such inclinations does not constitute a sin, at least to the extent that they are beyond one's control. Acting on such inclinations, however, is always wrong." "Ministry to Persons," 6, citing "On the Pastoral Care," no. 11.

23. Benedict XVI, *Caritas in veritate*, no. 18.

24. For further discussion of these and related points, see the works cited in note 6, above.

25. The introduction to our companion volume, *Inquiry, Thought, and Expression*, discusses at length the history of Catholic magisterial and theological discourse concerning homosexuality.

26. Cf. the strong reactions worldwide evoked by Pope Francis's remark during a July 28, 2013, press conference: "If a person is gay and seeks the Lord and has good will, well who am I to judge them? The *Catechism of the Catholic Church* explains this in a very beautiful way, but says . . . [that] these persons must not be marginalized for this, they must be integrated into society." *Catholic News Agency* (Vatican City, August 5, 2013), http://www.catholicnewsagency.com/news/full-transcript-of-popes-in-flight-press-remarks-released/.

27. The emphasis on and attention to "experience" in contemporary Catholic theology and ethics is warranted in official teaching by the oft-noted "turn to the subject" and "turn to historical consciousness" that was a hallmark of the approach taken in the documents of Vatican II, in particular by the Pastoral Constitution on the Church in the Modern World (*Gaudium et Spes*), where the term "experience" is used over fifty times. Catholic theologians' engagement with human experience is both intellectually critical and ecclesially situated. Far from assuming that either unexamined "experience" or unexamined "tradition" provides automatic answers concerning what is true or good, they labor to analyze, to interpret, to discern, and to articulate to the best of their ability the truth and value discoverable in the dynamic encounter between Catholics' faith traditions and their embodied, historically and culturally situated experiences and practices. See, e.g., Karl Rahner SJ, "Reflections on the Experience of Grace," in *Theological Investigations* (London: Darton, Longman, and Todd, 1967), 3:86–90; Monika Hellwig, *Whose Experience Counts in Theological Reflection?* (Milwaukee, Wis.: Marquette University Press, 1982); Ellen Leonard CSJ, "Experience as a Source for Theology," *Proceedings of the Catholic Theological Society of America* 43 (1988): 44–61; Francis Schussler Fiorenza, "Systematic Theology: Tasks and Methods," in *Systematic Theology: Roman Catholic Perspectives*, 2nd ed., ed. Francis Schussler Fiorenza and John Galvin (Minneapolis: Fortress, 2011); Aidan Nichols OP, "Aid to Discernment: Experience and Magisterium," in his *The Shape of Catholic Theology* (Collegeville, Minn.: Liturgical Press, 1991), 235–247.

28. Complementing and at times contesting contemporary Catholic theology's treatment of *experience* has been the emergence of a diverse, ecumenical field of study focusing on *practices* as constitutive of Christian life. Along with Tom Beaudoin's contribution from a practical-theological perspective in the afterword of this volume, see, e.g., David Tracy, "The Foundations of Practical Theology," in

Practical Theology: The Emerging Field in Theology, Church, and World, ed. Don Browning (New York: Harper and Row, 1983), 62–82; David Tracy, "A Correlational Model of Practical Theology Revisited," in *Religion, Diversity, and Conflict*, ed. Edward Foley, International Practical Theology 15 (2011), 49–61; Bonnie Miller-McLemore, ed., *The Wiley-Blackwell Companion to Practical Theology* (West Sussex: John Wiley and Sons, 2012).

29. In this sense, one might think of the present volume as the first stage in an exercise in developing a practice-based theology of sexual difference. Richard Osmer, in *Practical Theology: An Introduction* (Grand Rapids, Mich.: Eerdmans, 2008), identifies the collection of data about theologically informed practices as the starting point for practical-theological investigations. On this point, see further Tom Beaudoin's and Brad Hinze's afterword to this volume.

30. Reviewing the rosters of speakers from the four conferences, we discovered that at least two important constituencies were not represented: the Catholic bishops of the United States and young people, namely, teenagers and college students. We therefore invited essays from two individuals who did not participate in the More than a Monologue conferences: Thomas J. Gumbleton, a Catholic bishop from Detroit, who has written a moving essay on the development of his own views on sexual diversity, and Jeanine Viau, a doctoral student in the field of Christian ethics who has contributed a chapter, based on her dissertation research, on the experiences of queer students in Catholic colleges and universities in the Chicago metropolitan area.

31. Here we offer a brief overview of the sections of this volume; the essays themselves are introduced at the opening of each section.

32. Adolfo Nicolás SJ, "Depth, University, and Learned Ministry: Challenges to Jesuit Higher Education Today," Mexico City, April 23, 2010.

33. Association of Jesuit Colleges and Universities, "The Jesuit, Catholic Mission of U.S. Jesuit Colleges and Universities" (Washington, D.C.: Association of Jesuit Colleges and Universities, 2010), 6.

34. Pope Francis, address to writers of the Jesuit journal *La Civiltà Cattolica*, June 14, 2013: "The break between Gospel and culture is undoubtedly a tragedy (cf. *Evangelii nuntiandi*, 20). You are called to give your contribution to heal this break, which passes also through the heart of each one of you and of your readers. This ministry is typical of the mission of the Society of Jesus. . . . Your proper place is the frontiers. This is the place of Jesuits. That which Paul VI, taken up by Benedict XVI, said of the Society of Jesus, is true for you also in a particular way today: 'Wherever in the Church, even in the most difficult and acute fields, in the crossroads of ideologies, in the social trenches, there was and is the confrontation between the burning exigencies of man and the perennial message of the Gospel, the Jesuits have been and are there.' Please, be men of the frontier, with that capacity that comes from God (cf. 2 Corinthians 3:6)."

1. This Catholic Mom: Our Family Outreach

DEB WORD

1. Then archbishop, now Cardinal Timothy Dolan of New York directed this comment to Eternal Word Television Network's Raymond Arroyo when he appeared on his show on November 28, 2011.

2. This statement, made in an interview with a Chicago television station, was reported in the *Huffington Post*. See "Cardinal George: Chicago Gay Pride Parade, LGBT Movement Could 'Morph Into Ku Klux Klan,'" *Huffington Post* (December 22, 2011), http://www.huffingtonpost.com/2011/12/22/cardinal-george-gay-pride-kkk_n_1165179.html. See also Manya A. Brachear, "Cardinal Apologizes for Remarks Comparing Gay Rights to KKK," *Chicago Tribune* (January 7, 2012), http://articles.chicagotribune.com/2012-01-07/news/ct-met-cardinal-george-apology-20120107_1.

2. O Tell Me the Truth About Love

EVE TUSHNET

1. Christopher C. Roberts, *Creation and Covenant: The Significance of Sexual Difference in the Moral Theology of Marriage* (New York: Continuum, 2008).

2. Wesley Hill, *Washed and Waiting: Reflections on Christian Faithfulness and Homosexuality* (Grand Rapids, Mich.: Zondervan, 2010).

3. David Morrison, *Beyond Gay* (Huntington, Ind.: Our Sunday Visitor, 1999).

4. Melinda Selmys, *Sexual Authenticity: An Intimate Reflection on Homosexuality and Catholicism* (Huntington, Ind.: Our Sunday Visitor, 2009).

5. Frederick S. Roden, *Same-Sex Desire in Victorian Religious Culture* (New York: Palgrave Macmillan, 2002).

6. Aelred of Rievaulx, *Spiritual Friendship*, ed. Marsha L. Dutton, trans. Lawrence C. Braceland (Collegeville, Minn.: Cistercian Publications, 2007).

4. Mother, Father, Brother, Sister, Husband, and Wife

HILARY HOWES

1. "Strong Majorities Favor Rights and Legal Protections for Transgender People," Public Religion Research Institute (November 3, 2011), http://publicreligion.org/newsroom/2011/11/news-release-strong-majorities-favor-rights-and-legal-protections-for-transgender-people/.

2. Jeff Israely, "The Pope's Christmas Condemnation of Transsexuals," *Time* (December 23, 2008), http://www.time.com/time/world/article/0,8599,1868390,00.html.

3. Thomas Merton, "The Inner Experience: Notes on Contemplation (1)," *Cistercian Studies Quarterly* 18 (1983): 7.

4. John Norton, "Vatican Says 'Sex-Change' Operation Does Not Change Person's Gender," Catholic News Service (January 14, 2003), http://ai.eecs.umich.edu/people/conway/TS/CatholicTSDecision.html.

5. Patrick B. Craine, "Fired 'Trans' Activist Rejects Settlement from Catholic School Board," http://www.lifesitenews.com/news/fired-trans-activist-rejects-settlement-from-catholic-school-board/.

6. "Strong Majorities Favor Rights and Legal Protections for Transgender People."

5. A Call to Listen: The Church's Pastoral and Theological Response to Gays and Lesbians

THOMAS GUMBLETON

1. An earlier version of this essay appeared in Patricia Beattie Jung with Joseph Andrew Coray, eds., *Sexual Diversity and Catholicism: Toward the Development of Moral Theology* (Collegeville, Minn.: Michael Glazier / Liturgical Press, 2001), 1–21. Used with permission.

2. Thomas H. Stahel, " 'I'm Here': An Interview with Andrew Sullivan," *America* 168, no. 16 (May 8, 1993): 11.

3. "Letter to the Editor," *America* (October 17, 1992): 286.

4. National Conference of Catholic Bishops, "To Live in Christ Jesus: A Pastoral Reflection on the Moral Life" (Washington, D.C.: USCCB, 1976), no. 19.

5. *Catechism of the Catholic Church*, no. 2358.

6. National Conference of Catholic Bishops, "To Live in Christ Jesus."

7. National Conference of Catholic Bishops, "Human Sexuality: A Catholic Perspective for Education and Lifelong Learning" (Washington, D.C.: USCCB, 1991), no. 55.

8. Stahel, " 'I'm Here,' " 7.

9. Ibid.

10. Ibid.

11. Pope Gregory I, "Epistle 64," in *Patrologia Latina*, ed. Jacques-Paul Migne (Paris, 1849), 77:1196–1197.

12. Irenaeus of Lyons, *Against the Heresies*, 4.20.

13. Stahel, " 'I'm Here,' " 8.

14. Ibid., 6.

15. National Conference of Catholic Bishops, "Always Our Children" (Washington, D.C.: September 10, 1997), 8.

16. Second Vatican Council, Pastoral Constitution on the Church in the Modern World, *Gaudium et Spes*, in *The Documents of Vatican II*, ed. Walter M. Abbott (New York: Guild, 1966), 80, 294.

6. From Closet to Lampstand: A Pastoral Call for Visibility
M. SHEILA NELSON

1. In many parts of the country, the message given to GLBT parishioners is clear: *You are welcome here as long as you don't make a point of your sexual orientation; it's no one's business but yours. We don't want you to scandalize anyone or give anyone ideas.* In the "Pastoral Care" section of "Ministry to Persons with a Homosexual Inclination: Guidelines for Pastoral Care" (United States Conference of Catholic Bishops, November 14, 2006), the document advises: "For some persons, revealing their homosexual tendencies to certain close friends, family members, a spiritual director, confessor, or members of a church support group may provide some spiritual and emotional help and aid them in their growth in the Christian life. In the context of parish life, however, general public self-disclosures are not helpful and should not be encouraged" (17). This document also emphasizes the danger of participation in "gay subcultures" or any LGBT groups that do not promote the official teaching of the church. The document states: "Persons with a homosexual inclination should not be encouraged to define themselves primarily in terms of their sexual inclination, however, or to participate in "gay subcultures," which often tend to promote immoral lifestyles. Rather, they should be encouraged to form relationships with the wider community" (22).

Similarly, in the 2011 document from the Episcopal Commission for Doctrine of the Canadian Conference of Catholic Bishops, "Pastoral Ministry to Young People with Same-Sex Attraction," the bishops discourage the use of the words "gay" and "lesbian" as words that "do not describe *persons* with the fullness and richness that the church recognizes and respects in every man or woman. Instead, 'gay' and 'lesbian' are often cultural definitions for people and movements that have accepted homosexual acts and behaviors as morally good" (1, emphasis in the original). Again the bishops ask those who work with youth to "help them avoid involvement in a '"gay culture"' opposed to the church's teaching" and, when talking about counseling, advise parents: "Ensure that professional counselors or psychologists who see young people are distinguished by their sound human and spiritual maturity. They must be committed to the Christian vision of the human person and sexuality, as well as the church's teaching on homosexuality and chastity" (6).

2. Matthew 5:14–16 (The New English Bible).

3. John 10:10 (NEB).

4. Particularly relevant passages of the *Catechism of the Catholic Church* (Vatican: Libreria Editrice Vaticana, 1997) include paras. 2332–2333 and 2337–2338.

5. United States Conference of Catholic Bishops, Secretariat for Family, Laity, Women, and Youth, "Always Our Children: A Pastoral Message to Parents of Homosexual Children and Suggestions for Pastoral Ministers" (Washington, D.C.: United States Catholic Conference, 1997): 6.

6. Jeremiah 31:33–34 (New American Bible).

7. I conducted an online survey of persons involved with the Catholic LGBT community: priests and pastoral ministers serving the community; LGBT Catholics and former Catholics; and their families and friends, allies, or others with an interest in this population. Respondents were recruited primarily through the major Catholic LGBT organizations: Dignity, New Ways Ministry, Fortunate Families, and CALGM, although respondents were encouraged to share the introductory letter and survey link with others who might be interested (local parish ministries, etc.). COURAGE Apostolate was also invited to participate but chose not to. I did, however, receive about forty responses from COURAGE members who learned of the survey from other sources. I received a total of 430 completed surveys. The quotes come from responses to the open-ended question: "What advice do you have for improving the relationship between each of the following groups (Bishops, Priests, Catholic LGBT Ministry Groups) and the Catholic GLBT population? If they approached you and asked for your advice, what would you say?" My analysis is not yet complete, but if you are interested in more information about this study, contact me at snelson@csbsju.edu.

8. COURAGE describes itself in this way on its website: "COURAGE, an apostolate of the Catholic Church, ministers to persons with same-sex attraction and their loved ones. We have been endorsed by the Pontifical Council for the Family and our beloved John Paul II said of this ministry, 'COURAGE is doing the work of God!' We also have an outreach called EnCourage which ministers to relatives, spouses, and friends of persons with same-sex attraction." The homepage states that through embracing celibacy, "one can move beyond the confines of the homosexual identity to a more complete one in Christ." The ministry rejects an understanding of sexual orientation as a central piece of one's identity that must be embraced and integrated. It utilizes instead a twelve-step process, modeled on Alcoholics Anonymous, that treats same-sex attraction as an addiction. Some COURAGE chapters, though not all, encourage reparative therapy. http://www.couragerc.org and www.couragerc.org/Twelve_Steps_of_Courage.html.

9. Luke 12:2–3.

10. While this is not common practice, there is debate about the appropriateness of baptizing the child of a same-sex couple. The policy of the Canadian Bishops Conference allows only one person in a same-sex marriage or relationship to sign the baptismal document as the child's parent; if the parents insist

that they both want to sign the document, they are denied baptism. See http://
www.catholicnewsagency.com/news/cccb_clears_up_confusion_about_baptism
_for_children_of_samesex_couples/. In the United States, it is normally left up
to the pastor to determine the likelihood that the child will be brought up
Catholic.

11. The most publicized recent case occurred in Boulder, Colorado, in March
2010, when Father William Breslin informed a lesbian couple that their three-
and five-year-old daughters would not be allowed to return to Sacred Heart of
Jesus Parish School the following fall because of their mothers' relationship. See
Thomas C. Fox, "Boulder Pastor Says Jesus Turned Some Away," *National Catholic
Reporter* (March 17, 2010), http://ncronline.org/news/faith-parish/boulder-pastor
-says-jesus-turned-some-away.

12. Barbara Johnson was told by Fr. Marcel Guarnizo when she approached
the altar for Communion during her mother's funeral, "I can't give you Communion because you live with a woman, and in the eyes of the church, that is a
sin." The priest, claiming later that he was ill, left the sanctuary during Barbara's
eulogy to her mother, and he did not accompany the family to the cemetery for
the burial. Kate Childs Graham, "Communion Denied, Grieving Deprived for
Woman Spurned at Funeral Mass," *National Catholic Reporter* (February 29,
2012), http://ncronline.org/news/people/communion-denied-grieving-deprived
-woman-spurned-funeral-mass.

13. An additional problem for our church, which results from our current
polarization around issues of sexuality and sexual orientation, is that energy is
being sapped from other concerns that are arguably much more central to the
Gospel. How do our battles over sexuality distract us from unified efforts on
behalf of the poor or the work for justice and peace that cries out for our attention? The infighting, the harsh words, and the lack of trust within Christ's body
cannot help but interfere with our ability to reach out; they prevent us from
being the visible hands and heart of Christ at work in a hurting world.

14. John 6:68 (New American Bible).

7. Gay Ministry at the Crossroads: The Plight of Gay Clergy in the Catholic Church

DONALD B. COZZENS

1. Elisabeth Bumiller, "Out and Proud to Serve," *New York Times* (September
20, 2011).

2. These quotations are taken from the "Don't Ask, Don't Tell" law, which
until its repeal was 10 USC 654; quotations at 654(a)(15).

3. Donald B. Cozzens, *The Changing Face of the Priesthood: A Reflection on the
Priest's Crisis of Soul* (Collegeville, Minn.: Liturgical Press, 2000), 107.

4. Congregation for Catholic Education, "Instruction Concerning the Criteria for the Discernment of Vocations with Regard to Persons with Homosexual Tendencies in View of Their Admission to the Seminary and to Holy Orders" (November 4, 2005), nos. 5, 6.

5. David C. Trosch, "On Homosexuals in the Catholic Priesthood" (August 18, 2000), http://www.trosch.org/ant/gay_priests.html.

6. Mark Jordan, *The Silence of Sodom: Homosexuality in Modern Catholicism* (Chicago: University of Chicago Press), 160–161.

7. Donald Goergen, "Calling Forth a Healthy Chaste Life," *Review for Religious* 57, no. 3 (May-June 1998): 268.

8. Jeannine Gramick, *Homosexuality in the Priesthood and Religious Life* (New York: Crossroad, 1989), 148.

9. Jordan, *Silence of Sodom*, 159; Hanson, *Decadence and Catholicism* (Cambridge, Mass.: Harvard University Press, 1997), 7.

10. See Eve Tushnet's essay in this volume (Chapter 2).

11. Donald B. Cozzens, *Freeing Celibacy* (Collegeville, Minn.: Liturgical Press, 2006), 19–30, 65–74.

12. Hanson, *Decadence and Catholicism*, 297.

13. Jordan, *Silence of Sodom*, 159.

14. *Code of Canon Law* (Washington D.C.: Canon Law Society of America, 1987), 97.

15. Lisa Sowle Cahill, "Sexuality and Christian Ethics: How to Proceed," in *Sexuality and the Sacred*, ed. James B. Nelson and Sandra P. Longfellow (Louisville, Ky.: Westminster John Knox Press, 1994), 19.

8. The Experience of a Pastoral Advocate and Implications for the Church

BRYAN N. MASSINGALE

1. The line of argument I used and the ensuing controversy were covered in depth by the local newspaper. Bill Glauber, "Discussion or Dissent? Priest Offers an Alternate Take on Marriage Vote," *Milwaukee Journal Sentinel* (October 27, 2006), http://www.jsonline.com/news/milwaukee/29216494.html.

2. Indeed, Richard McCormick, arguably the most influential U.S. Catholic moral theologian of the twentieth century, noted over a quarter-century ago that "The modern need in the Catholic community is a pacific, unthreatened, open understanding and restructuring of sexual ethics. Whether this will or can occur is doubtful. Even modest attempts . . . are met with such *panic, fear, and denunciation* that scholars can only be discouraged from the attempt." Richard McCormick, *Health and Medicine in the Catholic Tradition* (New York: Crossroad, 1984), 104; emphasis added.

3. This is a riff off of a formulation I developed in a recent work that contends that in U.S. (and global) Catholicism, "Catholic" = "white." For this discussion, see Bryan N. Massingale, *Racial Justice and the Catholic Church* (Maryknoll, N.Y.: Orbis, 2010), 79–82.

4. For example, this is the deepest implication of the current prohibition against ordaining men with "deep-seated same-sex attractions." See Congregation for Catholic Education, "Instruction for the Criteria for the Discernment of Vocations with Regard to Persons with Homosexual Tendencies in View of Their Admission to the Seminary and to Holy Orders" (2005), no. 1, http://www .vatican.va/roman_curia/congregations/ccatheduc/documents/rc_con_ccathe duc_doc_20051104_istruzione_en.html.

5. For example, even a document that condemns all same-sex genital expression as manifesting self-indulgence at the same time counsels that gay and lesbian persons are to be treated with dignity and respect. See Congregation for the Doctrine of the Faith, "Letter to the Bishops of the Catholic Church on the Pastoral Care of Homosexual Persons" (1986), nos. 7, 10, http://www.vatican.va/roman _curia/congregations/cfaith/documents/rc_con_cfaith_doc_19861001_homo sexual-persons_en.html.

6. This conviction, despite current ecclesial practices to the contrary, is attested to in the magisterium's own documents. See *The Compendium of the Social Doctrine of the Church*, heading for no. 144: "The Equal Dignity of All People"; the *Compendium* then declares "the radical equality . . . of all people." What this volume intends, I believe, is to promote and stimulate dialogue on the practical and doctrinal implications of this belief in the "radical equality of all people."

10. A Delicate Dance: Utilizing and Challenging the Sexual Doctrine of the Catholic Church in Support of LGBTIQ Persons
TERESA DELGADO

1. "Iona College opened its doors in 1940, with nine Christian Brothers and six lay faculty greeting the first class. The Christian Brothers named the College after Iona, an island off the west coast of Scotland, home to the monastery of St. Columba. The Congregation of Christian Brothers was itself founded in 1802 by Blessed Edmund Ignatius Rice in Waterford, Ireland." http://www.iona.edu. Iona College is governed completely separately from the hierarchy of the Roman Catholic Church, unlike the Catholic University of America (CUA), which, "as the national university of the Catholic Church in the United States, founded and sponsored by the bishops of the country with the approval of the Holy See, CUA is committed to being a comprehensive Catholic and American institution of higher learning, faithful to the teachings of Jesus Christ as handed on by the Church." http://www.cua.edu.

2. In his book *The Pope's War: Why Ratzinger's Secret Crusade Has Imperiled the Church and How It Can Be Saved* (New York: Sterling Ethos, 2011), Matthew Fox dedicates the appendix of this volume to the many theologians who have been silenced, expelled, and banished under Cardinal Ratzinger, later Pope Benedict XVI. He states, "As one editor of a Catholic newspaper wrote me: 'Some theologians are not publically disenfranchised but nevertheless are marginalized and in effect banned. Friends in these jobs tell me moral theology is basically dead in RC institutions because of the chill.' It is a strange organization indeed that fires its thinkers and leaders, those who respond to the 'signs of the times'" (238).

3. Alice Walker, *In Search of Our Mothers' Gardens: Womanist Prose* (San Diego, Calif.: Harcourt, 1983), xi.

4. Margaret Farley, *Just Love: A Framework for Christian Sexual Ethics* (New York: Continuum, 2006).

5. See, for instance, Ivone Gebara, *Out of the Depths: Women's Experience of Evil and Salvation* (Minneapolis, Minn.: Augsburg, 2002).

11. Do Not Quench the Spirit: Rainbow Ministry and Queer Ritual Practice in Catholic Education and Life

JOHN P. FALCONE

1. John Fortunato's *Embracing the Exile: Healing Journeys of Gay Christians* (San Francisco: Harper and Row, 1982) speaks eloquently to the psychology and spirituality of this position.

2. John P. Falcone, "The Catholic Church and Sexuality: If Only the Hierarchs Would Listen and Learn," *Huffington Post* (November 14, 2011), http://www.huffingtonpost.com/john-falcone/catholic-church-sexuality_b_1085243.html.

3. As the Student Organization Manual states, Boston College forbids officially recognizing student groups "whose mission and purpose encourages advocacy of positions that are not consistent with the mission" of the university. I was told that my article had engaged in such "advocacy" and so—by extension—had GIFTS. In addition, my article had misrepresented the nature of the STM by calling it a "seminary." To call the STM a seminary is to imply that Catholic seminaries welcome and affirm gay students—which, of course, they must not.

4. Bible translations are from the New Revised Standard Version.

5. See Michel Foucault and Joseph Pearson, *Fearless Speech* (Los Angeles: Semiotext[e], 2001).

6. Stanley B. Marrow SJ, "Parrhēsia and the New Testament," *Catholic Biblical Quarterly* 44, no. 3 (1982): 431–446.

7. For some incipient examples of this thinking, see the rising scholar Justin Ernest Crisp, "Rending the Chasuble: A Genealogy of the Anglican Crisis" (Hon-

ors Thesis Project, University of Tennessee, 2011). See also James Bernauer SJ and David Rasmussen, eds., *The Final Foucault* (Cambridge, Mass.: The MIT Press, 1988).

8. See Michael Welker, *God the Spirit*, trans. by John F. Hoffmeyer (Minneapolis: Fortress, 1994).

9. See the essays collected in Michael Welker, ed., *The Work of the Spirit: Pneumatology and Pentecostalism* (Grand Rapids, Mich.: Eerdmans, 2006). Especially relevant to the question of emergence are John Polkinghorne, "The Hidden Spirit and the Cosmos," 169–182; Amos Yong, "*Ruach*, the Primordial Chaos, and the Breath of Life: Emergence Theory and the Creation Narratives in Pneumatological Perspective," 183–204; and Michael Welker, "The Spirit in Philosophical, Theological, and Interdisciplinary Perspectives," 221–232. Polkinghorne is a scientist and Anglican theologian; Yong is a Pentecostal thinker and a disciple of the late Jesuit theologian Donald L. Gelpi; Welker is a German Evangelical.

10. Welker, *God the Spirit*, 40.

11. *Sacrosanctum Concilium (Constitution on the Sacred Liturgy)*, no. 14, in *Vatican Council II*, vol. 1: *The Conciliar and Post Conciliar Documents*, ed. Austin Flannery (Northport, N.Y.: Costello, 1975).

12. Calling Out in the Wilderness: Queer Youth and American Catholicism

JEANINE E. VIAU

1. Eve Kosofsky Sedgwick, *Tendencies* (Durham, N.C.: Duke University Press, 1993), 3.

2. The interviews cited in this essay were part of an original, qualitative study approved by Loyola University Chicago's Institutional Review Board. In order to protect the confidentiality of my collaborators, personal names have been replaced by pseudonyms, and personally identifiable information has been removed.

3. Here I refer to a string of suicide completions that received widespread public attention after the internationally syndicated columnist Dan Savage led a media mobilization to bring these stories to center stage. Victims reported in this rash include Justin Aaberg, 15; Billy Lucas, 15; Tyler Clementi, 18; Seth Walsh, 13; Asher Brown, 13; and Raymond Chase, 19. See reports from the *New York Times*, *Advocate*, *ABC News*, and local news agencies, among others. Also note Dan Savage's attention to these tragedies in his column "Savage Love" and the initiation of his social media campaign, the It Gets Better Project, http://www.itgets better.org.

4. For an overview of studies and findings regarding suicide and related risk factors, see, within an extensive literature, Stephen T. Russell, "Sexual Minority Youth

and Suicide Risk," *American Behavioral Scientist* 46, no. 9 (2003): 1241–1257; and R. C. Savin-Williams, "Suicide Attempts Among Sexual-Minority Youths: Population and Measurement Issues," *Journal of Consulting and Clinical Psychology* 69, no. 6 (2001): 983–991. For recent data concerning transgender youth, see Arnold H. Grossman and Anthony R. D'Augelli, "Transgender Youth and Life-Threatening Behaviors," *Suicide and Life-Threatening Behavior* 37, no. 5 (2007): 527–537.

5. See the school climate studies conducted biennially by the Gay, Lesbian, and Straight Education Network (GLSEN) since 1999, e.g., "The 2009 National School Climate Survey: The Experiences of Lesbian, Gay, Bisexual and Transgender Youth in Our Nation's Schools," GLSEN (September 14, 2010), http://www.glsen.org/cgi-bin/iowa/all/news/record/2624.html. As the sample size and geographical reach of the survey has grown, the results have been consistent from year to year.

6. For example, Melissa Wilcox, as a social science researcher, prefers to use "LGBT" in order to be sensitive to many people's negative experiences with the term "queer." As another example, in an activist context, the Illinois Safe Schools Alliance instructs teachers and administrators not to use this term unless asked to by a student. Even then, persons outside (and in) the community have to be careful about how and when it is appropriate to invoke queer language.

7. The turn to ethnography is a growing methodological shift in the field of Christian ethics. See, for example, Christian Scharen and Aana Marie Vigen's recent project, *Ethnography as Christian Theology and Ethics* (New York: Continuum, 2011).

8. The language of intervention is well attested to in feminist and gender critical literature. Intervention refers to methodological innovations, to a researcher's primary contribution to a discussion in her field, and, in the case of socially and politically engaged scholarship, the implications of her work for social beliefs and practices.

9. "Cisgender" designates persons whose gender identities correspond, in accordance with cultural expectations, to the sex they were assigned at birth. So a cisgendered male is a person of the male sex who identifies as a man. Trans-aware activists and researchers use this designation to displace the normativity of sex-gender correspondence, revealing that this too is a particular location in the strata of gender and sexual differences, a location that carries certain expectations, privileges, and assumptions.

10. CCD stands for the Confraternity of Christian Doctrine, which is now used to refer to the religious teaching program of the Catholic Church.

11. Dorothy Smith, *Institutional Ethnography: A Sociology for People* (Lanham, Md.: AltaMira, 2005), 41.

12. See David Gibson, "Gay Bullying and Catholic Responsibilities," *dotCommonweal* (October 8, 2010), http://www.commonwealmagazine.org/blog/?p=10364.

Gibson's blog post includes links to several articles about the bishops' statements concerning antigay bullying legislation, specifically the video campaign of Archbishop John Nienstedt of Minneapolis-St. Paul and statements by the Catholic bishops of North Carolina against including language about sexual orientation in antibullying legislation.

13. See, for example, the letter that the United States Conference of Catholic Bishops (USCCB) sent to Congress regarding the Employment Nondiscrimination Act (ENDA), May 19, 2010. Full text is available at *America* magazine's *In All Things* blog, "USCCB Letter on Same-Sex Marriage and ENDA," http://www.americamagazine.org/blog/entry.cfm?blog_id=2&entry_id=2923.

14. See original reports from the *Boston Globe*, http://www.boston.com/globe/spotlight/abuse/extras/coverups_archive.htm. See Rachel Martin, "Abuse Scandal Still Echoes Through Catholic Church," National Public Radio (January 11, 2007), http://www.npr.org/templates/story/story.php?storyId=6765175, for an overview. Also see nine years of reporting in the *Boston Globe*, *New York Times*, and other major news publications across the country.

15. See "Introduction" and "2. Homosexuality and the Ordained Ministry" in Congregation for Catholic Education, "Instruction Concerning the Criteria for the Discernment of Vocations with Regard to Persons with Homosexual Tendencies in View of Their Admission to the Seminary and to Holy Orders" (Rome, November 4, 2005), http://www.vatican.va/roman_curia/congregations/ccatheduc/documents/rc_con_ccatheduc_doc_20051104_istruzione_en.html.

16. PRRI/RNS Religion News Poll, conducted by Public Religion Research Institute in partnership with Religion News Service, "Less Than 1-in-5 Give America's Places of Worship High Marks in Handling Issue of Homosexuality," Public Religion Research Institute, Religion News Survey, http://publicreligion.org/research/2010/10/less-than-1-in-5-give-americas-places-of-worship-high-marks-on-handling-issue-of-homosexuality/.

17. Peter Steinfels, "Further Adrift: More Catholics Are Jumping Ship," *Commonweal* 137, no. 18 (October 22, 2010): 20. Also see the Pew Forum on Religion and Public Life, *2008 U.S. Religious Landscape Survey*, http://religions.pewforum.org/, as cited in Steinfels, "Further Adrift." The sample size of the Pew study is much larger than the PRRI/RNS sample, 35,000 as opposed to just over 1,000.

18. The Pew Forum on Religion and Public Life, *2008 U.S. Religious Landscape Survey*, Portraits, Catholics, Social, and Political Views (2008), http://religions.pewforum.org/portraits.

19. PRRI/RNS Religion News Poll.

20. Transgender refers to individuals whose gender identity does not match the sex assigned to them at birth. This is often used as an umbrella term to describe a range of identities that do not conform to cultural gender roles, expectations, and correspondence to biological sex. Genderqueer and gender variant are

newer terms. Both describe gender nonconforming identities. These terms provide a sense of the gender fluidity, performance, and binary resistance that stabilized identifiers, even trans- identifiers, cannot name. It is important to note that there is a broad spectrum of individuals and communities characterized by a broad spectrum of gender expressions who claim these identifiers. Also, gender identifications do not necessarily have anything to do with sexual orientation.

21. "Folks" may seem informal, but its usage is strategic. It shows how theological ethical reflection should be informed by the practical, informal, everyday wisdom of the community, meaning the activists on the ground, the people in the pews, the youth hanging out on the street corner.

13. The Stories We Tell
KATE HENLEY AVERETT

1. Gargi Bhattacharyya, *Tales of Dark Skinned Women: Race, Gender and Global Culture* (London: Routledge, 1998), 36.
2. Published in *From the Pews in the Back: Young Women and Catholicism* (April 14, 2010), http://fromthepewsintheback.com/2010/04/14/done/.

15. A Voice from the Pews: Same-Sex Marriage and Connecticut's *Kerrigan* Decision
MICHAEL A. NORKO

1. *Kerrigan v. Commissioner of Public Health*, 957 A.2d 407 (Conn 2008).
2. Ibid., 433.
3. Connecticut Catholic Public Affairs Conference, "Connecticut Catholic Conference, on behalf of the Catholic bishops, clergy, religious, and laity of the State of Connecticut, condemns today's Connecticut Supreme Court decision on same-sex 'marriage'; calls for a 'Yes' vote on a Constitutional Convention" (October 10, 2008), http://www.ctcatholic.org/Statement-of-Bishops-on-Court-Same-sex.php.
4. Robert P. Jones and Daniel Cox, *Roman Catholics and LGBT Justice Issues* (Washington, D.C.: Public Religion Research Institute, 2008), 6.
5. See, for example, Jeannine Gramick and Francis DeBernardo, "A Catholic Case for Same-Sex Marriage," *Washington Post* (February 14, 2012), http://www.washingtonpost.com/local/a-catholic-case-for-same-sex-marriage/2012/02/13/gIQAl4cwDR_story.html.
6. Connecticut Catholic Public Affairs Conference, 2008.
7. *Lumen Gentium* (Dogmatic Constitution on the Church), November 21, 1964, in Austin Flannery OP, ed., *The Basic Sixteen Documents: Vatican Council II Constitutions, Decrees, Declarations* (Northport, N.Y.: Costello, 1996), 1–96.

8. *Gaudium et Spes* (Pastoral Constitution on the Church in the Modern World), December 7, 1965, in Flannery, ed., *The Basic Sixteen Documents*, 163–282.

9. *Apostolicam Actuositatem* (Decree on the Apostolate of the Laity), November 18, 1965, in Flannery, ed., *The Basic Sixteen Documents*, 403–442.

10. *Lumen Gentium*, no. 35.

11. Ibid., no. 37.

12. Ibid., no. 41.

13. *Lumen Gentium*, no. 37.

14. *Gaudium et Spes*, no. 43.

15. Ibid., no. 44.

16. Ibid., no. 62.

17. Ibid.

18. *Apostolicam Actuositatem*, no. 2.

19. Ibid., no. 10.

20. References to Vatican II documents in this letter are printed here as in the original letter, without additional citation in endnotes, which would be unnecessarily repetitive.

21. The letter ended with a postscript attempting to convey my seriousness of thought and purpose in corresponding: "As an example of my desire to bring Catholic thought into dialogue with medicine and social issues, I am attaching a copy of an article published a few months ago on the subject of the death penalty." In that article I praised John Paul II's teaching on the death penalty in *Evangelium Vitae* and its worth to public discourse and the promotion of genuine human flourishing. See Michael A. Norko, "The Death Penalty in Catholic Teaching and Medicine: Intersections and Places for Dialogue," *Journal of the American Academy of Psychiatry and the Law* 36 (2008): 470–481.

22. Code of Canon Law, promulgated 1983, canons 208–223: "The Obligations and Rights of All the Christian Faithful," http://www.vatican.va/archive /ENG1104/__PU.HTM.

23. Ibid., canon 208.

24. Ibid. Canon 212.2 reads: "The Christian faithful are free to make known to the pastors of the Church their needs, especially spiritual ones, and their desires." Canon 212.3 follows: "According to the knowledge, competence, and prestige which they possess, they have the right and even at times the duty to manifest to the sacred pastors their opinion on matters which pertain to the good of the Church and to make their opinion known to the rest of the Christian faithful, without prejudice to the integrity of faith and morals, with reverence toward their pastors, and attentive to common advantage and the dignity of persons."

25. *Apostolicam Actuositatem*, no. 1.

16. At a Loss
DAN SAVAGE

"At a Loss," from AMERICAN SAVAGE: INSIGHTS, SLIGHTS, AND FIGHTS ON FAITH, SEX, LOVE, AND POLITICS by Dan Savage, copyright © 2013 by Dan Savage. Used by permission of Dutton, a division of Penguin Group (USA) LLC.

1. Garry Wills, "Contraception's Con Men," *New York Review of Books* (February 15, 2012), http://www.nybooks.com/blogs/nyrblog/2012/feb/15/contraception-con-men/. Copyright © 2012 by Garry Wills, used by permission of The Wylie Agency, LLC.

2. PFLAG stands for Parents and Friends of Lesbians and Gays.

3. Rachel K. Jones and Joerg Dreweke, *Countering Conventional Wisdom: New Evidence on Religion and Contraceptive Use* (New York: Guttmacher Institute, 2011), http://www.guttmacher.org/pubs/Religion-and-Contraceptive_Use.pdf.

4. Humphrey Taylor, *The Harris Poll* no. 78 (2005), http://www.harrisinteractive.com/vault/Harris-Interactive-Poll-Research-New-Finds-Different-Religious-Groups-H-2005-10.pdf.

5. Catholics for Choice, "Catholics Voters' Presidential Preference, Issue Priorities, and Opinion of Certain Church Policies," survey, Belden Russonello Strategists, 2012, http://www.catholicsforchoice.org/news/pr/2012/documents/CFC-BRS_2012_Election_Study.pdf.

6. David Morris, "U.S. Catholics Admire, Disagree with Pope," *ABC News* (October 15, 2012), http://abcnews.go.com/WNT/story?id=129364&page=1.

7. *Catechism of the Catholic Church* (Vatican City: Libreria Editrice Vaticana, 1993), 2352.

8. Ibid.

9. Wills, "Contraception's Con Men."

10. Christopher Ryan, "What Rick Santorum Doesn't Know About Sex," *Psychology Today* (January 6, 2012), http://www.psychologytoday.com/blog/sex-dawn/201201/what-rick-santorum-doesn-t-know-about-sex.

11. Ibid.

Afterword: Reflections from Ecclesiology and Practical Theology
TOM BEAUDOIN AND BRADFORD E. HINZE

1. "Dogmatic Constitution on the Church," *Vatican Council II: Constitutions, Decrees, Declarations*, ed., Austin Flannery (Northport, N.Y.: Costello, 1996), no. 37; on the baptismal inheritance of all the faithful to participate fully in the mission of the church, ibid., nos. 11–13, 32–33; on the promotion of councils and synods and dialogue with the laity, see the "Decree on the Pastoral Office of

Bishops in the Church," nos. 27 and 36. See Bradford E. Hinze, "Synodality in the Catholic Church," *Theologische Quartalschrift* 192 (2012): 121–130; Bradford E. Hinze, "The Reception of Vatican II in Participatory Structures of the Church: Facts and Friction," in Canon Law Society of America, *Proceedings of the Seventieth Annual Convention* (Washington, D.C.: Canon Law Society of America, 2008), 28–52.

2. For the denial of Eucharist to LGBT persons and baptism to their children, see the essay by M. Sheila Nelson, Chapter 6 in this volume.

3. For LGBT persons in lay ministry, see the essay by Jamie L. Manson, Chapter 14 in this volume.

4. As it is stated by the Congregation for Catholic Education, in "Instruction Concerning the Criteria for the Discernment of Vocations with Regard to Persons with Homosexual Tendencies in View of Their Admission to the Seminary and to Holy Orders" (November 4, 2005), "this Dicastery . . . believes it necessary to state clearly that the Church, while profoundly respecting the persons in question, cannot admit to the seminary or to holy orders those who practice homosexuality, present deep-seated homosexual tendencies or support the so-called 'gay culture'. Such persons, in fact, find themselves in a situation that gravely hinders them from relating correctly to men and women." http://www.vatican.va/roman_curia/congregations/ccatheduc/documents/rc_con_ccatheduc_doc_20051104_istruzione_en.html.

5. Dialogical processes of ecclesial discernment and decision making include parish and diocesan pastoral councils, parish assemblies, and diocesan synods.

6. Yves Congar, *True and False Reform in the Church*, trans. Paul Philibert (Collegeville, Minn.: Liturgical Press, 2011); the four conditions are found on 215–228.

7. Ibid., 229–264.

8. Ibid., 265–290.

9. Ibid., 291–307.

10. The U.S. bishops have written, "To the extent that a homosexual tendency or inclination is not subject to one's free will, one is not morally culpable for that tendency. . . . A considerable number of people who experience same-sex attraction experience it as an inclination that they did not choose." United States Catholic Conference of Bishops, "Ministry to Persons with a Homosexual Orientation: Guidelines for Pastoral Care" (2006), http://www.usccb.org/about/doctrine/publications/homosexual-inclination-guidelines-page-set.cfm. This line of argument was introduced by the Congregation for the Doctrine of the Faith, "*Persona Humana*: Declaration on Certain Questions Pertaining to Sexual Ethics" (December 29, 1975), no. 8. "A distinction is drawn, and it seems with some reason, between homosexuals whose tendency comes from a false education, from a lack of normal sexual development, from habit, from bad example, or from other

similar causes, and is transitory or at least not incurable; and homosexuals who are definitely such because of some kind of innate instinct or a pathological constitution judged to be incurable." http://www.vatican.va/roman_curia/con gregations/cfaith/documents/rc_con_cfaith_doc_19751229_persona-humana _en.html.

11. See Chapter 5 in this volume.

12. Jordan summarizes the argument thus: "Current Roman Catholic teaching on the priesthood is many things, some of them quite beautiful. Whatever else it is, it is also a teaching about gender—about the necessary correlation of culturally available ideals of masculinity with a particular form of priestly power. To allow priests in the Roman Rite to marry would change this power and this masculinity. So too, more decisively, would the ordination of women. The peculiar geometry of this form of male-on-male power—its demands for absolute certainty, its attraction to regimented purity, its tastes in humiliating surveillance—depends on the exclusion of women." See Mark D. Jordan, "Talking About Homosexuality by the (Church) Rules," in *More than a Monologue: Sexual Diversity and the Catholic Church*, vol. 2, *Inquiry, Thought, and Expression*, ed. J. Patrick Hornbeck II and Michael A. Norko (New York: Fordham University Press, 2014), chap. 2.

13. Bradford E. Hinze, "Ecclesial Repentance and the Demands of Dialogue," *Theological Studies* 61 (2000): 207–238.

14. Theologians writing about Catholic morality, and the Catholic Church more broadly, have made substantial inroads toward fresh theological thinking. See, for example, James Alison, *Faith Beyond Resentment: Fragments Catholic and Gay* (New York: Crossroad, 2001); Margaret A. Farley, *Just Love: A Framework for Christian Sexual Ethics* (New York: Continuum, 2006); Mark D. Jordan, *The Silence of Sodom: Homosexuality in Modern Catholicism* (Chicago: University of Chicago Press, 2000); Todd A. Salzman and Michael G. Lawler, *The Sexual Person: Toward a Renewed Catholic Anthropology* (Washington, D.C.: Georgetown University Press, 2008).

15. These are key themes of *Gaudium et Spes*, the "Pastoral Constitution on the Church in the Modern World." See Flannery, ed., *Vatican Council II*. These themes are evident in both content and form throughout the Council documents. John O'Malley has argued that the rhetorical style of Vatican II, in its employment of "epideictic," marks a substantial break with conciliar language from the Council of Nicaea through the Council of Trent. See John W. O'Malley, "Vatican II: Did Anything Happen?" *Theological Studies* 67 (2006): 3–33.

16. See Karl Rahner, "Practical Theology Within the Totality of Theological Disciplines," in Karl Rahner, *Theological Investigations*, trans. Graham Harrison (London: Darton, Longman, and Todd, 1972), 9:101–114; Karl Rahner, "The Second Vatican Council's Challenge to Theology," in Karl Rahner, *Theological Inves-*

tigations, trans. Graham Harrison (London: Darton, Longman, and Todd, 1972), 9:3–27; Heinz Schuster, "Pastoral Theology," in *Encyclopedia of Theology: The Concise Sacramentum Mundi*, ed. Karl Rahner (New York: Seabury, 1975), 1178–1182; David Tracy, "The Foundations of Practical Theology," in *Practical Theology: The Emerging Field in Theology, Church, and World*, ed. Don S. Browning (New York: Harper and Row, 1983), 61–82.

17. *Gaudium et Spes*, no. 16.

Contributors

KATE HENLEY AVERETT is a graduate student at the University of Texas, Austin.

TOM BEAUDOIN is associate professor of theology in the Graduate School of Religion and Religious Education, Fordham University.

MARK ANDREW CLARK is assistant clinical professor of medicine at Columbia University College of Physicians and Surgeons.

DONALD B. COZZENS is writer-in-residence at John Carroll University.

TERESA DELGADO is associate professor of religious studies at Iona College.

JOHN P. FALCONE is a doctoral candidate in theology and education at Boston College.

THOMAS J. GUMBLETON is retired auxiliary bishop of Detroit, Michigan.

BRADFORD HINZE is professor and Karl Rahner chair of theology at Fordham University.

CHRISTINE FIRER HINZE is professor of theology and director of the Francis and Ann Curran Center for American Catholic Studies at Fordham University.

J. PATRICK HORNBECK II is chair and associate professor of theology at Fordham University.

HILARY HOWES is a member of the board of Gender Rights Maryland.

JAMIE L. MANSON is a journalist and columnist for the *National Catholic Reporter*.

BRYAN N. MASSINGALE is professor of theology at Marquette University.

M. SHEILA NELSON is associate professor of sociology at the College of St. Benedict, St. John's University.

MICHAEL A. NORKO is associate professor of psychiatry at Yale University School of Medicine.

JANET F. PECK and CAROL CONKLIN were plaintiffs in the case *Kerrigan v. Commissioner of Public Health*.

DAN SAVAGE is a columnist, activist, and author.

EVE TUSHNET is a writer and blogger in Washington, D.C.

WINNIE S. VARGHESE is rector, St. Mark's Church-in-the-Bowery, New York.

JEANINE VIAU is a doctoral candidate in theology at Loyola University Chicago.

DEB WORD is a member of the board of directors of Fortunate Families.

Index

CATHOLIC PRACTICE IN NORTH AMERICA